BY DESIGN

BY DESIGN

PLANNING RESEARCH ON HIGHER EDUCATION

RICHARD J. LIGHT
JUDITH D. SINGER
JOHN B. WILLETT

Harvard University Press
Cambridge, Massachusetts, and London, England

Library of Congress Cataloging-in-Publication Data

Light, Richard J.
  By design : planning research on higher education / Richard J.
  Light, Judith D. Singer, John B. Willett.
    p.   cm.
  Includes bibliographical references.
  ISBN 0-674-08930-8 (alk. paper).—ISBN 0-674-08931-6 (pbk. :
  alk. paper)
  1. Education, Higher—Research—United States. 2. Universities
  and colleges—United States—Evaluation. I. Singer, Judith D.
  II. Willett, John B. III. Title.
LB2326.3.L54 1990   89-36311
378'.0072073—dc20   CIP

PREFACE: YOU CAN'T FIX BY ANALYSIS
WHAT YOU BUNGLED BY DESIGN

We are seeing an explosion of interest in systematic research to improve the effectiveness of college. Parents and students ask what growing tuitions buy. Governors ask how to make public systems of higher education more cost-effective. Presidents and deans ask how they can attract better prepared students to their schools. Faculty members show a growing interest in innovation. How can teaching be strengthened? What are students learning? How long do students retain what they have learned?

For several years, we have been addressing these and other questions about higher education in the Harvard Seminar on Assessment. Initiated by President Derek Bok, the Seminar involves over one hundred faculty, administrators, and students from twenty colleges and universities. The Seminar gives us a wonderful opportunity to work

closely with colleagues from other campuses to plan and
conduct research on higher education.

Members of the Seminar agreed not only to explore
higher education as it stands now but also to work for its
improvement. As President Bok wrote in his inaugural
letter to Seminar participants:

I am beginning to think about how one might move from an
initial stage of arousing interest in assessment and demonstrating its potential to a further stage involving sustained effort to
learn how well we are doing and how we can do better in achieving certain major goals of education. My longer-term concerns
involve the possibility of devising a research strategy involving
a series of studies over time to increase our knowledge of how to
achieve some truly fundamental goals of education. Perhaps this
is too ambitious an objective. Yet I cannot help thinking that an
institution serious about improving the quality of its education
should develop some sort of sustained strategy of research along
these lines.

Seminar participants adopted, and indeed broadened,
Bok's call for systematic research. They identified potential
innovations, reviewed what was known already, and then
conducted research projects. Participants familiar with organizing research in universities organized their own projects. Others without a formal research background sought
the advice of colleagues. The three authors of this book
brought our own experience in program evaluation, education, and health policy research to the Seminar, and
worked with our colleagues to organize and carry out new
projects.

We want to share with a wider audience the lessons we
have learned about planning and implementing research
in higher education. Our experience is most extensive with
projects conducted at institutions participating in the Seminar, but the problems and challenges we faced are common
to many of America's colleges and universities. For example, faculty members at nearly every college wish to

strengthen the clarity and style of expository writing. Faculty members at nearly every college wish to understand the long-run effects of different courses, and what students retain over time, if anything. A core of such basic questions spans many campuses.

This book is written for anyone interested in investigating how American higher education works, and how research can be used to improve it. We try to strike a balance between general principles and specific details, between what we would like in a perfect world and what can be done in the real world, between theory and practice. We are convinced that good research is easier to carry out in higher education than in any other setting. Faculty, staff, and students in our colleges and universities understand the value of research. They are often willing participants in the process. Admissions records make sampling easier. The registrar's office can easily provide background information on participants in a project. Students are accustomed to being evaluated. Individual faculty members, and entire departments, enjoy a pedagogical autonomy that permits them to innovate. There is an all-pervading sense that *more information means a better job can be done.* Where is there a more supportive arena for high-quality research?

We hope that faculty, administrators, and students will all find this book useful. It requires only a modest technical background. There are no equations; readers need only be familiar with the concepts presented in a basic statistics course. Readers who want to design and implement projects of their own will find practical advice. Readers interested in commissioning research, or interpreting the research of others, will find suggestions about how to distinguish good research from bad.

We emphasize research design over measurement and analysis. This is because good design comes first. No matter how precise your measurement or how sophisticated your analyses, you risk failure if your research is not well planned. *You can't fix by analysis what you bungled by design.* Therefore, we discuss the basic principles of research design and illustrate our points with sixty real examples of recent research in higher education. Our examples come from private and public institutions, two-year and four-year, selective and not so selective colleges.

The book is organized around the questions we ask colleagues who come to us for help in planning their research. What do you want to know? What has been done before on your topic? What can you learn from it? Whom are you interested in studying? What measures will you use? Are they the best measures for this purpose? What predictors interest you? How many students must you include? Should you try out your project on a small scale? Each of these questions gives rise to a chapter in this book.

A key theme throughout is that improving the effectiveness of an institution takes time and requires using the results of research to change policies. Therefore, *organizing systematic research at any college is a long-term process.* Most of our colleagues pay close attention when an innovation, such as a new way of teaching, is found to work particularly well. Everyone is interested in especially successful outcomes, and in how they were achieved. But a big lesson from our Seminar on Assessment is that *by rewarding only successful innovations, a college may create an atmosphere that discourages widespread experimentation.* If each of three professors has a new idea for improving instruction, does anyone really expect all three ideas to be major breakthroughs? Of course not. We shouldn't be surprised if one or more of them don't work any better than the old way; indeed, we should be delighted if *any* of the new methods is an improvement. Yet, often only those colleagues with successful innovations are rewarded. Shouldn't all three professors be encouraged and commended because they tried a new idea and systematically evaluated how well it worked?

The best way to encourage new ideas and innovation, as well as careful evaluation and assessment of them, is to reward the *process* of systematic investigation. Administrators and faculty should be urged to try a change in procedure, to compare outcomes achieved with an innovation to outcomes achieved with older methods. *This means taking risks.* Not all innovations will work. But without risk-taking, and systematic evaluation of its results, innovation and improvement cannot flourish.

Rewarding the evaluation process has yet another strength—it sets the tone that research is an ongoing, cumulative activity, and that one of its benefits is to enhance the college experience for future generations of students. Any one project, whether it tries to improve teaching or to identify and help students who are struggling, is but one step in a long-run effort to strengthen higher education. A long-term policy of systematic innovation and assessment builds in a constant search for improvement, and rewards all those who participate in the search. It is a goal worth working hard to achieve.

ACKNOWLEDGMENTS

We would like to thank several individuals and organizations who helped to make this book possible. Substantial financial support for the Harvard Seminar on Assessment came from the Fund for the Improvement of Postsecondary Education, the Mellon Foundation, and the Sloan Foundation. This assistance was invaluable in allowing us and a devoted group of graduate students to work on both Seminar projects and this manuscript.

A number of individuals played special roles as we prepared for this book. President Derek Bok of Harvard initially called for the systematic use of research to strengthen higher education, and he has supported our work enthusiastically. His presidential leadership played a big role in getting the Seminar started, and he has consistently urged us to keep our eye on the concrete policy implications of each project.

Many colleagues at Harvard have been particularly helpful. We would like to especially thank Constance Buchanan, Catherine Krupnick, David Riesman, Daniel Burnstein, Harvey Cox, Ellen Sarkisian, Howard Gardner, William Fitzsimmons, John Fox, Warren Reed, Dean Whitla, Fred Jewett, Henry Moses, and David Pilbeam. Each of these has made substantial contributions to the development of ideas presented in this book.

Colleagues at other colleges and universities and professional organizations extended our perspective and offered a diversity of ideas that enhanced both the Seminar and the book. Special thanks to Worth David and Judith Hackman of Yale; Joan Gurgis and Fred Hargadon of Princeton; Jean Wu of Brown; Chris Jernstedt, Al Quirk, and Chris Strenta of Dartmouth; Michael Behnke and Ben Snyder of M.I.T.; Robert Grose of Amherst; Edgar Beckham of Wesleyan; Charles Karelis, Thomas Carroll, and David Holmes of the Fund for Improvement of Postsecondary Education (FIPSE); and Patricia Cross of the University of California at Berkeley.

Much of the work of the Assessment Seminar was carried out by students at Harvard, working as research assistants or carrying out research for doctoral theses. A first-class team was organized by Thomas Angelo, who was the assistant director of the Seminar for two years. In addition to organizing his own projects, he helped countless others with the day-to-day concerns of their work, and trained students in questionnaire design and interviewing skills. Doctoral students who made special contributions to the Seminar include Jan Civian, Kimberly Hokanson, Karen Hoelscher, Barbara Bushey, Belle Brett, Keith Light, Robin Worth, and Andrew Eisenmann. Leigh Weiss and Andrea Shlipak wrote their senior honors theses at Harvard College in connection with Seminar projects.

We got crucial help with earlier drafts of this book from Frederick Mosteller and David Pillemer. The book has been substantially improved by their suggestions. Each of these two colleagues kept pushing us always to do just a bit more, and we are grateful. We also extend our thanks to the many doctoral students in our courses on research design who encouraged us to write a book and offered helpful comments on what we presented to them. A special word of thanks goes to Beth Gamse, who read several drafts of the manuscript and gave us detailed editorial and substantive suggestions. Wendy Angus and Sandra Metts were most helpful in the preparation of the manuscript. At Harvard University Press, Michael Aronson was a joy to work with as an editor, and kept pushing this project along briskly. Camille Smith's many changes and suggestions improved the manuscript enormously. We appreciate the help and support from all these people.

Most of all, we want to thank our families. The three of us sometimes worked long and odd hours to finish this book, and our families always accepted this in good spirits. To Pat Light, Steve Gordon, and Jerri Willett—you helped to make this fun.

CONTENTS

BY DESIGN

WHY DO RESEARCH
ON HIGHER EDUCATION?

1

Is your college doing a good job of teaching undergraduates to think critically? Do your students write clear and gracious prose? Which professors are the most effective teachers? What do they do that makes them so effective? Could others become more effective by emulating them? Are students integrating modern technology into the way they work and the way they learn? Do students who use computers learn more than those who do not?

Such questions are not new. But many of our colleagues, including faculty, administrators, students, legislators, and parents, are asking them with new urgency. Perhaps this is because of increasing competition among colleges. Perhaps it is because of a renewed sense among faculty and administrators that, as tuition rises dramatically, they should work harder than ever to deliver the best education possible. Perhaps it is because consumers are demanding more value for their money. Whatever the reason, more campuses are initiating research and using the results to strengthen educational quality.

We hope to help by making methods for planning good research more easily accessible. We have written this book as a resource for those who want to conduct such research. If ever there was an ideal organization to encourage systematic research, it is the university. Faculty members are generally aware of what it means to do research, even if each professor is not an expert on every intricacy of the empirical method. Faculty members work hard to enhance students' learning, because, despite the cynical views of some of education's critics, most professors take pride in their teaching and work hard to do it well. Organizing systematic ways to use information to improve teaching and learning is a widely shared goal.

Many Questions, Many Options

Research on higher education can address diverse questions. Our goal is to help you design first-rate studies to answer them. We use three general paradigms, which we will call *descriptive, relational,* and *experimental* inquiry. Each leads to results with concrete implications for policy and practice.

Descriptive studies are used for doing exactly what their name implies—describing the way things are. They answer questions such as: How well do students write? What are the most popular courses on campus? How many graduates are accepted to medical school? How much money do our graduating seniors owe? Descriptive studies characterize the status quo; they do not tell you *why* things are the way they are.

Beth Schneider (1987) used a descriptive study to estimate the prevalence of sexual harassment at a major Eastern public university. She contacted a random sample of female graduate students, and of the 356 students who returned a mail questionnaire, 60 percent reported having been harassed in some way by a male professor at least once during their graduate career; 10 percent had been sexually propositioned. Schneider's startling results documented the need for university guidelines on sexual harassment and for educational programs designed to ameliorate the problem.

Glenda Rooney (1985) organized a descriptive study at the University of Wisconsin at Madison to profile minority students' participation in campus student organizations devoted specifically to minority concerns. She selected a stratified random sample of minority students, and of the 322 interviewed, 98 percent belonged to at least one campus organization. But fewer than 20 percent belonged to an organization specifically devoted to minority concerns. Rooney's results refuted a *Newsweek* poll suggesting that minority students restrict their campus involvement to minority student groups.

Relational studies are used to examine relationships between two or more factors. You can use them to answer such questions as: Are men more likely than women to persist in studying science? Do dropout rates differ by student socioeconomic status? Do varsity athletes learn as much as their classmates who don't play on a team? In a relational study, you examine natural variation in predictors and outcomes to figure out whether they are associated. Relational studies help you move beyond simple descriptions to understanding *why* things are the way they are.

Christos Theophilides, Patrick Terenzini, and Wendell Lorang (1984) organized a relational study at the State University of New York at Albany to examine the stability of students' choice of major and what characteristics are associated with the likelihood of change. More than 300 students completed a questionnaire during orientation week and follow-up questionnaires near the end of both freshman and sophomore years. By the end of sophomore year, 77 percent of the students had changed majors: 32 percent changed once and 45 percent twice. Students who changed had lower GPAs and less clear academic objectives than students who did not. Theophilides and his colleagues used these results to highlight the need for early student advising and to suggest methods for identifying students most in need of such services.

Ernest Pascarella, John Smart, and Corinna Ethington (1986) found a relational study helpful for examining the institutional and personal characteristics associated with the likelihood that students attending two-year colleges would eventually pursue and complete a bachelor's degree. Among a national probability sample of 825 students who entered college in 1971 and were followed up each year until 1980, 53 percent had obtained a bachelor's degree and 16 percent were still pursuing a degree. Students were more likely to persist if they were integrated into the academic and social systems of their college. Pascarella and his colleagues concluded that policies and practices that would enhance students' academic and social integration into campus life might increase the likelihood of long-term persistence.

Although relational studies allow you to identify an association between predictor and outcome, the type of relationship you can talk about is limited. With a relational study, you can only talk about *correlation,* not *causation.* Because you are examining *natural variation,* you can never be sure whether a predictor *causes* the outcome to behave the way it does, or whether the effect is caused by some other predictor that you failed to study. Does student integration into academic life cause long-term persistence, or does some other factor, such as prior academic preparation, cause both academic integration and long-term persistence? Both Theophilides and Pascarella and their colleagues used statistical analyses to rule out many of these rival explanations. But as both teams of researchers concede, relational studies cannot establish causation.

You also can use relational studies to compare the effects of naturally occurring treatments or programs, but the problem of causal attribution persists. Kathleen Berg (1988) conducted a relational study of the association between residence arrangements and eating disorders among 584 female undergraduates at the University of Western Ontario. Fifteen percent of the women met standard criteria for bulimia. Those living on coed floors of coed dorms displayed more bulimic symptomatology than their peers living in women-only residence halls or on women-only floors in coed dorms.

Does coed living *cause* bulimia? It is hard to say, because the students Berg studied chose their own living arrangements. How will we ever know whether it was the living arrangement, and not some other characteristics of their backgrounds associated with choice of living arrangement, such as sex-role development, that caused the increased prevalence of bulimic symptomatology? But even without pinning down a causal link, Berg's compelling results on the prevalence of bulimia across *all* dormitory settings at Western Ontario led to a training program for residence-hall staff on the detection and treatment of eating disorders.

To establish a causal link, you must conduct an *experiment*. In an experiment, you implement a specific treatment, or set of treatments, for the explicit purpose of learning about its efficacy. You intervene in the system, control the experiences of everyone you study, and watch what happens. The statistical principle of random assignment helps you to rule out rival predictors that might "explain away" your findings, eliminating the shadow that always looms large over relational studies. Of the three research paradigms we discuss, only experimental inquiries allow you to determine whether a treatment *causes* an outcome to change.

John Belland and his colleagues (1985) designed an experiment to determine whether a moderate amount of external pacing improved a microcomputer-based instructional program for teaching undergraduate biology. They randomly assigned 100 freshmen at Ohio State University among three instructional programs and a control group. Comparison of student knowledge after completion of the instruction revealed that, while all three experimental groups differed from the control group, students working with a moderate level of external pacing learned the most. Because they conducted an experiment, the researchers were able to conclude that external pacing *caused* the improved performance.

Larry Weber, Janice McBee, and Jean Krebs (1983) conducted an experiment at Virginia Polytechnic Institute to investigate the effects of test administration ("in-class closed book" versus "in-class open book" versus "take-home") on student achievement. Sixty-four students were randomly assigned to three groups, and each group took three tests, one of each type. When students took the take-home tests, their scores on knowledge items were higher and their levels of anxiety were lower than when they took the in-class tests. No evidence of rampant cheating was found with any test format. Because the researchers conducted an experiment, they were able to conclude that differences in test format *caused* the differential results.

The beauty of experimental studies stems from the strong, clean inferences you can draw from their results. An experiment reduces ambiguity. Causal attribution is clear. Of course, not all research questions can be addressed experimentally—you can't randomly assign students to different sexes, for example—but when experiments are feasible, they are preferable to relational studies.

Our Philosophy of Research Design

Through our own research experience and work with colleagues, we have developed several principles for designing research. We offer four maxims to reveal our biases and to foreshadow the type of advice we give throughout the book.

Our basic tenet is that *your study's design is the single most important factor that determines whether your findings will be scientifically first-class.* When colleagues seek us out for assistance, they often have their data in hand and they ask us to suggest appropriate statistical analyses. We nearly always find that their entire project would have yielded more useful and more convincing results if they had thought through their design more carefully before collecting data. Elaborate statistical analyses rarely, if ever, can retrospectively correct weak project design. Taking extra care at the design stage is well worth the extra effort.

A corollary is that you should *explore many design options before adopting any plan, especially a weak one.* When practical constraints prevent you from implementing the ideal design, don't say: "If I can't do it right, it doesn't really matter how I do it. I'll just do something quick and dirty." Research designs form a hierarchy and, if your first-choice design isn't feasible, there is often a second choice distinctly preferable to an entirely uncontrolled investigation. Explore all the possibilities, and then decide.

Our third maxim—*pay enormous attention to detail*—may seem trivial, little more than common sense, but, as we constantly remind ourselves and our colleagues, the little details determine the ultimate credibility of a project. If you want to evaluate a new curriculum, for example, you can choose among many different designs, several of which use randomization in the selection and assignment of students. But there are many different ways to randomize. Depending upon the method you choose, your ultimate analyses may have very high power or very low power, all at the same cost and with similar numbers of professors and students involved. Paying attention to detail always has a high payoff.

Our final maxim urges an attitude for approaching research in higher education. Most of this research requires student participation, and administrative and faculty cooperation too. You should continually remind yourself, as well as your administrative and faculty colleagues, that *research must respect collaboration and cooperation.* This attitude has an important implication: treat people's participation with respect, don't settle for a weak research design. Otherwise, in Frederick Mosteller's words, you will be doing little more than "fooling around with people."

How This Book Is Organized

This book is written in the format of a discussion with colleagues. In its pages we ask the very questions we ask colleagues who come to us for advice on research design. They are questions you should ask yourself when planning your study. The answers should guide you toward an effective plan. One good way to use this book is to read it with a concrete research problem in mind. If you don't have a specific problem, you may still find it useful for assessing the work of others. Although you can read any chapter on its own, we believe you will get the most from the book if you read it sequentially.

In Chapter 2, we ask: *What are your questions?* Before you can design your project, you must decide exactly what you want to know. Well-crafted research questions guide the systematic planning of research; without research questions, you will not be able to manipulate those facets of design that increase your ability to learn what you want to know. In this chapter, we suggest specific strategies for writing research questions and show how to use previous research to refine those questions.

In Chapter 3, we ask: *What groups do you want to study?* To select a sample of individuals, you must specify precisely whom you want to investigate. Are you interested in students in general, or just freshmen and sophomores? What about faculty members? How you specify your target population determines the generalizability of your study—the extent to which your results are applicable to other persons, places, and times. In this chapter, we discuss how to decide whom to study, and how to select a sample of people who meet your criteria.

In Chapter 4, we encourage you to identify the factors or programs you want to study by asking: *What predictors do you want to study?* Good research designs incorporate and manipulate the predictors of primary interest, the ones you will build into your work, thereby facilitating the detection of their effects. Organizing a first-class design requires you to identify the important predictors *before* collecting data. In this chapter, we present strategies for identifying predictors and for incorporating them into a design.

We devote Chapter 5 to a special kind of predictor—one distinguishing a program or treatment group from another group receiving no special treatment—when we ask: *Compared to what?* People in the comparison group are a baseline or standard against whom you compare people in the treatment group. The particular comparison group you choose determines how well your inferences will hold up. In this chapter, we present the pros and cons of eight alternative comparison groups, and show how you can choose the best one for the research question you want to answer.

In Chapter 6 we ask: *What are your outcomes?* College changes people in many different ways. Students learn new facts, new ways of thinking, and new ways of viewing the world. Which of these outcomes do you want to focus on? In addition, do you want to emphasize students' status at a particular point in time, or changes in their status over time? How do you know you are measuring what you *think* you are measuring? In this chapter, we describe how you can determine how valid your measures are for your specific purposes.

In Chapter 7, we ask: *How can you improve your measures?* The more reliable and precise your measures, the stronger the "signal" they convey and the weaker the "noise" obscuring their true information. High-quality measures give you a better chance of detecting relationships between predictors and outcomes. Should you use long questionnaires or short ones? Should you use 4-point, 5-point, or 10-point scales for measuring student attitudes? Should you obtain one measure of each variable or more? In this chapter, we offer several ways to increase the precision of your measures. We also discuss how you can incorporate opportunities to estimate precision directly into your design.

Chapter 8 poses the query we are asked more often than any other: *How many people should you study?* How many are enough? Will a well-chosen sample of a dozen students give a clear picture, or do you need several hundred to be really sure? This decision about sample size is crucial. It affects the power and the cost of your project in a big way. If you want to be absolutely sure you do not miss detecting a real improvement, use an enormous sample—in fact, include everyone in the population. But be prepared for an FDIC bailout, because large samples can break the bank. In this chapter, we discuss the crucial tradeoffs that you must make when choosing your sample size. We also show how you can increase your study's power when you are limited to small sample sizes.

In Chapter 9, we ask: *Should you try it out on a small scale?* The advantages of small-scale projects are clear: they are less expensive and they can help to shape and strengthen later, more elaborate work. The disadvantages are also clear: your results will be less generalizable than if you had organized a full-blown study and you will run a greater risk of not finding any effect at all. You have to weigh the costs against the benefits. In this chapter, we identify the circumstances when a small-scale study is a superb and efficient idea, and when it is a waste of time. We suggest particular ways to design small-scale studies that will yield the strongest findings.

In Chapter 10, we ask: *Where should you go from here?* If you want to initiate a project on your campus, what are some different ways to begin? How can you capitalize on existing resources and make the most of data that are available now? We offer several suggestions both from our experience at Harvard and from activities on many other campuses, to help start new research in an effective manner.

2

Anecdotal reports of sexual harassment fill the student newspaper. Formal charges have been brought against two professors, and an accompanying editorial implies these two are just the tip of the iceberg. The president asks the assistant dean for student affairs to "study the problem" of sexual harassment on campus. How should the dean begin?

Three years ago, faced with a declining number of applications, the dean of admissions recommended relaxing admission standards. Without this change, she argued, the size of the entering class would decline. The faculty reluctantly agreed. The registrar now reports that more students dropped out last year than ever before. Is this the result of lowered admissions criteria, or of some other cause? How can the dean find out?

Each of these scenarios identifies a broadly stated *re-*

search theme—a dilemma to investigate. The research theme in the first example is the extent of sexual harassment on campus; the research theme in the second example is the link between admissions criteria and student persistence. Both themes are good candidates for detailed investigation.

How can you take a broad theme and actually plan a study in detail? What is the first step you should take? Identify available data? Ask experts for advice? Ask colleagues on other campuses what they know? Send a research assistant to the library to review past literature?

Information-gathering is essential, but it should not be your first step. Your first step should be to *articulate a set of specific research questions.* Good design flows from clear goals. Do you want to know how many undergraduates have been sexually harassed? Conduct a confidential student survey. Do you want to know whether the problem is worse at the graduate level? Include graduate students as well. Do you want to know whether a workshop for faculty and students would decrease the incidence of harassment and increase the chances that people who were harassed would come forward? Offer a workshop and evaluate what happens. *Well-crafted questions guide the systematic planning of research. Formulating your questions precisely enables you to design a study with a good chance of answering them.*

It is challenging to move from broad research themes to specific research questions. Many prospective researchers say: "I'm just interested in the general topic; I don't have specific questions. I need to collect some data; the questions will arise from those data. If I knew the questions, I wouldn't need to do the research." Although you should always be open to new ideas generated by data, these views are a woefully inadequate basis for *planning* research. If your research is not grounded in specific questions, you court the serious risk of not finding anything. Your design won't be targeted to a precise purpose. If questions are not posed, you have no basis for manipulating features of your project's design to help you find answers.

Moreover, when pressed, most researchers actually do have specific questions in mind. Something—an *observation* about the world, a *theory* or *hypothesis* about how the world works, or the need to know about the effectiveness of a *new policy*—led them to pursue a project. These observations, theories, hypotheses, or policies lead to specific questions. The goal of this chapter is to help you move from the generalities of research themes to the specifics of research questions. In subsequent chapters, your research questions will provide the foundation for making decisions about your design. By the end of this chapter, you should have some ideas about how to:

- *Articulate clearly specified research questions* linked to hypotheses, theories, observations about the world, or problems in practice. Research questions form the basis for making subsequent design decisions.
- *Understand the link between research questions and methodology.* Although some research questions can be addressed using a variety of research designs, others require the use of particular types of designs.
- *Learn from the work of others and refine your research questions accordingly.* Review other people's research on the questions you want to address. Learn from their successes and from their failures. Knowing what has gone before helps you to avoid pitfalls and to identify new directions.

Why Are Research Questions So Important?

To design a project you must make some decisions. Time and time again, you will have a choice and you will have to determine the best course of action. Whom do you want to study—freshmen, all undergraduates, or doctoral students? How should you collect data—using registrar's records, tests, independent evaluations, or interviews? What time frame is appropriate and feasible—the past, the present, or the future? The quality of your decisions shapes the quality of your study. Make good decisions, and your study will be first-rate; make poor decisions, and your study will be second-rate at best. The dilemma you face is: On what bases should I make these decisions?

We believe that clearly specified *research questions are the only basis for making sensible planning decisions.* Think about what you want to know. Ask yourself: "If I make Choice A, will I be able to answer my research questions? What if I make Choice B?" Every design decision has consequences—some trivial, some monumental. Considering your research questions, and understanding the ramifications of your decisions, can help you make intelligent choices.

To illustrate how research questions help inform design decisions, suppose your broad research theme is concerned with the effectiveness of your college's faculty advising system for undergraduates. You want to know more about the present system and to consider the possibility of a new, intensive mentoring system. You have yet to specify precise research questions. How will these questions shape subsequent design decisions?

Research questions identify the target population from which you will draw a sample. Should you study both students and faculty? Freshmen and sophomores only, or juniors and seniors, too? You should decide whom to study only after considering exactly whom you want to make policy decisions about. If you do not identify the people you are most interested in before collecting data, you risk omitting important respondents from your study.

Research questions determine the appropriate level of aggregation. Should you measure efficacy at the level of student, advisor, department, or institution? Are you interested in the characteristics of advisors that make *them* particularly effective, or in the characteristics of students that make *them* particularly easy to advise? Research questions can be framed at different levels of aggregation. If you do not think about the issue of aggregation before you collect data, you risk not having enough data at a crucial level of aggregation to answer your research questions.

Research questions identify the outcome variables. What do you mean by the effectiveness of advising? Are you interested in student perceptions or in objective measures, such as the number of student-advisor contact hours? In short-term or long-term success? You can determine appropriate outcomes only after considering exactly what you want to know. If you do not define the outcome variables before data collection, you may fail to collect data on the most important outcomes.

Research questions identify the key predictors. Does efficacy differ by student gender? By advisor gender? By the match between advisor and student gender? By the advisor's academic rank? You can determine the important predictors only after thinking about all the things that might be associated with your outcomes. If you do not think about predictors before data collection, you may fail to measure essential variables.

Research questions determine how much researcher control is needed and whether a descriptive, relational, or experimental study is most appropriate. When the influence of mentoring is compared to traditional advising, will you study the new system the first year it is implemented or after it has been in place for three years? Can you randomly assign students to advising systems, or must you study them after they have selected the system they prefer? If you have a great deal of control over the research setting, you can draw strong inferences. By not deciding how much control you need, you risk not having enough.

Research questions identify background characteristics

that might be related to the outcome. Should you account for differences in faculty burden due to different numbers of advisees per advisor? Should you incorporate different students' goal orientation? Random assignment of students to advisors will eliminate most potential biases, but if you cannot use random assignment, differences in background characteristics such as faculty advising loads may distort your findings. Disentangling the effects of different predictors is often very difficult during analysis. It is much easier to control background influences by design.

Research questions raise challenges for measurement and data collection. Are there published instruments that assess advisor effectiveness? Do they require individual administration? Can they be mailed, or must they be filled out in person? Are the measures appropriate for the students and faculty members at your school? Is one measure of effectiveness sufficient, or should you use several? Data collection is expensive, so spend your resources wisely. If you do not think about measurement and data collection at the outset, you may never gather the key information you require.

Research questions influence the number of people you must study. Not only is research design guided by your questions, so is statistical analysis. Different questions require different analyses which, in turn, require specific sample sizes to ensure adequate statistical power to detect effects. Once the data have been collected, it is too late to add respondents—you have to make this decision in advance.

Our message is simple: *Research questions determine every facet of research design.* If your questions are not precisely stated, you have little basis for making crucial decisions. Today's naive choices may have dire consequences tomorrow. If you plan your study with your research questions in mind, you can ensure that your project will be able to answer those questions at the end.

EXAMPLE: *Linking research questions to design decisions: Geographic mobility for academic men and women.*

The conventional wisdom of academic life suggests that (1) career advancement often requires geographic mobility, and (2) women advance more slowly and occupy less prestigious positions than men. Rachel Rosenfeld and Jo Ann Jones (1987) asked whether these phenomena are related. Can sex differences in mobility explain sex differences in career progress?

Rosenfeld and Jones developed three specific research questions: (1) Does geographic mobility differ by sex? (2) Does the relationship between mobility and career attainment differ by sex? (3) Have these patterns changed over time? Based on a random sample of 311 women and 311 men, they found that (1) early in their careers, women are less mobile than men, but later on, this differential diminishes; (2) although geographic mobility is related to career advancement, this relationship does not differ by sex; and (3) these patterns have not changed over time.

These findings are persuasive because Rosenfeld and Jones linked their research design to their questions in six specific ways. First, because of interest in "academics," their target population was men and women who received a doctorate and who worked at a college or university immediately after receiving their degree. Second, because they needed published data on career histories (to save money) and a sufficient number of women (to examine their questions), they studied psychologists. (Thirty percent of the members of the American Psychological Association are female and the membership directory includes extensive employment data.) Third, because of their focus on sex differences, they oversampled women and undersampled men, selecting equal numbers for their project. Fourth, because of their interest in changes over time, they did not restrict attention to psychologists who graduated in any one year, but included people who received a doctorate between 1965 and 1974. Fifth, because their questions emphasized career *progress,* not career *status at a given time,* they followed psychologists from doctoral degree until 1981, creating a study period as long as 16 years and as short as 7 years. Sixth, because of their focus on career success as measured by standard academic barometers, they used the Social Science and Science Citation Indices to determine the number of articles published each year, the National Union Catalog to determine the number of books published each year, and academic rank as a measure of career progress.

Getting Specific

Research questions rarely come in a single burst of inspiration. Do not expect to sit down for an hour and produce an elaborate list of specific questions. Although you must take the time to do just that—sit down and write—your initial list will not be your final list. Expect to iterate. A good set of research questions will evolve, over time, after you have considered and reconsidered your broad research theme.

Begin by asking yourself the simple question: "What do I want to find out?" Be as general as you like—the broader, the better. Do not worry about data collection; that comes later. Do not worry about measuring fuzzy concepts; that comes later, too. Imagine you have access to any resource you need. Is that really all you want to know? Have you left something out? Will you be content if that is all you can say? Write down all your ideas, however grandiose, however small.

Now comes the hard part: *Get specific*. Examine every outcome on your list. Define it. Refine that definition. Think about how you would measure it. Do the same for every predictor. Identify the target population of greatest interest. Should it include anyone else? Be as precise as you can—the clearer, the better.

Make sure your questions are not inward, incomprehensible to colleagues. After all, your findings must be persuasive to external readers, too. Ask colleagues to review your list. Do they understand every question? Do they see something you overlooked?

Be wary of the desire to push forward before going through this process. It is all too easy to write instruments, select respondents, and collect data before articulating specific questions. Many researchers believe they are productive only when they write interview schedules, gather data, or do statistical analysis. Don't fall into this trap. You may end up with long, rambling questionnaires and aimless interviews that alienate respondents. You may omit respondents who will be crucial later. Ultimately, you risk becoming stranded with key questions unanswered and key issues unresolved.

EXAMPLE: *Stating research questions: The effects of a career development course for undecided freshmen.*

One way to foster career development is to offer, for academic credit, a one-semester course in career choices. David Carver and David Smart (1985) examined the effects of one such course: "Career and Self-Exploration (CSE)" at the University of Northern Colorado.

The researchers' broad theme was an evaluation of "the effectiveness of the fall 1981 sections of CSE in promoting four major areas of student development: (a) academic and career decisionmaking; (b) career maturity; (c) positive self-concept; and (d) interaction between the student and the campus environment" (p. 38). But Carver and Smart did not stop there; they pushed themselves to become even more precise. Building upon a review of the literature, their specific research questions were:

> whether freshmen students completing CSE would score significantly higher than a comparison group in the following seven areas: (a) career decidedness (as measured by the CDS, Item 1), (b) academic major certainty (as measured by the CDS, Item 2), (c) reduction in academic and career indecision (CDS, Items 3–18), (d) maturity of career attitudes (CMI, Attitude Scale), (e) overall level of self-esteem (TSCS, total P score), (f) use of academic advising, personal counseling, career planning, placement, and tutorial services (as measured by the Student Involvement Survey), and (g) involvement in student organizations, university programming and student government (Student Involvement Survey). (p. 39)

CDS (Career Decision Scale), CMI (Career Maturity Inventory), and TSCS (Tennessee Self-Concept Scale) are standardized, widely available instruments.

Carver and Smart used their research questions to make many design decisions. Their questions guided their measurement choices; the instruments, and even specific items, are cited in the questions. The questions also guided their choice of a comparison group. Carver and Smart wanted a comparison group of students who did not take CSE, but were otherwise similar to the CSE group. They were especially concerned about differential motivation to explore career options. Random assignment was not possible because of the university's policy of admitting students to courses on a first-come, first-served basis. Their very good compromise for a control group was students who expressed interest in taking CSE but who could not enroll, because of schedule conflicts or because all sections were filled.

Building on the Work of Others

Having specified your research questions in as much detail as possible, you should spend time examining previous research on these and related questions. Reviewing and synthesizing the work of others can help both to clarify and to broaden your questions. A good literature review can identify unexamined target populations, important predictors and outcomes, and tried and tested measurement techniques. A thorough review has another advantage as well: by learning from the work of others, you can avoid repeating their mistakes.

The Goals of a Research Review

The primary purpose of a research review is to learn what is already known so that you can build on it. The most helpful reviews identify corroborating *and* conflicting evidence. Corroborating evidence suggests "facts" that you must take into account when designing your new project. Conflicting evidence generates new questions for future research.

Occasionally, every study you examine will suggest the same clear and unambiguous answers to your research questions. If this happens, think about exploring new uncharted territory, or modifying your questions. Why conduct yet another study documenting for the eleventh time what has already been replicated ten times?

But unanimous agreement is rare. All the studies in a group of studies probably used different research methods, and may have reached somewhat different conclusions. They may have sampled different target populations, used different measuring instruments, applied different analytic techniques, or simply found different answers. But whatever the differences are, you can learn from them. These differences, and any systematic patterns in them, can tell you a lot about how to design any new study. In fact, although conflicting findings prevent unambiguous answers from shining through, they actually tell you more about future design than you would learn from a world where there was unanimous agreement. You can use conflicting evidence to generate new, more fine-grained questions and to construct more powerful research designs.

EXAMPLE: *What can you learn from previous research? The effects of financial aid on student persistence.*

Does financial aid help students to stay in, and eventually graduate from, college? Tullise Murdock (1987) examined more than 500 studies of the effect of financial aid on persistence. She carefully synthesized a subset of 62 of these, and found that students receiving financial aid were slightly more likely to persist than similar students without aid. Specifically, "financial aid could be expected to move the typical person from the 50th to the 55.2 percentile of persistence for the nonfinancial aid population" (p. 84).

From a research design standpoint, Murdock's findings on the variation across studies of the impact of financial aid were even more informative. Her review showed that the impact of financial aid differed depending upon the following factors: (a) *The type of institution:* effects were larger at two-year schools than at four-year schools, and larger at private colleges than at public colleges. (b) *The definition of persistence:* effects were larger if persistence was defined in terms of graduation, as opposed to reenrollment from semester to semester or year to year. (c) *Student enrollment status:* effects were larger for full-time students than for part-time students. Murdock's careful review turned up another critical finding: effects differed depending upon whether differences in academic ability between recipients and nonrecipients were controlled. In the seven studies that matched groups of students by ability, financial aid had no effect on persistence.

Does Murdock's review establish definitively that financial aid and persistence are related, and therefore that no additional research is needed? She found a "small" effect. Because money woes make it difficult for needy students to persist, and because financial aid converts this considerable disadvantage into a slight advantage, you might argue that even a small effect "in the right direction" establishes the efficacy of financial aid. But this conclusion may be premature. Effects differed across institutions, students, and measures, and the seven studies that controlled for academic ability found no positive effect on persistence. Additional research would certainly help to clarify these issues.

What direction might new research take, and how can it build upon the thorough review? Murdock addresses this very question:

> For more accurate measures of financial aid effect on persistence, researchers should try to include part-time students, transfers, and stopouts in their study population. These three groups compose a large percentage of the total student population, and how a study treats their persistence mediates the effect size. To adopt this recommendation, studies will have to measure persistence over a longer period of time than just one semester, one year, or even two years. Only thus will the true effect of financial aid on the total student population be determined.   (p. 96)

A good "next" study could build upon Murdock's work by including a broader cross-section of students and by collecting data for a longer period of time. Her careful review has refined the design of future research.

How to Conduct a Review

Carol Weiss has said that, until the 1970s, the best practical advice on how to review an extensive research literature was: read everything you can find, think carefully, and be smart. In a survey of 39 books, 87 review articles, and 2050 article abstracts discussing methods for reviewing the literature, Gregg B. Jackson (1980) concluded that systematic procedures were rarely presented or recommended.

What Jackson describes is the classic, narrative literature review. Narrative reviewers collect as many studies of a particular research question as they can find and try to synthesize the disparate results into a coherent story. Sometimes reviewers present lists displaying each study's results, often restricting these lists to studies that meet specific criteria, such as those with true experimental designs, those supporting a specific point of view, or those carried out by particularly highly respected investigators. Narrative reviewers use common sense to distill essential findings from the literature. Conflicting findings are pitted against each other. Often a reviewer simply declares a few very well-done studies "the winners" and encourages her readers to believe only them.

But is this the best way to carry out a narrative review? Just because the review is qualitative, must it be nonsystematic? Obviously not. A good narrative literature review is like any other piece of research: if it is to be successful, it must be methodical and systematic. Without systematic procedures for identifying existing studies and comparing their findings, the biases of any particular reviewer will affect the overall conclusions. Another reviewer examining available reports on the same research question could reach an entirely different conclusion.

You should be as systematic in your narrative research as you are in your regular research. Your review should adhere to the same high standards and adopt the same systematic strategies. The only difference is that your unit of analysis is "study," not "respondent." Try to be as objective as possible; do whatever you can to avoid letting your own biases influence your findings. Your review should include at least *five* steps. You should: (1) establish one or two questions that will drive your review; (2) examine a representative sample of studies from the full "population"; (3) record the study findings and characteristics; (4) "analyze" the recorded "data"; (5) interpret your "analyses."

Questions. Focus your review on two types of questions: questions about *substantive detail* (e.g., What student characteristics are related to persistence?) and questions about *research design and methodology* (e.g., What characteristics of research design are related to each study's findings about persistence?). You are reviewing the literature to learn about both *substance* and *method.*

Sampling. Be sure to include in your review a representative sample of all the studies that have been carried out (the population of available studies). Do not restrict your attention to published research. Because of journal acceptance and rejection practices, published research has an overabundance of "statistically significant" findings, and by examining only published results you can overestimate the frequency of truly positive findings. Take the time to track down unpublished studies, dissertations, technical reports, and internal memoranda. There is much research done in higher education at the institutional level that is never even submitted for publication. You should examine this too. *Fugitive documents* balance the picture of what has been done and what has been learned.

Data collection. In tables, charts, and lists systematically code and record the characteristics of every study and its findings. Pay special attention to methodology—who was sampled, how they were assigned to groups, what measures were used, what background influences were controlled, and so on. The relationships between different research designs and different findings provide valuable information for you when you design your study.

Data analysis. Examine the recorded "data" and try to generalize across studies. Synthesizing the literature is never easy. Findings will vary considerably. Use conflicts between findings to examine the effects of methodology. Examine the strengths and weaknesses of the studies, determine whether similarly labeled programs or treatments differ in important ways, and assess the impact of differences among the studies in settings and respondents. Take special care before concluding that an answer is "known."

Interpretation. Use your research review in several ways. First, consider the *focus* of previous research. Identify areas that have been thoroughly investigated versus those that need additional work. Direct your research to uncharted areas or to areas where conflicts still exist. Try to predict how your study will fit into an accumulating knowledge base when the next person reviews the literature, next year. Second, consider the *strengths and weaknesses* of previous research. Learn from both mistakes and successes. Were findings more impressive when certain types of measures were used? Be sure to ask why. Were findings larger for certain types of respondents? Be sure you understand why. Don't reinvent the wheel; improve it. Third, use *discrepancies* among studies to generate new hypotheses for your work. Have studies at public colleges found larger effects than similar studies at private colleges? Why do you think this differential exists? Is it attributable to different organizational structures? To admissions criteria? To curricula? Do you think that private colleges could learn something from what public colleges are doing? The other way around? Perhaps you should include these new hypotheses in your project.

EXAMPLE: *How to review the literature systematically: Developing a model of nontraditional undergraduate student attrition.*

Why do nontraditional students—older, part-time, and commuter students—drop out of school? Is it because they cannot find the on-campus supports they need, or because their off-campus commitments present major obstacles to persistence?

John Bean and Barbara Metzner's (1985) work on attrition of nontraditional students is an excellent illustration of how to review the existing literature for a specific research question. Noting that the literature on nontraditional students was sparse, Bean and Metzner carefully searched books, articles, dissertations, and ERIC clearinghouse documents. They identified 56 useful studies. They constructed tables summarizing the substantive findings and methodological details of each study. Their summary gives information on each study's location, target population, sample size, definition of "dropout," and statistical method.

Then, in a series of narrative sections, Bean and Metzner describe the relationship between the decision to drop out and five sets of "predictors"—intent to leave, and academic, psychological, environmental, and background factors. Each set of predictors includes several specific variables. For example, the environmental cluster includes information on finances, hours of employment, outside encouragement, opportunity to transfer, and family responsibilities. The authors discuss the effects of each predictor in turn, describing studies that focused on it, noting what was found, and identifying discrepancies among studies and relating them to the type of institution or analytic method.

Borrowing from theoretical models of attrition among traditional students, Bean and Metzner synthesize their findings into a comprehensive model of nontraditional student attrition. Within this model, they comment specifically on the limitations of previous research—they identify, for instance, that "more than half of the 40 studies from two-year colleges were exit or autopsy studies . . . [in which] control groups of persisters and tests of statistical significance were lacking" (p. 528).

Bean and Metzner's careful attention to the needs of future research makes their review particularly helpful to anyone planning a new project. For example, they argue that research at commuter schools should not emphasize variables measuring social integration, but rather students' external environment. They discuss the need to distinguish between part-time and full-time students and between older and younger students. They also suggest that the variables associated with persistence will differ depending upon student demographics. They stress how future researchers must be sensitive to these demographics. Their comprehensive review, and their suggestions for future research, are an asset for researchers planning to investigate attrition for nontraditional students, and an example to those intending a narrative literature review.

Meta-Analysis

In recent years, methodologists have developed more rigorous ways of *coding* and *analyzing* the evidence collected in a literature review. The new approach, which uses the power of *quantitative methods* to systematize the narrative review, is called *meta-analysis* (Glass, McGaw, and Smith, 1981; Cooper, 1984; Light and Pillemer, 1984; Rosenthal, 1984; Hedges and Olkin, 1985).

Rather than creating narrative tables of summary findings and then informally synthesizing these "data" by counting the number of studies "for" and "against" a particular finding, meta-analysis summarizes each study *numerically*. Study findings—either the relationship between predictor and outcome, or the differences among treatment groups—are recorded as "effect sizes." Study characteristics are recorded as categorical and continuous variables. Then, over all coded studies, meta-analysis uses descriptive and inferential statistical techniques to explore the dependency of effect size on the study characteristics. Larry Hedges and Ingram Olkin (1985) provide a compendium of useful strategies.

Two types of effect size are most common. If most of the studies you review have estimated correlations between predictor and outcome, then the *correlation coefficients* themselves can be used as effect sizes to summarize the study finding. Bigger correlations indicate stronger relationships. On the other hand, if most studies have compared means for groups of respondents, say students getting a new curriculum versus students getting an old one, then a *standardized mean difference*—the difference between the two group averages, expressed in standard deviation units—is the appropriate effect size. Bigger effect sizes usually indicate more successful innovations or curricula or treatments. Whether you compute the summary effect sizes as correlation coefficients or as standardized mean differences is largely irrelevant, because each of them can be converted into the other by simple arithmetic manipulation (see Glass, 1976; Hedges, 1983; Hedges and Olkin, 1985).

Once you have coded the effect size and study characteristics for each of the studies, you can begin the "analysis" phase of your review by exploring your coded data from study to study. What type of analyses should you perform? The typical quantitative research synthesis will address four questions.

1. *Are effect sizes consistent across studies?* If not, how do they vary? You can examine the empirical distribution of effect sizes over studies. Do they follow a recognizable pattern? Are they centered around zero or around some non-zero value? Is the distribution of findings dispersed or tightly clustered? Is it symmetric or asymmetric? (Light and Smith, 1971; Rosenthal and Rubin, 1986.)

2. *What is the average effect size over studies, and is it different from zero?* If the empirical distribution of effect sizes does not have an unusual shape, or worrisome outliers, then the average effect size across all studies may be a useful summary statistic. It gives you an overall impression of the relationships or group differences that other researchers have found. If it is non-zero, the new curriculum you are looking at is better, or worse, than the old. If it is approximately zero, the collective evidence is that the innovation you are examining is no different from the "old way." Take special care if the effect sizes have an unusual distribution. In these instances, the average effect size is less useful and must be interpreted extra carefully. For example, perhaps an innovation works especially well for freshmen but not for seniors; the empirical distribution of effect size may be bimodal.

3. *Are the effect sizes related to study characteristics?* When study findings conflict, their effect sizes differ. Are there some very large or very small effect sizes? Is there

anything unusual about these particular studies? Are differences in effect sizes related to how studies were designed? Do effects differ at private colleges versus public colleges? At four-year colleges versus two-year colleges? For freshmen versus upperclassmen? Do well-controlled studies show a stronger or a weaker impact for a new curriculum or advising system? (Light, 1979; 1984).

4. *Does publication bias exist?* Publication bias can seriously affect the findings of your review. If you synthesize results from published studies only, you will be excluding, unintentionally but systematically, all those studies that never found their way into print.

If findings in the "omitted" papers are similar to the findings in those that were published, you will be fine. If they are not, then looking only at published work means you are reviewing a biased subset of findings. Typically, this will cause you to overestimate effect size. This is because *statistically significant* findings are more likely to be submitted to, and accepted by, a refereed journal than *nonsignificant* findings (Greenwald, 1975; Rosenthal, 1978).

You should take two steps to deal with possible publication bias. First, because publication bias arises when only those studies that appear in journals are reviewed, we urge you to include unpublished work in your review. Second, you should estimate the size of the publication bias. You can separate published from unpublished sources in your review, and explore whether one type of source reports noticeably different findings from the other. If it does, then you should think hard about informally "adjusting" the recommendations of your reviews.

The strength of meta-analysis is its systematic nature. Another reviewer using meta-analysis to synthesize the same literature should arrive at the same results as you (Light, 1983).

EXAMPLE: *Using meta-analysis to refine your questions: The effectiveness of special programs for high-risk and disadvantaged college students.*

Since 1894, when Wellesley College implemented what may have been the first remedial course for college students, many colleges have instituted programs designed to help students who might have problems. Given all the resources expended, just how successful are such programs?

Chen-lin Kulik, James Kulik, and Barbara Shwalb (1983) conducted a meta-analysis of research on college programs for high-risk and disadvantaged students. They focused on programs defining risk in terms of low test scores, low high school achievement, low college achievement, or membership in a socioeconomically disadvantaged group. Using computer searches of three major bibliographic databases, they identified 504 available documents. Sixty studies that systematically compared similar groups of students who participated and did not participate in an intervention program were selected for meta-analysis.

Effect sizes were computed to summarize group differences (membership in remedial program versus no membership) on two outcomes: achievement (college GPA) and persistence (reenrollment during the study period). The authors also coded 12 study characteristics: 3 describing the program (e.g., intervention mode), 2 describing the setting (e.g., type of college), 5 describing the design (e.g., random assignment), and 2 describing publication history (e.g., published or unpublished document). We describe results for the 57 studies reporting data on GPA.

Effect sizes varied from a low of $-.41$ to a high of 1.00, and their empirical distribution was fairly symmetric with no unusual values. The mean effect size was .27, indicating that in the average study, students getting special help had GPAs .27 standard deviations higher than students not getting such help. Kulik and her colleagues translate these effect sizes back into GPAs as follows: "In the typical report, the GPA for students from the special programs was 2.03 in the latest semester studied; the GPA for control students was 1.82. Although positive and statistically reliable, the overall effect of special programs on GPA was therefore clearly small in size" (p. 401).

Examining the large amount of variation among effect sizes, the authors explored relationships between study findings and the 12 study characteristics. They discovered four systematic patterns. Effects were *smaller* among established programs, programs that looked at long-term GPAs, and programs that used remediation. A potential publication bias also was discovered: unpublished studies had a lower mean effect size (.07) than published studies (.31) and dissertations (.30).

What can a researcher interested in evaluating the effects of special-help programs learn from this meta-analysis? First, remedial programs can help, although their impact may be smaller than an administrator might hope. Second, different kinds of programs have different effect sizes. Programs using guidance sessions had the largest mean effect size (.41); programs using academic training and comprehensive support services followed (mean effect sizes of .29 and .26); and programs emphasizing remedial studies were the least successful (mean effect size of .05). Third, be sure to look at both long-term and short-term success. Short-term evaluations give an overly optimistic picture of efficacy; follow students for several semesters if you want to learn whether the program is really effective.

Correlation versus Causation

Many research questions in higher education ask about the association between predictors and outcomes. Joseph Seneca and Michael Taussig (1987) studied the relationship between an offer of financial aid (the predictor) and the decision to enroll at Rutgers University (the outcome). Sophia Mahler and Dan Benor (1984) examined the relationship between attending a teacher-training workshop (the predictor) and instructional behavior of faculty members (the outcome). Larry Weber, Janice McBee, and Jean Krebs (1983) examined the relationship between the type of examination given—in-class versus take-home—(the predictor) and the amount of "rampant cheating" (the outcome).

What does it mean to examine the relationship between a predictor and an outcome? When you speak of relationships, do you mean *correlation* or *causation?* Do you want to know whether the predictor and outcome are simply associated or whether a change in the predictor will actually change the outcome?

If you could observe a correlation only when variables were causally linked, this distinction would be unnecessary. Questions about causality would be answered by examining correlations. But for years, nonstatisticians such as George Bernard Shaw (1911) have pointed out that many things in life that are correlated are anything but causally linked:

It is easy to prove that the wearing of tall hats and the carrying of umbrellas enlarges the chest, prolongs life, and confers comparative immunity from disease . . . A university degree, a daily bath, the owning of thirty pairs of trousers, a knowledge of Wagner's music, a pew in church, anything, in short, that implies more means and better nurture . . . can be statistically palmed off as a magic-spell conferring all sorts of privileges . . . The mathematician whose correlations would fill a Newton with admiration, may, in collecting and accepting data and drawing conclusions from them, fall into quite crude errors by just such popular oversights.

The moral: correlation does not imply causality.

Yet, if your work is to influence policymaking, then it must examine causal linkages. Does a generous offer of financial aid *cause* students to enroll in our school? If it does, we might change our school's financial aid policy with the hope of improving our yield rate. Does teacher training *cause* professors to teach better? If it does, we might require all professors to participate in workshops with the hope of improving their performance.

At other times, we want to know only whether a predictor and an outcome are correlated, but we want to be sure the correlation is attributable to a direct relationship, not to other predictors we failed to study. We would want to be sure, for example, that the correlation between attendance at a teacher training workshop and performance in the classroom was not an artifact of differential attendance at the workshops caused by a tendency of professors who were better instructors to begin with to be more likely to participate in the training.

Establishing a Causal Link

Frederick Mosteller and John Tukey (1977) identify four conditions for demonstrating a causal link. First, you must show that a change in the predictor produces a change in the outcome: the outcome must be *responsive* to changes in the predictor. Second, you must show that there is *no plausible alternative explanation:* no rival predictor must be able to explain the correlation you have observed. One way to ensure this is to assign study respondents randomly to the various levels of the predictor. Random assignment makes this group membership uncorrelated with all other predictors, thereby ensuring that any effect you observe is attibutable to group membership. Without random assignment, you must systematically examine, and rule out, all plausible rival predictors. Third, you must have some idea what *mechanism* explains how a change in a predictor produces a change in an outcome. If you have a theory describing how the predictor affects the outcome, then when you find a relationship you can tell an appropriate story. Without a theory, you should not be looking for a causal link. Fourth, you must be able to replicate the correlation in different populations with different characteristics. If a link is found time and time again, the consistent pattern is far more compelling than each isolated result.

Can research on higher education meet these four criteria? The answer is yes. The challenge is to plan research that can uncover strong linkages supported by well-crafted theory. We address this challenge throughout this book.

When investigating causation, the key criterion is responsiveness. Responsiveness is the $64,000 question of applied research, especially policy research. It is not enough to show that a policy choice is *correlated* with an outcome. You should demonstrate that a *change* in policy— be it a change in teaching style, dormitory assignment, or class size—*changes* the outcome. After all, if a policy change will not change the outcome, why bother changing the policy?

Active intervention is the only way to demonstrate responsiveness. Relational studies cannot do so. Comparing the enrollment rates of students receiving financial aid with those of students who are not cannot tell us, with confidence, whether offering financial aid to more students would improve yield rates. Determining the effects of a policy change requires changing the policy and seeing what happens.

Because of the intimate link between causation and responsiveness, you should always *answer questions about causality, if at all possible, with randomized experiments.* When you conduct a randomized experiment, you are an "agent of change," intervening in the system and observing what happens. Randomization has another advantage as well; its "balancing" properties help rule out rival explanations of the correlation between predictors and outcomes. These properties combine to make randomized experiments the best, and to many methodologists the only, way to go.

EXAMPLE: *Establishing a causal link: Can you train teaching assistants to be better teachers?*

Widespread complaints about the poor teaching of teaching assistants (TAs) has led many colleges to offer programs designed to improve TAs' classroom skills. Kathleen Dalgaard (1982) evaluated the effectiveness of one such program by conducting an experiment with 22 graduate-student TAs in the business administration, economics, and geology departments of the University of Illinois, Urbana-Champaign. She divided the TAs by department and randomly assigned half from each department to a training group, which participated in six two-hour seminars and an individual videotape critique session with the seminar instructor, and half to a no-training group. All TAs were videotaped once before the training began and once five weeks later. Independent raters (unaware of group membership) gave TAs in the training group better ratings of overall teaching quality than TAs in the control group.

Dalgaard's study provides convincing evidence that TAs can be trained to teach better—that training causes improvement. By offering a program and randomly assigning TAs to groups, she acted as an "agent of change," intervening in the system and observing what happened. This allowed her to demonstrate responsiveness. Random assignment also ensured that the two groups of TAs were similar with respect to background characteristics such as initial teaching skill and motivation to participate in a training program. (Comparing initial teaching skill ratings for the two groups confirmed this comparability.) This helped Dalgaard eliminate plausible rival explanations of group differences. The training program was based upon well-known theories of teaching and teacher training. This helped her posit a mechanism whereby the training caused behavior to change. The only criterion she was unable to comment on was consistency, for her study was limited to 22 TAs. Replication was left to future researchers.

If randomized experiments enable you to make strong inferences about relationships between predictors and outcomes, why conduct relational studies at all? One reason is that some predictors simply cannot be manipulated. You cannot randomly assign participants to levels of sex, age, race, or class year, and so to learn about the relationships between these predictors and an outcome, you must examine them as they occur in nature. A second reason is that logistical, practical, or ethical constraints often preclude randomization. For example, you may not have enough dollars to randomly assign students to different financial aid packages. Without random assignment, you can only examine the statistical association between measures.

EXAMPLE: *Conducting a relational study: The effects of freshman orientation on student persistence.*

Many colleges and universities invite incoming freshmen to an orientation session held before the beginning of classes. Ernest Pascarella, Patrick Terenzini, and Lee Wolfe (1986) conducted a relational study at a private residential university to examine the impact of freshman orientation on decisions to drop out before sophomore year. The researchers studied 763 students who were part of a random sample of incoming freshmen, and who also filled out two questionnaires—one in early fall and one in late spring of freshman year. Information on persistence came from university records. Seventy percent of the incoming students attended orientation; 88 percent of them persisted until sophomore year. Orientation and persistence were strongly correlated: students attending orientation were more likely to continue than those not attending.

Had the researchers estimated only simple correlations, their results would not have been convincing, for common sense suggests that background characteristics of students, associated with the decisions to attend orientation and to persist in school, may have spuriously created this correlation. The authors also hypothesized that the effect of orientation on persistence might not be direct, but might operate by influencing social and academic integration, which in turn affect persistence.

To investigate these alternative hypotheses, Pascarella and his colleagues estimated a series of statistical models incorporating rival predictors, such as the students' gender, major, socioeconomic status, and academic preparation, and moderating predictors, such as freshman-year social integration, academic integration, and institutional commitment. They found that presence at orientation did not have a direct effect on persistence; the correlation between the two variables diminished after the other predictors were included. But orientation did have an *indirect* effect on persistence, through its strong relationship with social integration and institutional commitment, which, in turn, predicted persistence. They conclude that attendance at orientation has a positive, albeit indirect, effect.

Because attendance at orientation was voluntary, this relational study cannot demonstrate responsiveness, and as a single study, it cannot demonstrate consistency. But the researchers did an excellent job of considering the remaining two criteria. Their research was well-grounded in theories explaining the persistence decisions of traditional students, including the work of Vincent Tinto (1975), William Spady (1970), and J.P. Bean (1985). They clearly articulated and explored the mechanism whereby orientation affects persistence. Using sophisticated statistical analyses, they eliminated many *plausible alternative predictors,* thereby suggesting that the effects they found were not artifacts.

But the nagging question remains: Does orientation *cause* persistence? Pascarella and his colleagues are direct and to the point:

> Finally, and perhaps most importantly, the study has the obvious . . . problems inherent in correlational data. Students in the sample self-selected themselves into the orientation and nonorientation group. This necessitated statistical controls . . . While such analytical models are useful in portraying what the patterns of causal influence might look like, they do not provide the same order of control as that achieved by a randomized experiment . . . [T]he estimation of the effects of orientation experience . . . under more controlled experimental conditions is a fruitful area for future inquiry.   (p. 172)

Unfortunately, such speculation always haunts relational studies.

You must decide, early in the research planning phase, whether you are interested in correlation or causation. This decision, more than almost any other, determines much about your final design. If you want to establish causality, conduct an experiment. If you are content to establish an association, conduct a relational study.

The Wheel of Science

Throughout this chapter, we argue that effective empirical research must be guided by specific questions. You will not find what you have not sought. You will not be able to provide answers if you have not directly looked for them.

But isn't this premise a bit too simplistic? Isn't it possible to have tacit knowledge without having asked a question first? We often learn by direct experience unprovoked by interrogation. We observe first and then ask why. Can't we learn from data even if we haven't posed a specific question? Can't research proceed without questions?

Of course it can. At issue here, though, is how successful your project will be if you plan it without attention to specific questions. Research does not require the articulation of specific questions; the systematic *planning* of research does.

Philosophers of science distinguish between two modes of inquiry, one based on inductive logic and the other based on deductive logic. When you use inductive logic, you begin with observations and then explain what you have observed by generalizing. You move from particular instances to general principles, from facts to theories. In contrast, when you use deductive logic, you begin with a conjecture— a theory, hypothesis, or law—and then you collect data to test the accuracy of the conjecture. You move from general principles to particular instances, from theories to facts.

Is one mode of inquiry "better" than the other? Does "true science" require deduction? Is induction second-rate? For centuries, philosophers have pondered these questions, some arguing for induction, some arguing for deduction. Most agree that deductive research, so common in the natural and physical sciences, *is* scientific. But fewer agree about inductive research, so widespread in the social sciences. Some argue that induction cannot be scientific, others argue that as long as induction is accompanied by rigorous methods, it, too, *is* scientific.

We take a middle position. We believe that practical scientific inquiry blends deduction and induction, cycling endlessly between the two extremes. In the inductive phase, you reason from data; in the deductive phase, you reason toward data. Both modes of inquiry are essential. Induction helps us generalize and build new theories, which in turn generate new hypotheses for future deductive research. On and on the circle turns, new knowledge building on old in an endless spiral—theory to data, data to theory. Practical scientific inquiry becomes a wheel—the "wheel of science" (Wallace, 1971).

We do not argue that our position is the best possible one, but rather that it is practical and effective. *Inductive inquiry must precede and support your design plans.* Exploratory research focuses ideas and helps build theory. But by framing specific questions and testing particular hypotheses derived from theory you gain irrefutable knowledge about how the world actually works.

Even statistics, a field wedded to deduction and hypothesis testing, has spawned disciples of induction. John Tukey, the father of the movement known as Exploratory Data Analysis, has said: "We need both exploratory and confirmatory [research] . . . [new] ideas come from previous exploration" (1980, p. 124). Use data not only to *test* theory, but to *develop* theory. Good statistical analysis combines exploratory model-building and confirmatory testing of hypotheses.

A close reading of almost any empirical research report reveals an implicit acceptance of this position. Consider Carver and Smart's study of the effects of career classes on career development. This was a solid piece of deductive research, yet they based their study on theories of career development, vocational choice, and student-institutional fit that were exploratory results from previous studies. And Carver and Smart discuss new exploratory findings, such as the effect of a student's advisor on her career choice, that future researchers can reframe as testable hypotheses.

Our philosophy has two practical consequences. First, *design your study only after doing a healthy dose of exploratory work.* Use your eyes and ears. Use informal contacts with administrators, faculty members, and students. Use colleagues on other campuses. Use the research of others. *Be inductive.* Second, *design your study with clearly stated research questions in mind.* Questions are crucial to your project's ultimate success. They fuel the engine and turn the wheel of science. They may be broad in a descriptive study, or narrow in an experimental study, but they are still questions. *Be deductive.*

WHAT GROUPS DO
YOU WANT TO STUDY?

3

Before you can begin, you must ask: Whom should I study?
The answer comes directly from your research questions.
Suppose, for example, you want to examine the effectiveness of a new approach to teaching expository writing. To
supplement individual writing outside of class, each student will write collaboratively with a classmate for one
hour during each two-hour class. You hypothesize that collaboration will help students develop skills necessary for
revising and improving not only their joint writing, but
their individual writing as well.

At first glance, the goal here is to examine *students*. The
purpose of the innovation is to improve students' writing
skills, and the most direct way to assess improvement is to
study the changes in their skills over time.

But identifying a target group with a label as broad as

"students" is only the first step in selecting people for study. In which students are you *particularly* interested? All students enrolled in freshman writing classes? Only those who have poor writing skills, because they have the most to gain if the new approach is beneficial? Only those who have good writing skills, because they have the crucial foundation for advanced editing skills? The word "students" is a good characterization of the group you want to study, but it is only a starting point.

Taking a broader perspective, are you interested only in how students respond to the innovation, or also in how instructors respond? Does student collaboration free up some of the instructors' classroom time, enabling them to spend more time with individual students? Or does the need to orchestrate successful collaboration between students absorb even more instructor time, leaving less for individual students? Innovative programs may affect participants other than just the target group. Students enrolled in the freshman composition course may be your primary interest, but perhaps they should not be your sole interest.

A key step in designing research is to clearly specify, *before collecting any data,* which respondents are the focus of your study. In this chapter, we develop several themes to help you make this specification:

- *Provide a rationale for all your decisions.* You should have a clear justification for all decisions about the people you will study. Feasibility is important, but your respondents must be chosen because you are specifically interested in them.
- *Consider issues of generalizability.* Will others see your research as useful to them, or will your results be too specific to a particular set of places, persons, and times?
- *Consider different types of respondents.* Many interesting questions in higher education involve not just one type of respondent, such as students, faculty members, or departments, but the relationships between types of

respondents. How do student-faculty interactions affect students and faculty members? What characteristics of teacher behavior enhance student learning? Expanding the types of respondents will give you another window on the phenomenon under study. But beware: studies involving more than one type of respondent must be designed with special care.

Specifying the Target Population

The first step in identifying whom to study is to specify a *target population*. By doing this precisely, you can select a sample of respondents that is representative of that population. With an imprecise specification, you will never know how useful your results are.

How do you identify the target population? One way is to select a target population because of its *generalizability*. Researchers achieve generalizability by using target populations that include a *wide range of persons, places, and times*. The broader the definition of the target population, the more broadly applicable your results, and the more likely other researchers will see the relevance of your results to their interests. Donald Campbell and Julian Stanley (1963) refer to this feature as external validity—how well the findings of a study apply to external groups.

But broad applicability of results is not the sole reason for selecting a target population. Substantive questions also are important. You must decide on the particular group you wish to study. Whom is the new advising system designed to help? Who is at risk for dropping out? Who could benefit from teacher training? Research projects usually evolve from your observation, intuition, or need-to-know about a specific group. That group is your target population.

Generalizability and substance should be foremost in your mind when specifying your population. But as a practical matter, the target population must be delimited precisely by specific characteristics. You must identify which *persons,* which *places,* and which *times.* We have found that four sets of criteria help to identify a population: (1) inclusion criteria; (2) exclusion criteria; (3) expected effect size; and (4) feasibility.

Inclusion Criteria

The major question you should ask yourself when developing inclusion criteria is: Why? Why do I want to study these particular students? Why do I want to study what happened during this period of time? Why do I want to study what happened in this particular department? *You should have a sound rationale for identifying those individuals eligible to be included in the target population.* If you do not have such a rationale, redefine the target population until you do.

What constitutes a sound rationale? In the abstract, the adequacy of a rationale is in the eye of the beholder. But once your research is completed, the adequacy of your rationale will be judged by your audience, be it administrators, faculty members, policymakers, or even students. A sound rationale is thus one that is logical to your ultimate audience. It does not have to be elaborate.

To illustrate, suppose you are interested in investigating the relationship between financial aid awards to freshmen and the likelihood that a student will complete her degree. Your hypothesis is simple—a student who receives financial aid is more likely to persevere and complete a degree than one who doesn't. And as financial aid increases, so does the likelihood that a student will graduate.

What rationale can be used to specify a time horizon—the beginning and end points for your study? For a starting year, you might choose 1975 because of changes in financial aid policies in the mid-1970s. Financial aid data for students enrolled before 1975 may be noncomparable with data for students enrolled after 1975. Or perhaps you should limit your study to students who enrolled after 1982, the year the Reagan administration introduced dramatic changes in the Guaranteed Student Loan Program. Our point is not that certain years are "correct," but rather that you must articulate a defensible reason for selecting the characteristics that circumscribe your target population.

EXAMPLE: *Specifying the characteristics of your target population: How long does it take to earn a doctorate?*

Every year since 1938, the National Research Council has conducted the Survey of Earned Doctorates by sending a questionnaire to every person who received a doctorate from a U.S. institution. In addition to asking how long it took the student to complete his or her degree, the questionnaire includes items asking about academic topics (e.g., field of study, undergraduate school), financial topics (e.g., type and amount of financial support), and demographic topics (e.g., age, sex, race, citizenship, marital status).

Jamal Abedi and Ellen Benkin (1987) used these data to examine factors associated with the length of time it took graduate students at UCLA to earn doctoral degrees. Although data were available for every year from 1938 until 1985, the authors restricted their analyses to the 4,225 UCLA students (with complete data) who received their degrees between 1976 and 1985.

Why did they choose these beginning and end points? Abedi and Benkin explain: "We chose to limit our population to this 10 year span for two reasons: (1) During that decade there were no major external changes that would cause students to finish more quickly or more slowly, and (2) some of the items in the Survey of Earned Doctorates relating to the variables we wanted to study were changed in 1976 but have not been changed since that time" (p. 7). This justification blends a substantive rationale with a practical rationale.

Exclusion Criteria

When deciding whom to *include,* you are also deciding, explicitly or implicitly, whom to *exclude.* For example, the broad definition of the target population for the financial aid study excludes some potential participants because it restricts attention to incoming freshmen. With this definition, students who transferred to the school as upperclassmen would be excluded from the study.

Exclusion criteria should be stated as explicitly as inclusion criteria. As with inclusion criteria, exclusion criteria must be supported by a rationale. With the financial aid study, for example, you might argue that transfer students have a different time trajectory from that of incoming freshmen. The rationales for inclusion and exclusion help determine the soundness of your design.

Many beginning researchers incorrectly assume that the exclusion of some individuals from the target population limits the relevance of a study. This simply is not correct. Excluding people makes the choice of target population more focused and deliberate. When this happens, your research is more likely to be successful because extraneous factors, which might vary tremendously in a less controlled target population, are being "held constant." In essence, by excluding some individuals from the study, you can obtain better information, although on a narrower population.

EXAMPLE: *Excluding subgroups can improve your design: Modeling MBA student performance.*

Richard McClure, Charles Wells, and Bruce Bowerman (1986) studied the predictors of academic performance among MBA students at Miami University in Ohio, using as their initial target population students who began the program during a single semester. They then excluded three small subgroups. First, they eliminated students who had withdrawn from the program after completing only one, two, three, or four courses, arguing that such a small number of completed courses could not yield a good estimate of a student's GPA. Second, they eliminated international students, "because of the unknown impact on performance of learning in a language and culture that is not native and because of the difficulty in reconciling their undergraduate grade point averages and GMAT scores with the corresponding scores for American students" (p. 183). Finally, they eliminated part-time students, because they hypothesized that the academic performance of part-time students would be adversely affected by professional responsibilities. These three criteria led to the exclusion of 37 students from the sample, yielding a reduced sample of 89 students.

The exclusions paid off. Three previous studies of the relationship between undergraduate GPA/GMAT scores and graduate GPA had been inconclusive. But by excluding the three subgroups, the authors were able to detect a moderate relationship. The narrower definition of their target population allowed them to find stronger effects, although their results are now generalizable, in turn, to a narrower population.

Expected Effect Size

Some researchers choose a target population because of the size of the effect they expect to find. Choosing a group for which you expect to find a large effect is not uncommon or unreasonable. For example, you might target a new writing program to students who have weak incoming writing skills. There are two good reasons for such a strategy: (1) if you find an effect for *this* group, future research can see if it holds also for *other* groups; (2) if you do not find an effect for this group, chances are you will never find it for any other group.

When you choose a target population because of an expected effect size, the generalizability of your findings to other populations is not a concern; indeed, generalizability is usually sacrificed. Instead, the goal is to find evidence to support or refute your hypothesis for *some* group.

In what types of target populations are you likely to find

large effects? Effects tend to be larger within groups in greater need or at higher risk—in other words, those with the most to gain. A study of the relationship between financial aid and college persistence, for example, might focus on a target population in great need of financial aid— such as students with lower family incomes or smaller savings. For these students, adequate financial aid may be a major determinant of whether they graduate. If a broader cross-section of students were studied, one that included some wealthier students, financial aid might appear to have a smaller effect.

The decision to specify a target population in greater need, or at higher risk, may also direct you to certain institutions or periods of time. For the financial aid study, for example, you might collect data at a college where students come from poorer families. Or you might collect data only after the restrictions on the Guaranteed Student Loan Program were tightened. By limiting your focus in these ways, you diminish the generalizability of your findings. But you trade generalizability for an increased probability of detecting an effect. Limited generalizability may be a small price to pay if you can demonstrate an important relationship. A subsequent study can then determine if the detected relationship holds for other, broader, populations.

EXAMPLE: *Choosing a target population in which the effects are likely to be large: Helping college women "break the ice."*

Charlene Muehlenhard, Laurie Baldwin, Wendy Bourg, and Angela Piper (1988) investigated the efficacy of a computer program designed to help college women start and maintain conversations with college men. Rather than using all college women as their target population, they focused their energies on a special subgroup—shy heterosexual women. To identify this group, they administered the Survey of Heterosexual Interactions for Females (SHI-F) to 663 women enrolled in introductory psychology classes at Texas A&M University, and then selected a sample of 45 women with especially low SHI-F scores, which indicate shyness.

These 45 women were randomly assigned to one of three groups: (1) a group that used a computer training program designed to help women initiate and maintain conversations with men; (2) a group that read a written training manual with the same goal; and (3) a no-intervention control group. The researchers also selected 15 women with average SHI-F scores as a "not-shy" control group. The 60 women filled out the SHI-F two more times— once immediately following treatment, and once four months following treatment.

Both the computer program and the written intervention worked. The women in these groups had much higher SHI-F scores at both posttest and follow-up than they had at pretest. The women in the two control groups had relatively stable SHI-F scores, stably high for the not-shy control group and stably low for the shy control group. By using a shy target population, the researchers were able to demonstrate the effectiveness of their training program. Had they focused their efforts on all women, their program might have had little effect.

Feasibility

A study, however well designed, will never succeed if it cannot be implemented. Research projects formulated in a vacuum, without attention to institutional policies, practices, constraints, and philosophies, will not get off the ground. Practical issues such as access, rapport, and logistics must be considered carefully when specifying a target population. Carrying out a study without the formal cooperation of an institution and the informal cooperation of its staff is virtually impossible. Cooperation is part and parcel of applied research.

Feasibility is a necessary, *but not sufficient,* condition for choosing a target population. Some researchers use feasibility as the primary rationale for specifying a target population, and ignore more important considerations such as generalizability. This practice is reflected in the many research studies in higher education conducted in one institution or a single professor's class. Some of these researchers have chosen the particular target population simply because their own institution and their own classes provide an easy source of data. This is inappropriate if the students enrolled in a specific college or course are not the *real* target population.

Not all single-institution studies are inappropriate. The effectiveness of a new policy at your institution can be best evaluated at your institution. If your research question is specific to one college, then it is entirely appropriate to use that college, and that college alone, to provide the target population. This rationale underlies much of the internally sponsored institutional research conducted on the nation's college campuses. Our point is that if you want to make a *broader* statement about a policy, you should evaluate it in a more general setting. To answer the latter type of research question, choosing a single institution will not be sufficient.

Tradeoffs among the Different Criteria

Several of the criteria for specifying a target population conflict. If you choose a target population because you expect to find a large effect, you may sacrifice generalizability. If you choose a target population because of its generalizability, you may sacrifice feasibility. How can you reconcile these conflicts? Although no single answer is applicable in all research settings, we have several recommendations.

Taking a sound rationale as a given, what do we think about the other criteria? In general, we believe that generalizability takes precedence. The broader the target population, the broader the statements you will be able to make about the effects you have investigated. You will be able to figure out if the relationships you have found for the group as a whole hold up across subgroups, or if they are weaker in some subgroups and stronger in others.

There are some research situations in which maximizing the effect size, or ensuring feasibility, should take precedence. We recommend choosing a target population in this way when conducting small-scale research in which the success of your study will be restricted by other factors, such as sample size or the practical difficulties of doing field research. This is particularly true during the early stages of a research enterprise, when investigators have yet to demonstrate *any* effect, let alone a generalizable one that holds across colleges, persons, places, and times.

Where Should You Conduct the Study?

Within the United States, there are some 2000 four-year colleges and universities and 1000 two-year colleges. Each college has its own hierarchical structure of divisions, departments, courses, residence halls, and so on. So when deciding *whom* to study, you must simultaneously decide *where* to conduct the study. Over and above the practical questions of feasibility and access, you must make some substantive decisions. In the sections that follow, we suggest several ways to decide where to conduct a project.

Everywhere

To achieve results that are generalizable across the broad sweep of American higher education, you could argue that the "best" study would be conducted using students and faculty members from the entire pool of postsecondary institutions in the United States. If you collect data on a random sample of students or faculty members from these 3000 schools, the results are easily generalized to students throughout the country.

Using this definition, the series of studies conducted by the Cooperative Institutional Research Program (CIRP) are among the most generalizable higher education research projects. Initiated in 1966, CIRP collects data on randomly selected college students at approximately 300 schools, using a national probability sample. The specific institutions vary from year to year, but collectively, each year's data are generalizable to the college student population of the United States for that year. In addition, the CIRP data base includes longitudinal information on approximately 200,000 students at these schools.

The target population of the CIRP studies is broad, and the researchers use well-designed and stringently applied principles of probability sampling to select institutions and respondents. With such large amounts of data available, the researchers are able to compare findings across different types of persons (e.g., men versus women), places (e.g., private versus public institutions), and times.

Many Places

Many research questions can and should be studied using more narrowly defined target populations, such as groups of institutions meeting a set of specific criteria. For example, L. David Weller (1986) studied the attitudes of college deans toward grade inflation: Did deans perceive grade inflation as a problem on their campuses, and what factors did they identify as contributing to it? Instead of surveying the deans of all undergraduate institutions, Weller limited his study to two types of schools: liberal arts colleges and colleges of education. He identified all American schools in these two categories, and randomly selected 205 liberal arts colleges and 100 colleges of education for study. Seventy-five percent of the deans of liberal arts colleges and 71 percent of the deans of colleges of education stated that grade inflation was a current concern on their campus. Because Weller used good random samples, his results are generalizable to all liberal arts colleges and colleges of education.

Selected Places

Generalization requires you to specify a broad target population, and then randomly sample from that population. But often you cannot select a representative group of institutions. For example, the intense requirements of data collection within each school may make it impossible to collect data at more than a handful of convenient schools.

An alternative method for achieving generalizability is to identify a small number of locations or "sites"—schools, colleges, or departments—where you will collect data. Within each site, you collect data on many respondents. When analyzing the data, you determine the extent to which the findings are consistent across sites. Consistent results suggest that findings are generalizable to a broader group of sites, while inconsistent results suggest that findings may be specific to the sites you have studied.

The challenging question then becomes: "Which sites should I select?" Although it might seem that the best solution is to select a few sites at random, such a strategy is usually ineffective. A handful of sites rarely gives a good picture of the entire target population, so a better strategy is specifically to select sites that meet certain criteria. In other words, with only a limited number of sites, consider *purposeful selection,* rather than relying on the idiosyncrasies of chance. Two broad strategies are available for purposefully selecting a limited number of sites: choosing sites that seem "average," or intentionally choosing contrasting, extreme sites.

Average sites. The use of "average," "typical," or "modal" sites has a long and rich history. The Lynds (1926), in their famous study of the patterns of relationships in a community and in families, used a single site, Middletown, as the prototype of a small American town. Medical researchers at Harvard and Boston Universities have, since 1965, studied a cohort of 20,000 residents of Framingham, Massachusetts, to understand patterns of health and normal aging (Dawber, 1980).

The problem with selecting average sites is that it is difficult to identify and defend any particular typical site. Is Oberlin typical? Typical of what? Midwestern liberal arts colleges? How about Louisiana State? Typical of universities? How similar are UCLA and the University of Wisconsin? What precisely is meant by "typical"? If your research question focuses on what *most* students experience, then perhaps large public universities are modal. If your research question focuses on what the public believes a certain kind of student experiences, perhaps small private colleges are modal.

The key point is that *there is no such thing as a typical college, typical department, or typical residence hall.* If you decide to study one or two schools, departments, or residence halls, don't make grand claims of generalizability based on artificial typicality. Generalize your results only to the particular schools or departments you have actually studied.

Contrasting, divergent sites. An alternative strategy for choosing a few sites is to select sites that differ dramatically on characteristics you expect to influence your results. If you find similar patterns of findings across widely disparate sites, there is a reasonable chance they generalize beyond the few locations you have studied. If you fail to find similar patterns across disparate sites, your findings probably do not generalize; they are site-specific.

EXAMPLE: *Using disparate sites to achieve generalizability: Do attrition rates differ by race?*

Jack Bynum and William Thompson (1983) studied racial differences in the rates at which college freshmen persisted until graduation, stopped out temporarily, or dropped out permanently. Because the researchers expected that the educational trajectories of students would differ dramatically by institution, they examined the trajectories for 1120 freshman who entered four small American colleges in the fall of 1977.

To broaden the generalizability of their findings, Bynum and Thompson carefully selected the four schools to represent "sharply diverse educational philosophies, constituencies, students and environmental settings" (p. 41). Although they did not give the names of the schools, to preserve anonymity, they described them in broad outline. College A was a state university serving predominantly white, middle-income students; College B was a state school serving predominantly black, lower-income students; College C was a private university attracting middle- and upper-income students from all over the country; College D was a private school closely affiliated with a small Protestant denomination, whose white and black lower- and middle-income students came from the Southwest.

Attrition patterns differed dramatically by college: Colleges A, C, and D—which were disproportionately white—had substantially higher dropout rates for black students; College B—which was predominantly black—had substantially higher dropout rates for white students. A reader could interpret the inconsistent findings for the two racial groups as suggesting that the dropout patterns were school-specific. But the *consistent pattern* of racial differentials according to the majority or minority status of the racial group at the school suggests a generalizability that would have been missing had a single institution been chosen. Had Bynum and Thompson examined only predominantly white institutions, they would have (incorrectly) concluded that black students are always more likely to drop out.

The authors acknowledge the limitations of a four-site study, concluding their article by saying: "While these findings appear conclusive, the authors extend cautious generalizations beyond these four particular schools. We would welcome replication of our methodology and the reexamination of the same variables in freshman classes at other institutions" (p. 48).

Selecting Your Sample

Most researchers use one of two types of sample selection: probability sampling or convenience sampling. In a *probability sample,* every member of the target population has a known, nonzero probability of being included in the sample. Because all the probabilities of selection are nonzero, every member of the target population has some chance of being included. If the probabilities of selection are the same and independent for all members of the target population, the probability sample is called a *simple random sample.* If the probabilities of selection differ across subgroups of the target population, called strata, the probability sample is called a *stratified random sample.*

Probability samples are a paragon of high-quality research. When you study a probability sample of respondents, you can be confident your results will generalize to the target population from which you chose them. Only probability sampling procedures produce samples that truly "represent" the target population. Most statistical techniques assume that the observations being analyzed are a random sample from a target population. So if you are to interpret the results of subsequent statistical analyses correctly, you should use probability sampling methods.

Nevertheless, many researchers resort to studying *convenience samples.* A convenience sample is just what its name implies—a sample of respondents selected simply because they are easy to get. In a convenience sample, each member of the target population does not have a known, nonzero probability of selection. Some members are more likely to be selected, others are less likely to be selected, and still others have *no chance* of being selected. As a result, convenience samples are not representative of the target population, and results from convenience samples cannot be generalized to the target population. In technical terms, we say that convenience samples are *biased.*

What precisely is wrong with convenience samples? An extreme example illustrates the general problem. A professor wants to evaluate student opinion of her performance in a large lecture course. Rather than administer a questionnaire to a probability sample of students taking her course, she decides to ask all students who come to her office hours during a three-week period in the middle of the semester to fill out her questionnaire. Lo and behold, the students give her high marks for accessibility, openness, and willingness to talk to students. How useful are her results? Not useful at all, because her convenience sample is likely to have been severely biased. Students who come to a professor's office hours have already, perhaps implicitly, decided that the professor is accessible, for if she were not, why bother coming? By involving only those students who come to office hours, the professor is "stacking the deck" in her own favor. The biases in convenience samples are not always so obvious. But because they can be severe, we strongly discourage the use of convenience samples.

Sampling Frames

The first step in drawing a probability sample is to construct a list of all members in the target population. The list need not be elaborate, but it must be complete. It should list *all members of the target population, without exclusions or duplications.* After all, if a respondent is not on the list, she has a zero probability of selection, and this violates one of the crucial tenets of probability sampling.

Developing a sampling frame is one area in which higher education researchers have a great advantage over many other social scientists. Unlike researchers who study broadly defined community-based populations, a higher education researcher is typically interested in a narrowly defined target population—the student body, or the faculty, or the alumni. Detailed lists of the members of these target populations are usually available from the institution, often from routine management records. Registration, payroll, and admissions files, for example, provide ready-made lists of people eligible for sample selection.

Although omissions are probably the most common problem when developing a sampling frame, you should also check for duplications. Duplications can arise when a researcher uses two or more lists to develop a master sampling frame. For example, Seymour Sudman (1976) describes a study of students and staff conducted at the University of Illinois, Urbana-Champaign. From two published directories, one of students, one of staff, an initial sample of 1145 names was selected. Ninety-six names appeared twice, once as students, once as staff, so the sampling frame actually included only 1049 unique names. (Most of the duplicates were graduate students.)

Try to eliminate duplicates from the sampling frame. Otherwise, you may contact some people twice, wasting precious resources and producing an unintended decrease in the final sample size. Duplicate entries also distort the probability sampling mechanism. People listed twice have higher probabilities of selection than people listed once. Because the higher probabilities of selection are unknown, this violates the principles of probability sampling. When duplicates do arise, consult a book on sampling for advice on handling the duplication.

Different Sampling Strategies

With your sampling frame in hand, you can select a probability sample. Several excellent books on sampling describe the details of how to assign identification numbers to units in the sampling frame and then select respondents for study. In this section, we concentrate not on the details of drawing the sample, but on the principles for deciding whether to use a simple random sample or a stratified random sample.

Simple random samples versus stratified random samples. Table 3.1 presents the number of doctoral students at the Harvard University Graduate School of Education in December 1986. The students are classified by their department affiliation: Administration, Planning and Social Policy (APSP); Human Development, Reading and Counseling (HDRC); and Teaching, Curriculum and Learning Environments (TCLE). Across all departments, there are 801 students, with approximately equal numbers in the two largest departments (around 300 in each) and about half as many in the smallest department. Suppose you want to select a probability sample of 80 graduate students. The simplest approach is to select a simple random sample. Sample sizes for two such random samples are presented in the third and fourth columns of Table 3.1. Within the limits of sampling variation, both random samples are representative of the target population of doctoral students at the School of Education who were enrolled in academic year 1986–1987. This representativeness is guaranteed by the principles of probability sampling, and any uncontrolled sampling variation can be automatically accounted for in the subsequent statistical analyses.

TABLE 3.1. DOCTORAL STUDENTS, HARVARD GRADUATE SCHOOL OF EDUCATION, DECEMBER 1986. COMPARISON OF RANDOM SAMPLING, PROPORTIONAL ALLOCATION, AND EQUAL ALLOCATION STRATEGIES.

| Department | Number in population | Simple random sample | | Stratified random sample | |
		I	II	Proportional allocation	Equal allocation
APSP	326	30	36	33	27
HDRC	313	26	34	31	27
TCLE	162	24	10	16	27
Total	801	80	80	80	81

However, each of these simple random samples has a minor problem. Random sample I is disproportionately weighted toward students in TCLE. Although this is the smallest department, the sample (at random) included somewhat more TCLE students than their proportional representation in the population. Random sample II has the opposite problem—it is disproportionately weighted toward students in HDRC and APSP. It contains fewer students from TCLE than their proportional representation in the population. Despite these problems, *because both these samples are probability samples, any ultimate statistical analyses will lead to findings that can be generalized back to the target population from which they were drawn.* But we see that, with simple random sampling, there can be some imbalance in the proportion of respondents selected from each of the departments.

For these reasons, we suggest that you use *stratified random samples.* To select a stratified sample, you divide the sampling frame into discrete groups called strata. In Table 3.1, the strata are departments. In other examples, they might be colleges, schools within colleges, types of students, and so on. Each member of the target population must be classified into one, and only one, stratum. Thus, the strata are mutually exclusive and exhaustive categories.

Two types of stratified random sampling strategies are most common. *With proportional allocation, each stratum's sample size is proportional to the relative size of that stratum in the target population.* As shown in the fourth column of Table 3.1, APSP, the largest department, with $326/801 = 40.7$ percent of the target population, would get 40.7 percent of the sample, for a sample size of 33. HDRC, with $313/801 = 39.1$ percent of the target population, would get 39.1 percent of the sample, for a sample size of 31. The balance of the sample would go to TCLE, with 20.2 percent and a sample size of 16. Proportional allocation improves upon random sampling by ensuring that the sizes of the samples within strata *perfectly* reflect the sizes of the strata within the target population. Under proportional allocation, the TCLE sample would always have 16 students; no more, and no less.

With *equal allocation,* sample sizes within strata are predetermined to be equal, regardless of the sizes of the strata in the target population. A sample size of 81, for example, would include 27 students from each of the three departments. With equal allocation, APSP and HDRC are undersampled, while TCLE is oversampled. Equal allocation is the probability sampling strategy that ensures you will have sufficient people to answer your questions within each stratum.

When should you stratify? Stratified sampling is most helpful when the distribution of respondents in the target population is unequal across strata, as in our simple example. For example, stratifying by student gender when studying undergraduates at a college with an unbalanced sex ratio helps to ensure an adequate representation of both men and women.

The advantages of stratified sampling diminish when the target population has an approximately equal distribution of respondents across strata. For example, although it is easy to stratify a population of undergraduates by class year, it generally has little value, because most colleges have approximately equal numbers of students enrolled in each class year. So even a simple random sample of students would yield approximately equal numbers of students for each class year unless the sample is very small and erratic. However, *you will never be disadvantaged if you do stratify* providing you have the resources to do the job well. In fact, if information on substantively interesting stratifiers is available, we believe that you should *always* stratify. You cannot lose, and you *may* gain.

When deciding between equal and proportional allocation, you should examine the degree of imbalance in the sizes of the strata in the target population. When the strata are about the same size, the two stratified sampling strategies will yield approximately equivalent results, and so proportional allocation is preferable simply because it is easier. When the strata differ in size, equal allocation is more attractive. By using equal allocation, you can ensure that you will have enough data within each small stratum to be able to examine differences among subgroups.

However, the gains associated with equal allocation come at a cost. Because in equal allocation the number of people within each stratum of the sample is not proportional to the number of people within the corresponding stratum in the population, you must use sampling *weights* in all subsequent statistical analyses. Cases from oversampled strata get smaller weights and cases from undersampled strata get larger weights. Without weights, the sample data would disproportionately represent the oversampled strata. For a more detailed discussion of weighting, and how subsequent statistical analyses are affected by it, see the books by Richard Jaeger (1984) or Seymour Sudman (1976).

More Than One Type of Respondent

Answering some research questions will require data on more than just one type of respondent. For example, studying the improvement in writing among students enrolled in collaborative writing classes only tells you how the *students* respond to the innovation. To understand fully the effects of the writing program and to examine how it could be implemented on a larger scale, you need data from the *faculty* too.

Using several types of respondents reveals a broader perspective and allows you to answer questions about the *relationships* between the responses from different types of respondents. In the writing program, for example, you might examine how faculty techniques and student performance are associated. Do students learn more when the instructor actively encourages collaboration by working with students in class? Or do students learn more when the instructor is passive and leaves collaboration to the students? We call such questions *cross-level* because they focus on the relationships between data collected for different "levels" of respondents. Fundamental questions about how higher education actually functions are frequently cross-level. They often take the form: How do features of the institution and the classroom affect student learning?

When research questions involve several types of respondents simultaneously, deciding precisely whom to study becomes complex. It is harder than specifying a single target population and drawing one random sample of respondents. To study multiple types of respondents, you must specify the target population for *each* distinct type, and develop plans for selecting people from each population. Designing studies with several types of respondents therefore involves taking into account the hierarchical organization of respondents.

In this section, we describe two approaches for designing studies with more than one type of respondent: the selection of *unlinked samples* and *linked samples*. We describe each and outline its strengths and weaknesses.

Unlinked Samples

To select unlinked samples, you independently specify each of the several target populations. In an unlinked study of student and faculty views about academic advising, for example, you would specify two separate target populations: one of advisors, one of students. Each target population would have its own set of characteristics for specifying membership. You might try to make the specifications similar—for example, you might limit both target populations to certain schools or departments within your college—but such a correspondence is not necessary. To select the respondents, you draw two probability samples: one from each of the two target populations.

When different types of respondents are studied using unlinked samples, the data sampled from the different populations cannot be routinely linked together on a case-by-case basis. For example, if you ask each student for the name of her advisor, and you separately ask each professor for the names of her advisees, you will likely be missing detailed advisor data for some students and detailed advisee data for some faculty members.

Because the two samples are not coordinated, you must conduct two separate analyses: one for advisees, one for advisors. You might look for similar patterns, but you cannot compare each advisor's responses with her advisees' responses. Therefore, unlinked samples do not allow you to study cross-level questions.

Collecting data on several types of respondents with an unlinked design is tantamount to conducting independent studies of the same topic in different populations. Each study is designed to be optimal for describing the responses of a specific population. But because responses cannot be linked across samples, you cannot fully capitalize on the different sources of information to answer cross-level questions.

EXAMPLE: *Using unlinked samples: Attitudes toward advising.*

Gary Kramer, Norma Arrington, and Beverly Chynoweth (1985) conducted an unlinked study of the undergraduate academic advising system at Brigham Young University. Three distinct target populations were identified: students, faculty, and administrators. For each target population, the researchers selected a stratified random sample of respondents: students were stratified by academic level and college; faculty were stratified by academic rank and college; and administrators were stratified by college. Each type of respondent received the same questionnaire, thereby allowing the researchers to compare aggregate responses from each type. For example, they report that "twenty-seven survey items [out of 49] produced significant differences among all subpopulations . . . Students consistently rated survey items lower than did faculty or administrators" (p. 27). Because the samples were not linked, however, the researchers could not determine whether student-advisor pairs were likely to share the same views.

Linked Samples

To draw linked samples, you collect data on "related" respondents with the goal of analyzing the relationships between their responses. In a linked study of academic advising, for example, you would collect data on advisee-advisor pairs, so that you could not only profile responses for advisees and advisors separately but also study the assocation between the two sets of responses.

Linked designs yield much more information than unlinked designs. Because respondents are linked, you can address both single-level and cross-level questions. For example, you can describe not only student views and faculty views but also the relationship between the two. However, this additional information comes at a cost. Designing a linked study of multiple respondents is much more difficult than designing an unlinked study. The major difficulty lies in the selection of the base target population, and the way you subsequently identify the linked respondents.

The crucial question to consider when designing linked samples is: *Which type of respondent should be the base target population?* In the advising study, for example, should you first select a target population of advisees and then collect data on their advisors, or should you first select a target population of advisors and then collect data on their advisees? There is no single correct answer to this question. Different approaches are best for addressing different types of research questions. The problem is that although each approach is optimal for some questions, it is suboptimal for addressing others. Thus, choosing the base target population is a crucial decision. It requires you to decide which types of research questions are most important to you.

To understand the consequences of choosing different base target populations, compare two linked samples for the advising study. Suppose your primary interest is in the advisors' viewpoints. Then you should select a target population of advisors, such as all faculty members in the college of liberal arts. You might stratify this target population by department, and select a proportionately allocated random sample of advisors from each department. Your sample would include more people from departments with larger faculties. It would represent the target population of advisors—faculty members in the college of liberal arts—very well.

How should you select a linked target population of advisees? The best approach is to identify all advisees assigned to each advisor in your sample. Then select a sample from this target population by taking either all advisees assigned to the selected advisors or a random sample of advisees assigned to the selected advisors. The key point is that, either way, the advisee sample is explicitly linked with the advisor sample. This design is excellent for describing advisors, and for comparing their responses to their advisees' responses.

If you are most interested in the viewpoints of advisees, use a different approach. Select a target population of advisees, such as all juniors and seniors in the college of liberal arts. You might stratify this target population by department, and select a proportionately allocated random sample of advisees from each department. Your sample would include more students from the more popular departments. It would represent the target population of advisees—students in the college of liberal arts—very well. To obtain a linked sample of faculty, select the advisors of all the sampled students. This design is excellent for describing advisees, and for comparing their responses to their advisors' responses.

Nonresponse Bias

In Chapter 8, we discuss how big a sample you need to take for a particular project. Yet the best-laid plans can lead to disaster if you fail to reach all the people you target. We have seen response rates vary enormously, from a low response of 2 percent in an alumni survey, to a 94 percent response rate in a study of extracurricular activities and part-time work at Harvard (Angelo, 1989).

The biggest threat to your results when many people in your target sample don't respond is nonresponse bias. You face such bias if the people you reach give different answers, on average, from what those you didn't reach would have told you. Since it is hard to know with any confidence what nonrespondents would tell you, you face an unknown level of bias when nonresponse is high (Hoaglin et al., 1982).

Before we worry about bias, what can cause nonresponse to a survey? Here are some possibilities:

- People are not at home (or at work, or in the dorm, or in class) when the interviewer visits or telephones.
- People are at home but choose not to respond.
- People are unable to respond—the respondent may be ill, or not understand your question.

- People are not found. They have moved, for example, or dropped out of a degree program.

How to Fix It

The best strategy for dealing with nonresponse bias is to work to minimize it at every stage in your survey. In Chapter 9, we argue that a pilot study is a wonderful tool for trying out questions, refining your survey instrument, and even field testing your ability to reach respondents in your target sample. We recommend you use a pilot study to make sure your instrument is clear, and that you will reach the students or alumni or faculty you hope to reach. But even good surveys will have some nonresponse. What can you do to deal with nonrespondents? Here are three steps.

Callbacks. These are common. If you want to do a personal interview with many students who live in campus dormitories, you probably won't get them on the first try. A student may be out. She may be at class. She may be busy with another activity. So calling back will involve going back a second, third, fourth time. If this seems like an extraordinary amount of work for little payback, you will be heartened that the statistician Leslie Kish (1965) has pointed out that, while the first call yields the most responses, the second and third calls often have higher rates of response per call.

Sampling nonrespondents. You can take a small random sample of nonrespondents, and work very hard to track down their responses. In an alumni mail survey, for example, this strategy will be especially effective. You can use personal interviews with a small sample of nonrespondents, and generalize your findings to all nonrespondents. This procedure will reduce bias dramatically.

Replacing nonrespondents. Professional survey organizations use nonrespondents from earlier surveys as replacements for people who are nonrespondents in a current survey. This procedure is especially useful if you conduct repeated surveys and maintain files of nonrespondents from past surveys, as alumni and development offices often do. The idea behind this procedure is that nonrespondents to different surveys at least have nonresponse in common. A good fallback strategy for estimating what a nonrespondent would have said in the current survey is to coax a nonrespondent from an earlier survey to respond this time.

EXAMPLE: *Reducing nonresponse bias in an alumni survey.*

While abstract claims about nonresponse bias are common, few researchers have examined how common such bias is, or estimated its size. Roseann Hogan (1985) has done this, and her findings are fascinating.

Hogan examined annual surveys conducted on the graduate cohorts of thirteen junior colleges in 1980 and 1981. The two surveys were done in dramatically different ways. The 1980 effort surveyed alumni by mail. No follow-ups were conducted. Cover letters were not included at all colleges. Return envelopes and postage were not provided. The response rate was 35 percent.

In contrast, the 1981 alumni survey was far more intense. Three mailings were conducted. The first consisted of a cover letter, questionnaire, and stamped, addressed return envelope. The second mailing was a postcard reminder. The third was a remailing of all the original material complete with stamped return envelope. The response rate nearly doubled, to 67 percent.

Hogan then asked how responses to each survey compare with known data for all alumni. She found that women are far more likely to respond than men (in both surveys); younger students are more likely to respond than older students (in both); whites are more likely to respond than blacks (in both); and the mean GPA of respondents was consistently higher than mean GPA for all graduates. Just as she expected, the 1981 survey generated responses that were much closer to known population values than did the 1980 survey.

Hogan reports one big surprise. Both surveys found just about identical correlations between variables. For example, the correlations between educational goals and salary, time it took to get a job, and employment characteristics are nearly identical for the two surveys. Hogan concludes her report by speculating that while lower response rates may lead to response bias for estimates of sex, race, income, or GPAs, the bias in estimating correlations between pairs of variables, such as GPA and salary, may be low even when response rate is low.

WHAT PREDICTORS
DO YOU WANT TO STUDY?

4

Researchers are seldom interested solely in the average value of the outcome in their sample. They are more likely to investigate *systematic variation* in the outcome. They might ask, for instance: Are men more likely than women to succeed in the study of mathematics? Are students with better school grades more likely than less able students to be satisfied with the college experience? Would a mentoring program increase the chance that freshmen who choose a major in science will graduate? Each of these questions expresses interest in the *connection between a particular predictor* (gender, school grades, membership in a mentoring program) *and an outcome* (success in math, satisfaction with college, graduation). Whether the predictor defines a characteristic of the individual (gender, school grade) or describes something that is done to the individual (membership in a mentoring program) the question is the same: What is the relationship between predictor and outcomes?

Many predictors are likely to be associated with any given outcome. How can you decide which of the dozens of potential predictors you should concentrate on? How can you ensure that your study will be able to demonstrate a causal link between predictor and the outcome if there is one? How can you decide when a relationship you observe between predictor and outcome is not attributable to other effects that you simply failed to examine? How can you refine your definitions of predictors to maximize your chance of finding potential effects?

In this chapter, we show how you can make these decisions. In your study, you should:

- *Acknowledge that different types of predictors require different strategies for detecting their effects.* Many different predictors may be associated with your outcomes. Carefully select those you are most interested in and design your study with them in mind.

- *Rule out rival explanations for observed relationships between predictors and outcomes.* Some apparent effects can actually be attributable to other predictors you did not examine. Learn how to identify alternative explanations, and how to design your study to eliminate them.

- *Maximize variation in the predictors.* The greater the variation in the predictors, the more likely that your study will be able to detect a relationship between predictor and outcome.

- *Consider statistical interactions among predictors.* The relationship between a predictor and an outcome may not be the same for all people; it may differ according to levels of another predictor. To detect such statistical interactions, you must include both predictors in your design.

Types of Predictors

The term *predictor* is a broad one. It encompasses all the potential variables that you might relate to whatever outcomes you are studying. Some predictors describe membership in treatments or innovations, such as a new course or a new method of teaching. Others describe respondent characteristics, such as number of hours of students' part-time work, or achievement test scores, or attitudes toward college success. You examine these characteristics as they occur naturally in the population. Any research project may involve either or both types of predictor.

Membership in an Innovation

Begin with an innovation or a new program. You usually evaluate its effect by comparing what happens to respondents in the program with what happens to those who are not in the program. A new curriculum, new advising system, new financial aid package, or new living arrangement is an innovation.

Categorical variables describing membership in an innovation are popular predictors, and their effects on the outcome are often relatively easy to evaluate. This ease stems from the large degree of *researcher control*. If you design your evaluation of an innovation *before* the program begins, you have control over many aspects of the research—who gets the treatment, how much of the treatment they get, how long they receive the treatment, what else happens to them while they are getting the treatment, and so on. Equally important, you also have control over who does *not* receive the treatment. When you have this control, you can apply it by using a totally impartial mechanism: random assignment. The actual process of random assignment can use coin flips or a table of random numbers.

The big point about random assignment is that an unbiased independent arbiter, *not the researcher and not the study participants,* determines who gets assigned to which treatment. In Chapter 6, we discuss methods of assigning people to levels of a predictor describing treatment, and comment further on the tremendous advantages that random assignment confers on your research.

EXAMPLE: *Innovations as predictors: Evaluating the efficacy of self-paced computer instruction.*

Microcomputer-based instructional programs are enjoying increasing popularity on college campuses. One reason for this popularity is the hope that these computer programs can adapt to individual differences in students' abilities, learning styles, and learning strategies, thereby allowing students to learn at their own pace. Ideally, self-paced instruction should promote student learning.

One hundred first-term freshmen at Ohio State University participated in a randomized experiment conducted by John Belland and his colleagues (1985), on the effectiveness of a self-paced software program for teaching about the systolic and diastolic operation of the heart. The researchers hypothesized that while some degree of self-pacing was good, some *external* pacing, whereby students moved forward in the program regardless of how well they were doing, would be even better.

Students were randomly assigned to one of four groups: three with differing levels of self-pacing and external pacing, and one no-treatment comparison group. The predictors in this experiment were the categorical (or dummy) variables describing the membership of each student in one or another of these treatments. The research question—whether knowledge of the operation of the heart differed by treatment group—simply asks whether the categorical membership variable is a good predictor of student learning.

For the three treatment groups, the researcher's control over the research setting was remarkable:

The study was conducted during two consecutive days. Four two-hour time periods were blocked off during which subjects reported to one of two separate microcomputer based laboratories. All subjects in a particular laboratory at a particular time experienced the same instructional program . . . The groups were not aware of any differences in the programs experienced by the other groups, nor were they aware that requests for feedback and overall time for instructional program completion were being monitored. When subjects completed the instructional program, they were sent to another room to take the five achievement tests . . . All three instructional program pacing groups received the same instructions and received their achievement tests in the same order.   (p. 193)

Because the treatment was a one-time use of a computer program, the investigators were able to control each student's experience fully. Students who were not learning the material using the microcomputer program could not go to the library and supplement their learning with a textbook. Nor could they ask their roommates or a professor for help. Students in all groups had identical experiences except for the degree of pacing of their software program. And because of the random assignments, the investigators could be sure that, on average, groups were similar in their abilities, learning styles, and learning strategies.

Respondent Attributes

Characteristics of people, such as their sex, race, date of birth, or year of entry into school, are beyond your control. You cannot change them. Yet such characteristics may be the most powerful predictors of many higher education outcomes, so the value of asking questions about them is high.

Without control over *who* has *what* features, whether a predictor is "truly" related to an outcome is difficult to establish. Critics can argue that other predictors you failed to examine are really what produced the effect. A classic example of such a "spurious" relationship was described by the English statistician George Yule (1926). He found a strong positive correlation between membership in the

Church of England (the predictor) and the annual suicide rate (the outcome). Of course, no one believed this association was causal (Yule himself called it nonsense); it was attributed instead to a third variable—the passage of time—that had simultaneously produced changes in both church membership and suicide.

Critics can also argue that self-selection of respondents into "groups" created nonequivalencies between the respondents and led to your findings. For instance, consider the relationship between years of education (the predictor) and salary (the outcome) for graduates of an economics department. The observed correlation may be *negative*—the more education a graduate has, the lower his or her salary! However, perhaps another predictor—employment sector— has confounded the relationship between education and salary. Graduates with bachelor's and master's degrees generally choose to work in the corporate sector (which pay higher salaries), while graduates with doctorates choose to work in academics or government (which pay lower salaries). On the surface it appears that education is *negatively* correlated with salary, when in fact, controlling for employment sector, the variables are positively associated.

Rival explanations always loom large as alternatives that might explain away such findings. The challenge for designing good research is to presumptively rule out as many rival explanations as possible.

Alternative explanations of relationships among predictor and outcome are not always easy to rule out, and this makes the problem very serious. For example, Rick Schrager (1986) studied fraternity members at the University of Illinois at Urbana-Champaign and found a correlation of .60 between students' college GPA and their reports of the fraternity's emphasis on academic achievement. Did the fraternity's emphasis on academic achievement *cause* students to perform better? Or did the better students select academically oriented fraternities because they thought they would fit in better? It's difficult to say, but both explanations probably have an element of truth.

EXAMPLE: *Studying respondent attributes: The effect of same-sex and cross-sex role models on the subsequent academic productivity of scholars.*

Elyse Goldstein (1979) reported on the relationship between the gender of doctoral degree recipients, the gender of their advisors, and their later research productivity. Her study provides a good illustration of the problems inherent in examining the effects of respondent characteristics. Goldstein collected data on 110 students who earned their doctorates between 1965 and 1973 at New York University, City University of New York, or the New School for Social Research. Twenty-six were men who had female advisors, 29 were men with male advisors, 30 were women with male advisors, and 25 were women with female advisors. Students with advisors of the same sex wrote more articles (an average of approximately 2 articles during a four-year postgraduate period) than did students with advisors of the opposite sex (who had an average of approximately .5 articles during this period). The effect was consistent for both men and women.

What can we conclude about the relationship between gender of advisor and later research productivity of the students? Correctly, Goldstein interprets her results with caution: "A causal relationship between scholar/advisor sex and academic productivity cannot be inferred. We have no way of knowing whether male and female subjects in same-sex groups would have performed even more successfully had they had opposite-sex advisors" (p. 409). She points out how participant selection bias may have influenced the findings—more ambitious or more able students may have sought out same-sex advisors, hoping to establish a long-term mentoring relationship. As long as students are free to choose their advisors and advisors free to choose their students, selection bias cannot be ruled out. Without random assignment of students to advisors, we will never be able to determine whether findings such as these are attributable to the sex matching of advisors and students, or to other, unexamined characteristics of the advisors and students.

The Important Role of Variation

Bigger things are usually easier to detect than smaller things. This simple principle applies not only to everyday life but to research as well. When a predictor is related to an outcome, the magnitude of the outcome will be detectably different at different levels of the predictor. The stronger the relationship, the larger the differences in outcome among levels of the predictor.

The relationship between part-time work and student performance illustrates this. Before you can conclude that these variables are related, part-time work must have a sufficiently adverse affect on student grades; the grades of students engaged in different levels of part-time work must be detectably different. If the effect of part-time work on grades is dramatic, and is noticeable even among students who only work a few hours per week, a study to detect the effect would be easy to design. For instance, you could compare the GPAs of working and nonworking students, and because the effect is so large, it would be noticeable even with a modestly sized sample. But if the effect of part-time work on grades is small, then a study to detect the effect would be harder to design. You could still compare the GPAs of working and nonworking students, but you might not be able to separate real effects from sampling variation.

The key message is that, unless there is variation in *both* the outcome and the predictors, no effects can be detected. Or conversely, if you ensure large variation in the outcome and the predictors, then any effects that are present are more likely to be detectable. Therefore, you should always plan your study so that, by design, as much variation as possible is built in to both the outcome and the predictors. Or, at least, so that none of the variation that occurs naturally *in the population* is unknowingly sacrificed *in the sample* by poor design.

Stratifying to Ensure Representative Variation

You can build adequate representative variation into your sample by using stratified sampling (Chapter 3). Whether your predictor is categorical—perhaps describing an innovative treatment—or continuous, the strategy is similar. Simply stratify according to values of the predictor and draw separate random samples within each stratum. Stratifying the predictor ensures that the sample contains a full range of different sorts of students. Drawing the sample randomly from within each stratum then ensures a representative variation in the outcome. Thus, the likelihood that a given effect will be detected is increased.

EXAMPLE: *Stratifying to ensure variation: Minority students' involvement on campus.*

Glenda Rooney (1985) used a stratified sample to examine minority students' involvement in minority student organizations at the University of Wisconsin at Madison. Because she expected that student involvement would differ for the specific minority student organizations on campus, she stratified the target population into four groups: Afro-Americans, Asian Americans, Hispanics (Chicanos and Puerto Ricans), and Native Americans. Noting that the sizes of the groups in the target population were very different, and wanting to be sure that she could compare responses across minority groups, she oversampled the smallest stratum (Native Americans) and the combined stratum (Hispanics), to ensure adequate representation of all five minority groups. The stratified sampling paid off. It was the Native American students who had the highest participation rate. Because they were the smallest subgroup, she might have not been able to detect this effect had she not used a disproportionate stratified sample.

Sometimes information on the stratifiers is not easily available. In that case, consider using a *screening sample*. First select a large sample from the target population. Then, for each participant, collect information on the stratifiers and stratify the screening sample. Then select a subsample for in-depth data collection.

If the target population is accessible, such as students in your classes, a screening approach may be feasible. But because a screening sample must be much larger than the final sample, screening costs can be high. When a screening sample is not feasible, because of logistics or resources, consider stratifying by an another variable, highly correlated with the one you want. For example, if you want to stratify freshmen by writing ability, instead of collecting writing samples for a large screening sample, use data from English achievement tests. These scores are not perfect predictors of writing ability, but they are sufficiently correlated with it. Stratification based on these tests would ensure representation of people with different writing skills in your sample. The achievement test scores are for sampling purposes only, and measures derived from actual writing samples become predictors in your subsequent analyses.

Don't Restrict the Range

If, for any reason, the range of values of the predictors or the outcomes are restricted in any way, then their net variability will be decreased and the likelihood of detecting an effect will be diminished. In practice, you can restrict range in at least two ways: (1) by using measuring instruments with coarse, limited scales so that "observed" scores do not adequately represent "true" values; (2) by studying unnaturally restricted or homogeneous samples. The first of these is relevant to all empirical research and can be ameliorated by the building of better and more reliable measures (see Chapter 7). The second—the problem of enforced homogeneity—is a particular problem in higher education.

Many studies examine the relation between academic qualifications of incoming freshmen and college GPA. In a 1977 report issued by the Educational Testing Service, Susan Ford and Sandy Campos summarize the results of 827 such studies. They found median correlations of .32 (for SAT math), .37 (for SAT verbal), and .52 (for high school record). But when Ford and Campos estimated the same correlation coefficients using a subsample of 84 studies where the median verbal SAT score of the students was 550 or greater, the median correlations dropped to .26 (for SAT math), .33 (for SAT verbal), and .45 (for high school record). Why? Because the more select subsample was more homogeneous and led to a restriction of range in both the predictor and the outcome. A strong relationship in a *heterogeneous* group is diminished in homogeneous subgroups.

Range restriction gets worse as the sample becomes more homogeneous. As a result, single-institution studies, which are limited to students who met the institutional criteria for admission, are especially susceptible. Paul Schaffner (1985) examined the predictive validity of high school academic qualifications among students at Bowdoin College, which since 1970 has not required applicants to submit SAT scores. Approximately 31 percent of students who matriculate at Bowdoin do not submit SAT scores. Using data from the remaining 69 percent, Schaffner examined the relationship between freshman GPA and the same three characteristics examined by Ford and Campos. He found correlations of .28 (for SAT math), .36 (for SAT verbal) and .37 (for high school record). Schaffner comments that although the correlations for the two types of SAT scores were similar to what Ford and Campos found for selective institutions (such as Bowdoin), the correlation for high school record was lower than expected. Schaffner speculates that Bowdoin's optional-SAT policy, which emphasizes high school records, may have inadvertently restricted the range on this variable even more than might be the case at other selective schools.

EXAMPLE: *The effects of range restriction: Does coaching improve students' SAT scores?*

Dean Whitla (1988) describes a study conducted in 1987 among freshmen enrolling at Harvard University. He asked students who took the SAT *twice* to report whether they had attended a coaching program. Students who reported attending coaching programs gained an average of 94 points between tests; students who reported not attending coaching schools gained an average of 67 points. The 27-point difference between the two groups was well within the standard error of measurement, and thus Whitla was unable to decide whether coaching made any difference.

Can we conclude that coaching has *no* effect? This is a complex question, involving issues of statistical power (Chapter 8), generalizability of findings at an institution such as Harvard to other colleges (Chapter 3), and the accuracy of self-reported measures of coaching courses (Chapter 7). But let us ask about restriction of range here. Whitla points out that since students admitted to Harvard are a selected group, it is more difficult to detect an association between their SAT scores, or changes in their SAT scores, and any predictor, such as attending an SAT coaching class. To investigate the true effects of coaching on SAT performance, a research design should include students with a broad range of SAT scores.

Continuous versus Discrete Measures

Many predictors are, by their very nature, discrete and categorical. Either a student receives the new curriculum or she receives the old one. She majors in the humanities, the physical sciences, or the social sciences. She lives in a sorority house, a dormitory, or off-campus. Each category of these predictors simply names the group to which a student belongs. Variation in the values of these predictors over people is fixed once the levels of the variable have been decided.

Other predictors are measured along an underlying quantitative continuum. Incoming qualifications measures, such as SAT scores, achievement test scores, high school GPA, and high school rank, are all continuous predictors, as are student age, number of credits taken per semester, and amount of financial aid. On no account should perfectly good continuous predictors like these be artificially reduced to a small number of discrete categories. Incoming students should not arbitrarily have their SAT scores classified as "high," "medium," or "low." Amount of financial aid should not be dichotomized into "no aid" and "some aid." The very act of categorization reduces the intrinsic variation in the predictor and throws away information.

In fact, some predictors often treated as discrete should always be reconceptualized as continuous if that is possible. For example, the class enrollment of a single student can be measured categorically (enrolled versus not enrolled). But a better representation might include hours of attendance at class or level of participation, both of which are continuous and consequently much more informative. Participation in intramural athletics is usually treated as categorical (participant versus nonparticipant). But number of hours spent in practice, number of games played per year, and number of sports played are all continuous variables and may better represent the student's commitment to intramural athletics.

Continuous predictors are all around us. But if they are so common, why are so many studies designed to incorporate only discrete predictors? The answer is simplicity. When planning a project, many researchers find it easier to conceptualize their predictors as discrete so that they can regard their research as comparing the "haves" with "have-nots." You can always improve your research by treating your predictors as continuous variables. The improvement arises not only from being able to design more variation "into" your predictors but also from being able to take advantage of more powerful statistical techniques to handle your analyses (see Chapter 8).

A consideration of the effects of part-time work on academic achievement illustrates this point. Rather than designing a study of part-time work as a comparison between two groups, you should define part-time work as a continuum, measured in number of hours per week. Combining all students who work part-time into a single, monolithic group is inefficient. Because the number of hours worked per week is reasonably easy to measure, it is *the* predictor to use. Maximize the sample variation in this predictor by including in your sample as many students as possible who work very few hours, and many who work lots of hours.

Planning to use continuous outcomes and predictors has a great side benefit: nonlinear relationships between the predictor and the outcome become easier to identify. Suppose, for example, you want to examine the relationship between the number of hours students spend studying and their performance on exams. Literature on preparation and stress suggests that the relationship is nonlinear: for modest amounts of time, the more a student studies, the better her performance; but once a student exceeds an "optimal" number of hours, performance drops. How can you detect nonlinearity? By examining students who have studied for various numbers of hours, you derive a better picture of the relationship between preparation time and exam performance. If you categorize preparation time by grouping students into predefined hourly ranges, then you may uncover a less interpretable pattern.

Just as it makes no sense to artificially categorize a

perfectly good continuous predictor, neither does it make sense to select out groups that are *extreme* on the predictor ("very high" and "very low") for comparison (on the outcome). Unfortunately, this strategy is very common and has an apparently convincing appeal. If you fail to find differences in outcome between these extreme groups, then it is hard to imagine exciting findings emerging from more ordinary comparisons. However, by choosing extreme groups, you are not only throwing away crucial information—the participants who fall between the extremes—with subsequent loss of power, but when you do detect differences in outcome across extreme groups, generalizing your findings can be chancy. Perhaps the students with the extreme values are simply "outliers." You could argue that if they are unusual with respect to the predictors, they might also be unusual with respect to the outcomes. Choosing to study only unusual, atypical cases is logically defective.

EXAMPLE: *Investigating extreme groups: Do low-achieving and high-achieving fraternities attract different kinds of students?*

Fraternities enjoy differing reputations, some emphasizing social life, others community service, and still others academic performance. Roger Winston, Steven Hutson, and Sue McCaffrey (1980) examined whether differences in orientation toward academics accounts for some of the variation in academic achievement across fraternities.

Two extreme groups of fraternities differed significantly with respect to emphasis on academic achievement, independence, and intellectuality. They did not differ significantly on SAT scores. Finding no differences in SAT scores among the two extreme groups, the authors conclude that "differences in academic abilities of members do not account for the differential academic performance of fraternities" (p. 452). But finding differences in social climate measures that one might expect to be associated with academic performance (academic achievement and intellectuality), they also conclude that in high-achieving houses, "there is not only concern for grades . . . but also concern for intellectual development beyond assigned classroom activities" (p. 453).

How does their selection of the six most extreme fraternities affect our confidence in their findings? Because they found no differences in SAT scores for these extreme groups, it seems reasonable to conclude that, at this university, there is no relationship between fraternity academic standing and incoming SAT scores. This is especially plausible because the relationship between academic standing and incoming SAT scores is unlikely to be nonlinear.

But the use of extreme groups may color your views about differences between high- and low-achieving fraternities. The authors find that 44 percent of the variation in academic achievement scores is attributable to a single categorical variable: fraternity type. Their use of extreme groups may give an exaggerated impression of the relationship between academic achievement scores and academic standing of fraternities.

Other Reasons for Selecting Predictors

Most predictors are included in your study because you want to learn about how they relate to particular outcomes. When you evaluate an innovation, for example, the categorical variable describing membership in the innovative treatment or control groups is the predictor. When you study the relationship between admissions data and college GPA, the admissions data are the predictors. The predictors are the "question variables": they are selected because you think they are substantively interesting or important.

But sometimes you should incorporate other predictors into your design for two other reasons: (1) *to disentangle the effects of the substantive predictors from the effects of other, less-important, "background" characteristics;* (2) *to determine whether two (or more) predictors interact in their relationship with the outcome variable.*

Predictors as Covariates

Some predictors are measured in a study simply as interesting background characteristics. They are then included in the eventual statistical analyses as covariates, so that the influence of the key substantive predictors on the outcome can be evaluated in the presence of the background effects. When you include covariates in your analyses, you are trying to distinguish the variation in the outcome that is attributable to the covariates from the variation that is explainable by the key substantive predictors. For example, examining the relationship between entering SAT scores and freshman GPA may make more sense when socioeconomic status has been included as a covariate so that the effects of SAT score and background can be separated.

If the covariates and the "substantive" predictors are only weakly related, or unrelated, to one another, this strategy works well. But when the covariates and the primary predictors are strongly related, the teasing out of the separate influences may be difficult, perhaps impossible. To illustrate, suppose you are investigating the relation between athletic participation and scholastic achievement, perhaps represented by college GPA. Does involvement in sports reduce college GPA? The crucial predictor is whether or not a student plays on a team. But many other things affect academic performance, and athletic participation is only one. So to disentangle how athletics affect academic performance, you must include covariates in your analyses.

Now suppose you collect data on just two predictors—incoming SAT scores and participation in athletics—planning to include incoming SAT as a covariate when you evaluate the relationship between athletic participation and college GPA. You will find it difficult to separate out the effects of incoming SAT and athletic participation on college GPA because these two predictors are strongly related to each other. Athletes often have lower SAT scores than nonathletes, so you often find an inverse relationship between athletic participation and incoming SAT scores. This correlation makes it difficult, perhaps impossible, to evaluate the unique effects of athletic participation on academic accomplishments.

Suppose on a simple graph you plot GPA as a function of both incoming SAT scores and whether or not each student participates on an athletic team. You will probably find two effects. First, students with higher incoming SAT scores have higher college GPAs. Second, athletes have lower GPAs than nonathletes. Can these two effects—the "athlete" effect versus the "SAT" effect—be disentangled? The dilemma is that, because athletes have lower SAT scores than nonathletes, a selection bias exists. Perhaps the poor academic performance of college athletes is attributable not to their participation in athletics but to their weaker academic preparation, which in turn is reflected in lower SATs. Perhaps these students would have low GPAs even if they had not played sports. And perhaps the non-athletes would have just as high GPAs even if they *did* participate in sports. You cannot tell, because you have too little data on athletes who enter well-prepared, and on nonathletes who enter poorly prepared. *The most sophisticated statistical analyses will not enable you to disentangle the effect of incoming SAT from the effect of athletic participation.*

When the effects of two predictors are hopelessly entangled in this way, we say the predictors are *confounded.* In this example, participation in athletics is confounded with incoming SATs. The two groups in our study (athletes and nonathletes) are too different with respect to a background characteristic (incoming SAT scores). Because of this, you are unable to separate the effects, to control for the selection bias.

Statistical techniques find it very hard to resolve this problem of confounding, for it is a problem of design, not a problem of analysis. Statistical techniques such as regression analysis will only be successful if the confounding variables are not highly correlated with the crucial predictors you most care about. If a covariate *is* highly correlated with a key predictor, there is no way to disentangle the effects by analysis. No, the problem can be resolved only by design. *You can reduce the high correlation between confounding variables by using the principles of stratified sampling.* For example, you could resolve the confounding of incoming SAT scores and athletic participation by stratifying the incoming class of 3000 students at a large state university by athletic participation (athlete/nonathlete) and combined SAT score (perhaps using three strata: below 900, 900 to 1100, and 1100 or more). This solution is illustrated in Table 4.1.

Notice that membership in one group (athlete versus nonathlete) is highly related to membership in the other

TABLE 4.1. DESCRIPTION OF PROPORTIONAL-ALLOCATION SAMPLE VERSUS EQUAL-ALLOCATION SAMPLE FROM A TARGET POPULATION: STRATIFYING TO ELIMINATE CONFOUNDING.

	SAT score			
	<900	900 to 1100	>1100	Total
Target population				
Athletes	300	150	50	500
Nonathletes	500	1000	1000	2500
Total	800	1150	1050	3000
Proportional allocation				
Athletes	30	15	5	50
Nonathletes	50	100	100	250
Total	80	115	105	300
Equal allocation				
Athletes	50	50	50	150
Nonathletes	50	50	50	150
Total	100	100	100	300

group (low, medium, or high SAT scores). In the target population, the majority of all athletes entering have SAT scores lower than 900, whereas the vast bulk of nonathletes entering is equally divided between the upper two categories of SAT. Your challenge is to select students into your sample to eliminate the confounding.

Suppose you can afford to select a sample of 300 students. You could use proportionate allocation, taking 10 percent of the students from each of the six strata defined in Table 4.1. But unfortunately, proportionate allocation replicates in the sample the confounding of SAT scores and athletic participation in the population. Of the 300 students in a proportional sample, only 5 would be athletes with SAT scores over 1100. Only 15 would be athletes with SAT scores between 900 and 1100. With these small sample sizes, incoming SAT and athletic participation would remain correlated and you could not disentangle the effect of athletic participation from that of incoming SAT on college GPA.

What changes with an equal-allocation sample? Athletic participation and SAT scores are no longer confounded in the sample. Athletes as a group are oversampled, and athletes with high SAT scores are oversampled even more. Nonathletes as a group are undersampled, and nonathletes with high SAT scores are undersampled even more. This over- and under-sampling unlinks the two predictors, enabling you to disentangle the effect of athletic participation from the effect of incoming SAT in subsequent analyses.

Interactions as Predictors

Researchers mostly ask questions about *main effects*. Does persistence in science differ by sex? By membership in a mentoring program? By the availability of a new financial aid package? However, there is sometimes a different relationship between a predictor and an outcome for different types of respondents. For example, the relationship between financial aid and persistence in science may not be similar for all sorts of students—it may differ depending on the student's financial need. Financial aid may have a larger impact among needier students than among less needy students. A new collaborative writing program may not be as effective for English majors as for nonmajors. When this happens—when the effect of one predictor, such as financial aid, or an outcome differs across levels of another predictor, such as need—we say that the two predictors *interact*. If you do not design your study to answer questions specifically about interactions, you may not gather enough data in each important subgroup to conduct the necessary statistical analyses later. For example, suppose only one-quarter of the students taking writing classes are not English majors. Then a small random sample of students in writing classes will have few nonmajors. There may not be enough of the nonmajors to allow you to figure out whether the program is particularly effective (or ineffective) for them.

Even when you collect data on many students in each subgroup, values of one predictor can be confounded with values of another. Suppose you want to evaluate the differential effectiveness of a writing program for two subgroups: (1) majors versus nonmajors, and (2) good writers versus poor writers. In the real world, you might expect English majors to have better writing skills than nonmajors. Of course, not all English majors are good writers, nor are all nonmajors poor writers. But suppose the two are strongly related. After collecting data on the writing programs, what will you conclude if the writing of the English majors improved more than that of the nonmajors? That the program is more effective for English majors? Or that it is more effective for students who are initially better writers? Because membership in one category (major) is confounded with membership in the other category (initial writing skill), you will have a difficult time disentangling main effects from potential interactions among these predictors and the treatment (the writing program) in the prediction of ultimate writing skill.

No amount of statistical analysis can solve these problems. To avoid them, *you should design questions about interactions between predictors directly into your study.* By specifying, in advance, the interactions in which you are interested, you can make sure you have enough students in each combination of predictor values. You can then be sure that when your data are analyzed, you will have enough students in each important stratum to seek out potential interactions.

Putting this recommendation into operation is similar to resolving the problem of confounding variables—you do it by stratified sampling. Stratify by the two predictors you think will interact, and then select separate random samples from each group.

This is precisely what Elyse Goldstein did when selecting her sample of doctoral students to investigate relationships between gender of student, gender of advisor, and later research productivity. Her initial target population was 481 doctoral degree recipients, divided into strata as shown in Table 4.2. By sampling approximately equal numbers of students within each of the four cells specified in the table, Goldstein was able to (1) ensure that she had enough students with female advisors; and (2) ensure that sex of advisor was almost unrelated to sex of student. This equal-

TABLE 4.2. MATCHING ADVISOR TO ADVISEE BY GENDER: GOLDSTEIN'S STRATIFIED SAMPLING STRATEGY.

		Advisor gender in target population		Advisor gender in stratified sample	
		Male	Female	Male	Female
Student gender	Male	260	35	29	26
	Female	155	31	30	25

allocation sampling prevented the gender of student and advisor from being confounded and enabled Goldstein to examine the interaction between the two predictors.

The Integrity of Your Treatment

When your key predictors describe participation in an innovative treatment group or a control group, there are additional issues that you must consider when designing your study. You must ensure that each participant receives the same "standardized" treatment. You must plan to monitor and measure the implementation of the treatment, perhaps with a view to accounting for any variation in implementation when analyzing your data and presenting your findings. You must be aware that uncontrollable outside influences may mediate the effects of the treatment, especially when the treatment is of long duration. We discuss each of these issues briefly below.

Standardizing the Treatment

In an ideal study, everyone in each treatment group has an identical, "standardized" experience. If the treatment is a new advising system, each student should have an advisor who does similar things. For example, each student should have the same number of hours of contact with an advisor. If the "treatment" is part-time work, each student should work a similar number of hours at a job with similar demands. Such levels of control are very difficult for researchers to achieve.

Short-term treatments are probably the easiest to standardize: the briefer the experience, the less opportunity for uncontrolled variation. When you are investigating longer-term programs, treatment standardization is more difficult if not impossible. Suppose you want to evaluate a new computer-based mathematics course for all entering freshmen who are not mathematics majors. The treatment, of course, is the new program. But this treatment will differ in many subtle ways among students. Not all students who enrolled will attend every class session. Not all students will complete every assignment. Not all students will pay equal attention in class. Not all students will spend equal time on the computer. Indeed, not all students will even complete the course. Although you want to evaluate "the course," different students are actually getting different treatments.

How can such a treatment be standardized? The guiding principle is to work hard to make the stimuli that form the treatment as similar as possible. If different instructors are implementing a new curriculum, make sure they have been similarly trained. Provide each instructor with a reading list, a set of homework assignments, and topics for unwritten assignments. Encourage them to use similar grading criteria. Ensure that each class has approximately the same number of students. If scheduling permits, make sure they meet at roughly the same time of day on the same day of the week. Require every student to spend at least three hours per week logged onto the computer. Higher education is an arena in which such standardization of treatment is often relatively easy to achieve.

The same principle applies to the comparison group: its experiences should also be standardized. The successful evaluation of a treatment's effect depends upon making an appropriate comparison (see Chapter 5). So the experiences of students in a comparison group should also be as homogeneous as possible. When comparing the new mathematics course with the old one, see if any students in the comparison group are taking another mathematics class. Check whether they are taking any related courses, such as computer programming or applied statistics, that may influence their performance. The goal remains the same: standardize your treatments whenever possible.

Monitoring Implementation of Treatment

Although standardization of treatment is a goal, it is not always attainable. No matter how much you control course materials and training, not all teachers are equally effective. Regardless of pressure to attend class, not all students will attend every meeting. And among those students who do, the degree of engagement will vary. Even in well-controlled studies, each participant will inevitably receive a slightly different treatment.

Because of this, you should *monitor implementation of treatment*. What should you do if you discover differences? Try to eliminate them where possible. Follow all participants—both instructors and students. Are they attending class on a regular basis? Are they fully engaged in the lectures? Are they turning in homework assignments? Are they logging onto the computers every week? You may have little control over their behavior, but you should be aware that the treatment is not necessarily being received by all.

The participants themselves can provide useful information on how well a treatment was implemented. As part of the overall data collection, ask them to reflect on what they felt were the most salient aspects of the treatment. Do they believe they fully received the treatment you were implementing? For example, suppose you want to study the effects on student learning of increased question-asking by instructors. You encourage several instructors in introductory economics classes to ask more specific questions during lectures. The instructors report that they have actually changed their behavior—they are indeed asking more questions during class. But perhaps the students do not perceive it that way. Perhaps they feel that while the professor now asks many questions, she is not open to receiving students' answers. There is a gap between the treatment planned and the treatment implemented. Before plunging into elaborate statistical analyses, you should know precisely what treatment has actually made it to the students.

Measuring Implementation of Treatment

Another way to resolve the problem of varying levels of implementation is to measure how well a treatment has taken hold and to use this information in your analyses. To this end, even using broad categories is better than assuming everyone received exactly the same treatment. For example, you would be better off classifying students as regular attenders and irregular attenders than assuming they all attended all class meetings. Information on the *amount* of treatment received can then be used during your analysis to figure out whether the amount matters. Was the new mathematics course more effective for students who attended class faithfully? Was it more effective for students who made greater use of the computer?

Adjusting the Definition of the Treatment

Sometimes implementation of treatment varies so much among participants that you cannot consider all members of the treatment group to be equivalent. If a student enrolls in the new mathematics course but rarely attends class, does she really receive the treatment? If a student signs up for the new advising system but never meets with her new advisor, does she really experience the new advising system?

One way to resolve this dilemma is to use your measurement of the amount of treatment more systematically. By including the *amount* of treatment as an additional predictor in your analyses, you can determine its relationship with the outcome variable.

Another approach is to narrow the definition of the treatment so that only those receiving at least a prespecified amount of it will be regarded as participants. For example, you might restrict the evaluation of the new mathematics program to those students attending at least half the class meetings. Or you might restrict the evaluation of the new advising program to those students meeting with their new advisor at least once during a semester.

Narrowing the definition of treatment is not especially helpful if it occurs *after* data collection. But if it occurs *before* data collection—during the design phase of a project—it can be valuable for targeting limited study resources. The relationship between part-time work and academic achievement illustrates this. Different students work different amounts of time each week—some work only 5 hours, others as many as 25. It seems likely a 5-hour work week would have a different influence on academic achievement from a 25-hour work week. The question is: Who should be included in the part-time work group?

You could include *all* part-time workers in the treatment group and measure the number of hours each student works per week. You would then use this measurement as a predictor in subsequent data analyses. But suppose your study resources are limited. Then perhaps you should narrow the definition of part-time work to students whose jobs require at least 10 hours of work per week. They would be classified as working part-time only if they met this criterion; the comparison group would still be those students who do not work at all. Within the smaller group of part-time workers, you would still measure the number of hours worked. But narrowing the definition would help you to standardize the treatment, and would ensure that differences between treatment and comparison groups would be clear.

Outside Influences

Many higher-education programs are long term. They involve semester-long, year-long, or even four-year-long experiences. Because they are long term, each student's experience is not entirely within the investigator's control.

Outside factors can, and usually do, influence the participants. You need to work hard to maintain the integrity of treatment over time, especially if the design includes randomization. When outside factors have not influenced students, you can be reasonably sure that any effects observed in a randomized experiment are a result of the treatment. But when outside factors have influenced students, such conclusions are difficult to draw because the outside influences—not the treatment—may have created the outcomes you have detected.

EXAMPLE: *The influence of outside factors: Modifying medical education.*

The influence of outside factors made it difficult for Rudy Mitchell (1989) to evaluate the Pathways program introduced at the Harvard Medical School in 1985. As part of the Pathways program, students met in small groups with a mentor and used medical cases to learn the traditional medical school curriculum. Among the 82 percent of the incoming class of 1989 who volunteered to participate in the Pathways program, half actually participated and the remaining half were assigned to the older, standard curriculum. But those not in the Pathways program began to hear about what was happening in the program. They formed their own study groups. They borrowed materials used by their friends. What began as a randomized experiment devolved into a messy comparative study, with steadily declining integrity of treatment. By the third year, Mitchell despaired of making valid comparisons, and came to rely more on anecdotes and student self-reports of their experiences.

Choosing Which Predictors to Study

We close this chapter with a question: Among all the predictors available for investigation, how should you select predictors you will design into your study? Borrowing from the work of Cox (1958), we present an exercise to assist you in identifying predictors worth including in your design.

With your research questions in mind, *make a list of all predictors you think might possibly be associated with your outcomes.* Your list should be extensive, including both obvious and less obvious predictors. It should include predictors you can easily measure and predictors that are more difficult to measure. Conduct brainstorming sessions with colleagues. Try to develop as comprehensive a list of potential predictors as possible. Then, with list in hand, *divide the predictors into four groups.*

1. *Those of great importance.* These are the predictors you are confident will be strongly associated with the outcome or whose effects you are interested in substantively. They are your "question" predictors.
2. *Those of moderate importance.* These are the predictors you suspect will be strongly associated with the outcome, but they are not a primary focus.
3. *Those of moderate importance, but that define small groups.* These are the predictors that you suspect will be strongly associated with the outcome, but which identify very small groups that are not a central interest.
4. *Those of little importance.* These are all the other predictors that might be associated with your outcome.

Predictors in group 1 are your highest priority. Design your study around them. Design your sampling strategy to incorporate these predictors. Predictors in group 2 are important, but not so important that you must design your study around them. These are predictors you will simply measure for all students in your study and possibly incorporate into your analyses. Predictors in group 3 are a special case. Because they define small subgroups, they are typically predictors whose effects on the outcomes you would like to eliminate. Consider redefining your target population to eliminate these small groups, using the techniques described in Chapter 3. This may diminish the generalizability of your findings, but the complexity of your design and analysis will also be reduced. If the groups you eliminate are small enough, the diminished generalizability will be small relative to your increased ability to pin down the effects of the predictors in groups 1 and 2. Predictors in group 4 have the lowest priority. If you have sufficient resources, collect data on them. But if sufficient resources are not available, simply choose not to measure them. There comes a time in every game when you have to make your bets and place your chips on the table.

5

How effective is the freshman advising system at your college? Does the expository writing program strengthen student writing? Is the need-based financial aid program working? How well are varsity athletes doing academically? None of these questions has a single, absolute answer. The answer depends upon the *baseline* you use to define effectiveness and success. So, when designing studies investigating such questions, you must ask: *Compared to what?*

Many research questions require comparisons. Sometimes you compare people with *different levels of a predictor*—freshmen with different SAT scores, applicants receiving different amounts of financial aid, faculty members assigned different numbers of advisees. Sometimes you compare people divided into *groups according to a predictor*—students using the new curriculum and students using the old, men and women, athletes and nonathletes. In Chapter 4, we discussed decisions you must make when selecting predictors. But when the predictors define groups, you must make another decision as well: What is the appropriate comparison group?

Different comparisons yield different answers. For example, if you compare writing samples from students currently enrolled in the expository writing program with samples from students ten years ago who had no program available, you may find a big effect. But is this the right comparison? Perhaps you should compare writing samples from current students in the program with samples from current students not in the program. Or compare them with samples from students enrolled in writing programs at similar colleges. Each comparison can give a different answer about program effects. You must decide which is most appropriate for your research questions.

What makes a comparison group appropriate? Are some suited only for particular types of questions? Are some so bad they should never be used? In this chapter, we show how to select the best comparison group for your purposes. By the end of the chapter, you should understand:

- *Why you need comparison groups.* Comparison groups are an essential feature of many research designs, yet many investigators fail to include them. Consider the problems this creates and why you should avoid them.
- *The advantages of randomization.* The best comparison groups are formed by randomly assigning people to groups. You can randomize in many different ways, each having strengths and weaknesses. Become acquainted with different strategies, how to implement them, and when to use them.
- *How to choose among the alternatives available when randomization is not possible.* Comparison groups can be formed using many other strategies, each having

strengths and weaknesses. Trade off the many possibilities, how to implement each, and when to use each.

Why Do You Need a Comparison Group?

Studies without comparison groups are among the weakest
possible research designs. Suppose, for example, you observe a group of students after they all have had the same
experience. For simplicity, we call the experience a *treatment,* but it could also describe a distinguishing personal
characteristic or a shared experience, such as being a member of a minority group or a psychology major or participating in intramural sports. You want to relate your after-
treatment observations back to the treatment. For instance, you might notice that students in small sections for
calculus rarely complain about the quality of instruction.
Or that students who use word processors write particularly well. Should you conclude that small sections improve
satisfaction? Should you conclude that word processors improve writing?

These hypotheses may be true, but you cannot know for
sure with "after treatment only" designs. Without a comparison group, you cannot rule out rival explanations of
the relationships you observe. Perhaps only experienced
instructors taught the small calculus sections: perhaps it
was not section size that created satisfaction, but instructor
experience. What would have happened if the students had
not written with word processors? Would they still have
written well? Because it is impossible to know, you cannot
definitively establish whether section size or word processors really make a difference. Because everyone received
the treatment, values of the predictor do not vary across
students. If you don't have predictor variation, you won't
be able to detect any relation between predictor and outcome (Pocock, 1983; Rutman, 1984; Dooley, 1984; Krathwohl, 1985).

A slight improvement on the "after treatment only" design is the "before and after treatment" design. Measure people twice—once before, and once after, the treatment. Then you can compare their "after" measurement with their "before" and see if they have changed. For example, you can see whether students write better after a semester of using a word processor. But attributing changes to the treatment remains difficult because you still have no comparison group. You have no way of knowing whether similar changes would have occurred had the participants not received the treatment. The changes may be attributable to nothing more than natural maturation. Students grow learn, and change, whether or not they receive any particular treatment. Perhaps they would have become better writers anyway, even if they had continued to write their papers by hand.

The perils of drawing inferences from studies without comparison groups are illustrated dramatically by Alexander Astin (1970). Astin tells the story of a colleague who was distressed to discover that nearly a third of students who entered a highly selective college as science majors switched to other fields before graduation. The colleague decided this dropout rate was too high and deserved immediate corrective action. He thought it reflected inadequacies in the science program, so he encouraged a curriculum reform committee to consider changes that might improve persistence. Astin pointed out that this dropout rate was actually much *lower* than the rates at almost any similar school. Astin argued that this college's program indeed may have been exemplary, worthy of imitation. Curricular changes actually might bring about adverse effects, perhaps increasing the dropout rate.

Because studies with no comparison groups are so weak, you should avoid conducting them at all costs. They appear less expensive because they require less primary data collection, but *you get what you pay for.* Why waste time collecting data that, at best, offer indecisive answers to your questions, and, at worst, might lead to erroneous conclusions? (Weiss, 1972; Bennett and Lumsdaine, 1975; Kleinbaum, Kupper, and Morgenstern, 1982.)

EXAMPLE: *The difficulties of drawing inferences without a comparison group: The efficacy of academic support services for high-risk students.*

Helene Abrams and Louise Jernigan (1984) collected data for 219 students who participated in Eastern Michigan University's PASS program (Promote Academic Survival and Success). Students enrolled in PASS have access to many services, including advising, workshops, and tutoring. Fifty-seven percent of the PASS students earned a freshman GPA of C or better. Those using more services had higher GPAs than those using fewer services. Reading skills improved as well, from a before-treatment mean of 11.10 (in grade equivalents) to an after-treatment mean of 11.52.

Should we conclude that PASS works? Based on this before-and-after-treatment study, it is hard to say. We do not know how the 219 students would have done if they had not participated in PASS. Perhaps they would have done as well, perhaps even better. We have no benchmark against which to judge these outcomes. Is 57 percent passing frighteningly low or amazingly high? Is a gain of .42 points in reading big or small? The authors are aware of this limitation:

> Tempering the study results [is the concern that] . . . there is no true control group, because no corresponding group of high-risk students was admitted and offered an identical experience but without access to the support services . . . The lack of a control group does preclude the claim that support services are the exclusive factor in success for these students. Yet, the data do portend a critical role for such programs, which should be confirmed or rejected on the basis of additional research. (pp. 271–272)

Studies lacking a comparison group will always be suggestive at best. Determining the true effectiveness of PASS would require further comparative research.

Randomized Control Groups: The Best Comparisons

Recognizing the need for a comparison group is the first step; the next is identifying a good one. What should you look for? A simple principle summarizes the technical idea: Compare what happens to people who received the treatment with *what would have happened to these very same people had they not received the treatment.* When scientists discover how to clone human beings, applied research will begin a new era, because it will then be possible simultaneously to observe the same people under different circumstances! For now, we must rely on a modified version of this principle and observe what happens to *similar* people. Therein lies the idea behind a good comparison group—*it is composed of people who are similar to the people in the treatment group in all ways except that they did not receive the treatment.*

This idea leads to the argument for random assignment to treatment and control groups. Random assignment ensures that, *on average,* the comparison and treatment groups will be equivalent to each other with respect to any and all background characteristics. The comparability comes not from links between specific members of the two groups—there is no one-to-one correspondence between members of the treatment group and members of the comparison group—but from average equivalencies across all members of each group. Once random assignment has been used to create groups, any remaining accidental differentiation between the groups can be attributed to sampling variation and will be handled automatically by the future statistical analyses. It is for this purpose that statistical analyses were designed! Because of the superior quality of comparison groups formed using random assignment, and the large amount of control you need to create them, such groups are called *control groups.* Studies using random assignment to form groups are called *experiments* (Riecken and Boruch, 1974; Cook and Campbell, 1979).

Is Random Assignment Really Feasible?

But will study participants resist random assignment? Might they argue, for example, that random assignment is inequitable and that people should be assigned to treatments on the basis of some other principle, such as need or merit? Fortunately, the available empirical evidence on this topic suggests just the opposite. For instance, when given a choice, it seems that college students actually prefer random assignment.

Evidence for this assertion comes from an experiment conducted by Camille Wortman and Vita Rabinowitz (1978) using 259 students enrolled in an introductory psychology course at Northwestern University. Early in the term, students were told about an innovative program covering "hot" topics not addressed in the regular curriculum, such as child abuse and biofeedback. Students interested in participating in the innovative program were asked to complete a take-home test that presumably assessed their prior knowledge of psychology.

One week later, each student received personalized information about the innovative program. Each was told that there were not enough places for all interested students, so the instructors had selected a subset for participation. However, different students were given different information about the selection process. One quarter were told priority had gone to students with the highest test scores (the merit principle). Another quarter were told priority had gone to students with the lowest test scores (the need principle). A third quarter were told priority had gone to students who handed in the test early (the first-come, first-served principle). The final quarter were told admission had been based on a lottery (the random assignment principle).

Then the researchers manipulated the students' self-interest under the different assignment criteria by randomly subdividing each group into four subgroups. Students in the merit group either were given no information about their test scores or were told they had done very well, average, or poorly. The idea was that students told they had done very well would have self-interest in the merit principle. Similar manipulations of self-interest were done for the other three groups by giving bogus test results (for the need group), bogus information on order of turning in exams (for the first-come, first-served group), or bogus information on lottery numbers (for the random assignment group).

Students were then asked about the fairness of the selection procedures, and told that their opinions would shape the next year's selection process. Across *all* experimental conditions, students rated random assignment as fairer than any other procedure. On a scale from 1 to 15, with 15 being fairest, the mean ratings were 10.5 for random assignment, 7.8 for need, 6.5 for first-come, first-served, and 5.8 for merit. And students who were told that selection would be based on random assignment rated this principle as fairest, regardless of whether they had a good chance of being selected because of their lottery number.

Wortman and Rabinowitz conclude that "some of the objections to random assignment that administrators expect from participants may never materialize, and that among the majority of students, random assignment is likely to be judged the fairest of them all" (p. 184). Of course, results at Northwestern may not generalize to other colleges at other points in time. But all higher-education researchers should note that *random assignment is often feasible, and when it is, students may actually prefer it to other methods of assignment.*

Types of Random Assignment

Once you have decided to assign people randomly to treatment groups, you must develop a strategy for carrying out your objective. In many situations, such as Wortman and Rabinowitz's study, implementation is straightforward—the students are simply randomly assigned to the different groups. In other instances, especially in studies of treatments that must be given to *groups* of people at the same time, implementation is not always so clear-cut.

Suppose you want to compare two methods for teaching expository writing. Method A is the traditional one; Method B incorporates detailed feedback on several drafts of the same manuscript during the term. Ten professors agree to participate and to use any assignment mechanism you want. You decide to assign randomly. What are your options?

One option is to ask each professor to assign students randomly to treatments *within her class*. Half the students will get Method A and half get Method B, with assignment within each class being random. Your analysis will then compare writing samples from the two groups of students, controlling for professor. This design is similar to conducting ten parallel miniexperiments.

A second option is to assign randomly five intact classes to use Method A and the other five to use Method B. In this case your analysis will compare students in the first five classes with students in the second five. This is also a randomized design, but randomization occurs at the level of *class* rather than *student*. It is easier to implement from the faculty's perspective, because each professor uses the same method for all her students. The only constraint is that a random number table determines the particular method she uses.

A third option is to assign all the potential students randomly to the ten sections. If five professors already use method A and the other five already use B, this design allows professors to continue teaching the way they always have. And it certainly builds in some random assignments. You are randomly assigning students to classes, but not randomly assigning professors to methods.

Each of these options has strengths and weaknesses. From a research design perspective, the first is clearly the best. Why? Because it randomizes people at the lowest possible level. By having each professor use both methods, the design controls for differences in outcomes that might arise from differences in instructional quality across professors. And by randomly assigning students to methods, it rules out selection bias: students cannot select the approach they like best and professors cannot select students for the method they think best matches the students' needs.

The drawback of this design is feasibility. It is the hardest to implement because each professor must use both methods in a single class. She must always remind herself which strategy to use with each student. If she is not consistent, the experiment falls apart. It may become too complicated to implement. But if the professors can carry out the procedures, this design yields the best information about the effectiveness of the innovative method.

The second design randomizes at the class level. It is easier to implement for both you and the faculty. Unfortunately, if you randomize at the class level, you need more classes to detect effects because you are dealing with effects in the aggregate. Five professors using each method may be too few.

This problem stems from two sources. Professors differ in many ways other than just teaching methods. Because each professor uses only one method, and only five use each, differential effectiveness between professors is hard to control for. You may be studying hundreds of students, but you are studying only ten professors. To get a handle on variation among professors, you need more professors using each method. In addition, if students have selected the professors they like, because of reputation or some other shared reason, students in the same class will be more homogeneous than students in different classes. In technical terms, students within classes will not be statistically independent. This violates an assumption of most statistical analyses, and the best way to compensate for it is to collect data on more classes, aggregate to the class level, and carry out your analyses at that level. The bottom line: *If you randomize at the class level, be prepared to study many classes.*

The third option randomizes at the class level too, but only in the assignment of students to classes, not in the assignment of faculty to method. It is clearly the easiest option to implement. Professors continue teaching the way they always have; the only way your study affects them is in the particular students enrolled in their classes. But this design is the weakest for answering questions about curriculum effectiveness. Not only do you have too few professors to control for differences in the quality of their teaching, you also may have a selection bias. Randomly assigning students to classes eliminates some potential bias, but because professors choose the method they want, some bias may remain. You cannot find out whether differences across classes are attributable to the method used or to other things the professors do.

All three of these options employ random assignment. But *some forms of random assignment are clearly better than others.* Our advice is to *randomize at the lowest possible level.* If you can, randomize people, not intact groups. If you must deal with intact groups, such as students in courses or residence halls or faculty in departments, randomize people *within* the groups. If you must assign intact groups, use more groups than you would if you randomly assigned individuals to the same treatments (Singer, 1982; 1987).

EXAMPLE: *Implementing a randomization strategy: The relationship between learning styles and teaching format.*

Do some students prefer instructor-centered (IC) courses while others prefer peer-centered (PC) courses? Is student preference related to learning style? John Andrews (1981) conducted a randomized experiment investigating these questions using four teaching assistants and 102 freshmen enrolled in an introductory chemistry course for nonmajors at the University of California, San Diego. Unaware that different sections would be taught using different techniques, students signed up for one of eight sections, simply on the basis of schedules and personal considerations. Each TA taught two sections, one using IC techniques and the other using PC techniques. At the beginning of the term, each student filled out a standardized instrument assessing her own learning style; at the end of the term, each student filled out a questionnaire eliciting her reactions to the course.

Compatibility between teaching format and learning style made a big difference—collaboratively oriented students gave PC sections high ratings, and competitively oriented students gave IC sections high ratings. Andrews used these results to refute the popularly held belief that all "students here [at UC San Diego] are too competitive—they will never work together or learn in small groups" (p. 176).

Andrews's fine study design reinforces our belief in his findings. Since students signed up for sections without knowing the section's TA or teaching format, it does seem likely that "there is no known bias relevant to the hypotheses under study" (p. 164). This is supported by the lack of differences between the groups with respect to the measures of learning style. And since each TA taught one section of each type, assigned at random, the study controlled "for differences in TA personality, teaching style, and preference for section format" (p. 165).

Two Caveats

Anyone thinking about using random assignment should be aware that it can let you down in two ways. First, the statistical theory underlying random assignment ensures that it works best for *large samples*. With small samples, groups may still differ substantially on some background characteristic. For example, if eight women and twelve men are randomly assigned to two groups of ten students each, it will not be astonishing if one group has six women and the other only two. And if gender of student is related to outcomes, this discrepancy may make a difference.

The best solution is to assign randomly within subgroups (strata). If you suspect that a background characteristic may affect responses, stratify the sample by that characteristic and assign within strata. For example, you might stratify the twenty students by gender and randomly assign four women and six men to each treatment. Stratification rules out potential imbalance. It is useful in many projects, but is especially helpful when you use small samples.

The second way random assignments can let you down is by occasionally leading to a "quirky" result, even when the process is carried out with integrity. All the rich students may end up in one group, or all physics majors may get the new treatment, or students who work especially hard may be assigned to large classes. Statisticians disagree about what to do when this happens. Some consider respect for the integrity of the randomization *process* more important than worrying about the effects of a "fluke" randomization. Others argue that if random assignment leads to groups that differ in some important way, you cannot ignore this nonequivalence. They suggest you start over, and randomly assign again. This has its appeal, but with modest-sized samples there will always be *some* difference between groups. The last thing any statistician would want you to do is to assign repeatedly until you "get it right." Repeated random assignment destroys the logic behind the process in the first place.

Philosophical debates aside, the practical issue remains: What should you do if random assignment results in groups that are clearly nonequivalent? Our advice is to respect the process and avoid repeated randomization. Stratify in advance if possible. But even when you cannot stratify in advance, always make a concrete analytic effort to see whether the groups you form differ in dramatic or important ways. At least you will know about differences that might matter, and you can interpret your findings with an eye to such differences.

EXAMPLE: *Randomizing within strata: Improving small-group discussion sections.*

Are discussion sections more effective when students prepare for them before class? Does the clear designation of a leader make a difference? Ernest Baxter (1985) found that the answer to both these questions was yes when he conducted a randomized experiment using 60 seniors enrolled in an educational psychology class at the University of Queensland, Australia. He examined two predictors: student preparation and designation of a leader. Four groups were created by pairing all the possibilities: prepared students with an assigned leader; prepared students with an emergent leader; unprepared students with an assigned leader; and, unprepared students with an emergent leader. Measures of verbal activity and inactivity were taken during eight section meetings.

Baxter was concerned that students' background characteristics would influence their participation. So he stratified the 60 students into 15 subgroups based on academic achievement and scores on the Eysenck Personality Inventory, the Taylor Manifest Anxiety Scale, and the Tennessee Self Concept Scale. Within each stratum, he randomly assigned students to the four treatment groups.

Baxter examined the success of the stratification in detail. He found no differences among the four groups according to the personality variables, academic achievement, or age. But the sex ratio differed slightly (but not significantly) across groups. Although the overall sample was 60 percent female, the percentage of women in the four groups ranged from 40 to 67. With only 60 students, such differences are expected; this slight imbalance shows just the type of variation you can expect when randomly assigning small numbers of people to groups. Sampling variation like this is accounted for automatically by the statistical methods used to analyze the data.

Requiring Informed Consent

To implement a randomized study you often need the informed consent of students or faculty members, and you must be able to answer several questions about what may happen if some don't participate.

The first question you will be asked in return is: "Does the new curriculum work?" You may respond by saying, "If I knew the answer for sure, we wouldn't be organizing this study. After the results are in I can answer your question." Yet your response will be stronger if you can assure the questioner that the "no worse" principle applies. That is, the questioner will become no worse off by participating in a randomized study. What makes giving such assurances hard is the difficulty you will have saying anything in the absence of reliable information. Even if you are confident that a randomized study won't harm any participants, you won't really know until you actually carry out such a study and analyze the findings. Yet it is hard to blame students for preferring to volunteer only when they know it won't hurt them. Since many students have strong views about what type of instruction is best suited to their particular learning style, most students prefer to choose which section of a course they join, and not to relinquish this control to you if they can help it.

EXAMPLE: *Innovative sectioning in a large core course.*

Barbara Bushey (1989) examined an innovative way to create sections in a large undergraduate course at Harvard University. Professor Harvey Cox's course "Jesus and the Moral Life" attracted 384 students in 1988. Each student was required to attend three lectures and one smaller section meeting per week. In the past, sections had involved 20 undergraduates led by a graduate student. Cox decided to organize an experiment, to see if smaller section sizes would lead to more student involvement and greater learning.

Each of the 384 students was given a choice at the beginning of the course: join a traditional section of 20 led by a graduate student, or join a "mentored cluster" of 5 students. In each mentored cluster, no graduate student would be present during sessions. Rather, 2 undergraduates out of the 5 would be responsible for leading each week's discussion. The 2 leaders would meet with a teaching fellow for in-depth preparation before their class, and then again afterward to debrief and to make the session a better learning experience. The pairs of student leaders would rotate so that each student would be paired with several other students, and each would lead several classes.

Free to choose, 304 students chose a traditional section, while only 80 chose the mentored cluster innovation. When asked why they made their decisions, most students choosing the traditional section said that they were hesitant to try an unknown format, and that they had heard the traditional larger-section format was perfectly good. Students who chose the small clusters, in contrast, reported that they were generally neither happy nor effective in larger, more passive groups. They were confident they would learn more from the smaller, more active, clusters.

Barbara Bushey collected data throughout the course on both concrete learning (test scores) and student participation in sections (videotapes). She found that while concrete learning was roughly the same in both formats, significant differences emerged in group participation for the different sections. Students in the mentored clusters improved much more in ability to function well as part of a group—fewer interruptions, more participation, more comments that moved an argument forward.

Does this show that smaller, student-led sections will improve group participation for *all* students? Probably not. Bushey concludes that the mentored clusters are a wonderful option for those students who choose them freely. Simply making the choice gives a signal that they prefer a small group, and are willing, indeed enthusiastic, to lead group discussion. Bushey observes that she has no information at all about how the other 304 students—more than 75 percent of the class—would have made out in the small clusters. She points out that only a randomized study would tell us that, and that she felt uncomfortable asking for consent for randomization when she had no evidence at all about the effectiveness of mentored clusters.

How to Fix It

There is a way to increase the chances that students will participate in a randomized study, yet still respect fully the right of each student to give informed consent in advance. It was originally proposed by Marvin Zelen (1979) for medical settings, and we adapt it here.

The standard randomized design requires you first to get each student's consent to participate. Students who consent are then randomized between, say, two curricula, A and B. Those who do not consent are dropped from the formal research entirely, and do not participate further.

Here is an alternative. It is especially useful when a course meets in many sections. Randomize all students into two classrooms before seeking any consent. Students randomly assigned to one classroom are not asked to consent to anything. They simply receive the current curriculum A. Students in the other classroom are asked whether they are willing to participate in a research study and to receive the new, experimental curriculum B. Those students who agree to try B stay in the room and get B. Those who decline are invited down the hall to a different classroom and given A, just like the original half who were randomly assigned to A.

If you use this design, you will ultimately compare all the students randomized to A with those randomized to B who stayed. There are two strengths to this approach. One is that each student knows exactly where she stands— whether she will get the old curriculum or the new—before participating. The second is that no student must ever give consent to the abstract process of randomization. She simply agrees to accept the new curriculum, or states she prefers the old and gets it. So this plan respects students' wishes to decline the new curriculum, and eliminates the need to ask students to agree to participate in any random assignment.

Volunteer Bias

To conduct a randomized study, you need some degree of investigator control over who gets what treatment. It is inappropriate to have some students voluntarily sign up for a new curriculum, for example, while others voluntarily sign up for the old.

If students are free to choose, you will never know if volunteer bias exists. Suppose the harder-working students tend to choose the new curriculum. Suppose the math hotshots choose the new one. Then students choosing to join the two curricula are simply different. You risk never knowing whether any differences in outcomes that you find later are due to the curriculum you are examining, or simply to who signed up.

To implement a randomized study you need control, and often you also need student consent. It is often unethical, or administratively inappropriate, to assign students randomly among treatments. Just as in medical research, where it is generally necessary to get patients' consent before assigning some to an old drug and others to a new one at random, research in college can require students' permission.

Now you face a dilemma. What happens if you want to implement a randomized design, you ask students (or faculty colleagues) for their agreement to participate, and they don't all agree? You can forge ahead anyway and conduct your research only on those who volunteer. But there is a serious downside risk. Students who volunteer may be different, in some important way, from those who don't. You can try to measure differences between students who volunteer and those who don't on features such as age, race, sex, SAT scores, or whatever other factors you can think of. But you won't think of everything. Neither will your colleagues. So doing a research study using only volunteers risks biasing your results.

Estimating Volunteer Bias

David Oakes and colleagues (1974) have proposed a constructive plan to estimate volunteer bias. If none turns up, you need not worry further. If bias exists, you can develop an estimate of how serious it is.

Oakes's proposal carries a third group for a comparative study. Assume you are comparing a new curriculum to an old one. In the early phases of study design, ask students whether or not they agree to participate in a randomized experiment. Some will say yes and others will say no. Those who say no are not part of your formal experiment—they simply sign up for either the old curriculum or the new one as they see fit. Those who do say yes, however, are then divided into two groups. All students in group one are invited to participate in the randomization, with some of them assigned to the old curriculum and others to the new. All students in group two are told, "Thank you for volunteering, but we simply have more volunteers than we need for the randomization. We chose participants for the actual randomization by lottery. You just go ahead and choose whatever you want, new curriculum or old, and you will be accommodated. Use your usual good judgment to choose."

What do you know about the students in group two? You know after the experiment that each chose the new curriculum or the old based on her own preference. So when choosing between curricula they behaved just like the students in group one who didn't give their consent to be randomized. They chose on their own. But the key is that we know these students were volunteers for the randomization, even though they weren't actually randomized.

Why is this design useful? Because by comparing outcomes for students in group two with outcomes for students who refused to be randomized, you can estimate the size of any volunteer effect. For example, if the new curriculum is modestly better than the old for both the group-two students and the nonvolunteers, you will be able to conclude that there is no big volunteer bias, and that the new curriculum is indeed modestly better. In contrast, if the new curriculum outperforms the old for the group-two students while the reverse is true for the nonvolunteers, there is strong evidence of a volunteer effect, and you cannot have much confidence that the new curriculum is truly better.

EXAMPLE: *How effective is a special enrichment program for high-risk freshmen?*

An experiment to evaluate a support system for high-risk students illustrates how this proposal can be used. Stayner Landward and Dean Hepworth (1984) organized and evaluated an academic enrichment program (AEP) at a large state university. Entering freshmen described as "high risk" were the target population. High risk was defined as a predicted GPA of lower than C. The program's key features were: (1) an advisor helping students intensively; (2) a college official meeting regularly with each student; and (3) organizing high-risk students into study groups.

The research design is in the spirit of Oakes's proposal. It has three groups. All 123 freshmen who indicated no interest in participating were called nonvolunteers. The 91 freshmen who did volunteer were randomly divided into two groups—30 who actually got the support program, and 61 who were not chosen to participate.

AEP assistance was offered to the 30 freshmen for ten weeks during the first semester. At the end of the semester, GPAs were computed for students in the three groups. The 30 freshmen getting AEP had a mean GPA of 2.14. The 59 (surviving from the original 61) volunteers for AEP who didn't get to participate had a mean GPA of 1.41. The 115 (surviving from the original 123) freshmen who had not volunteered had a mean GPA of 1.34.

What could Landward and Hepworth conclude? First, they decided that based on first-term results, AEP was successful. The freshmen in AEP outperformed those not in it. To any skeptic who asserts that the students in AEP would have done better even if they didn't get the extra help, because

they are the go-getters, Landward and Hepworth can point to the 59 freshmen who volunteered for AEP but weren't accommodated. They did far
worse than the AEP freshmen, yet they are the same go-getters in every
other respect. They were at risk upon arrival, and they also volunteered for
AEP. Finally, Landward and Hepworth note that there is a volunteer bias,
although it is slight—the 59 freshmen volunteers not in AEP outperformed
the 115 nonvolunteers with GPAs of 1.41 versus 1.34.

Comparison Groups without Random Assignment

You cannot investigate *all* research questions using randomized experiments. When studying effects of a program
that has already begun, or effects of personal characteristics not within researcher control, you cannot randomly
assign students or faculty to groups. Sometimes ethical,
logistical, or legal constraints make random assignment
out of the question. And because it may take a long time
to conduct a good experiment, sometimes an immediate
need for *some* information, even crude information, pre-
cludes the possibility of random assignment.

Various strategies are available for selecting comparison
groups when random assignment is impossible. Some lead
to comparisons that are very good indeed, while others lead
to comparisons that are so weak you should avoid them at
all costs. We now describe these several options and suggest
when each is particularly appropriate. Instead of exhaus-
tively cataloguing the many possibilities, we identify six
popular ones and give a flavor of issues involved in assessing the adequacy of others.

Outlining Your Options

Suppose you want to evaluate the effects of a recently
instituted study-skills course. Any freshman can sign up

for the one-semester no-credit course covering study skills and strategies. The treatment group is all freshmen enrolled in the course during the current academic year. Success will be measured by student GPA. You decide that random assignment is not feasible. To whom should you compare the enrolled students? Consider the following six possibilities:

A. All freshmen at your school during the previous ten years.

B. A simple random sample of current freshmen not enrolled in the course.

C. A stratified random sample of current freshmen not enrolling in the course, stratified by proposed major and ACT or SAT scores.

D. A sample of current freshmen not enrolling in the course, matched, on a person-by-person basis, according to proposed major and ACT or SAT scores.

E. A sample of current freshmen at high academic risk based on their incoming ACT or SAT scores and high school rank.

F. A sample of current freshmen expressing interest in the course, but who could not enroll because of scheduling difficulties.

Each of these six groups represents a possible comparison group. Because none was formed using random assignment, none allows you to determine absolutely whether the study-skills course *changes* academic achievement. But each gives you some handle on whether tutoring and achievement are *correlated*. We now discuss each in greater detail.

Historical Comparisons

Comparison using group A—the freshmen from the previous ten years—is a *historical comparison*. The distinguishing feature of a historical comparison is its reliance on data collected *at an earlier point in time*. Most historical comparisons are created using records kept at the same school as the current study. Others are created from data published in the literature or collected at other schools.

Historical comparisons are seriously flawed, for a simple reason: The equivalence of a previous cohort of students assessed using different data-collection strategies is hard to ensure. Any change occurring during the intervening years invalidates the historical comparison. Changes in admissions procedures, yield rates, grading practices, financial aid policies, or course requirements create uncontrolled differences. Sometimes the very process of doing research—with the extra attention given to participants and record keeping—not the intervention itself, affects performance. Was similar attention lavished on previous students not participating in a research project?

For these reasons, *we strongly discourage the use of historical comparisons*. But we do note that not all historical comparisons are equally weak. The worst are derived from published studies. Data culled from the literature provide helpful contextual information—where your college stands in relation to other colleges—but you should not use such data to make statements about treatment effectiveness. Your college differs from all other colleges in so many ways that arguing for true equivalence is futile.

Slightly better are historical comparisons based on records kept at the same school. Suppose, for example, that over the past ten years an average of 15 percent of freshmen failed each year, while among students in your new study-skills course only 5 percent failed. The course sounds very promising. But perhaps students in the course are so motivated to succeed that they would have been less likely to fail anyway. Or perhaps grade inflation has made the difference. With a historical comparison, it is hard to say.

The best historical comparisons come from a previous study at the same college. Using historical comparisons generated during previous research projects at a college ensures that data collection procedures are rigorous, records are kept in a similar way, and students and faculty are roughly equivalent. But while these biases are minimized, the groups are still distinguished by the passage of time. If any real change in other factors *has* occurred, it will destroy the quality of even this comparison.

EXAMPLE: *Using historical comparisons: Does the addition of plus and minus qualifiers improve the reliability of grades?*

In 1970 the University of California, Riverside, added plus and minus qualifiers to its grading system. To investigate the effects of this change on the reliability of grades, Royce Singleton, Jr., and Eliot Smith (1978) compared grades given in the six years after the change (1970 to 1975) with grades given in the five years before (1965 to 1969). The average correlation among the grades given to each student was used to estimate reliability.

Reliability estimates were different before and after the system change. Before the change, reliability was decreasing steadily; after the change, reliability began increasing, eventually exceeding the 1965 level.

Did the system change improve the reliability of grades? Or does use of historical comparisons make this conclusion untenable? Singleton and Smith's careful consideration of *other changes* occurring during the study period enhances the face validity of their results. With regard to admission standards, only one minor change occurred during the study period—a lower GPA requirement for junior college transfers. Because this affected only 50 students per year, the effect on reliability should have been small. With regard to the composition of the student body, the number of transfer students did increase during the study period, from 35 to 52 percent. But because this increase was steady during the period, while the trends for reliability reversed direction, this change could not have created the reliability pattern observed. The only other change was the addition of a pass/fail option in 1966. But because the percentage of courses taken pass/fail remained steady during the period, this change was unlikely to have caused the observed behavior of the reliability coefficients. Although historical comparisons are weak, the addition of plus and minus qualifiers does seem to have improved the reliability of student grades.

Simple Random Sample of Nonparticipants

Comparison using group B—a simple random sample of freshmen not enrolling in the study-skills course—is a major improvement over historical comparison. Examining students who matriculated in the same year at least rules out any differences that might arise from differences across time.

This comparison group is appealing for another reason as well. A representative sample of freshmen not enrolling in the course provides important contextual information. For example, you can ask nonparticipants why they chose not to enroll. This might help future targeting of resources. And by comparing the groups with respect to background characteristics, you can determine who is most likely to take advantage of a study-skills course.

But this very strength leads to the biggest flaw of comparison group B. After comparing the two groups, you are likely to discover that students enrolling in the course differ systematically from those not enrolling. They may be more motivated to succeed at college, they may feel at greater risk of failure, or they may simply be more willing to take advantage of free help. In advance of data collection, you will not know precisely how they differ, but they probably *do* differ in some way. Any such difference creates *selection bias*.

EXAMPLE: *Using a random sample as a comparison group: The effects of college football on social mobility.*

Does playing college football facilitate social mobility? Allen Sack and Robert Theil (1979) examined this question using data on 344 football players who graduated from the University of Notre Dame between 1946 and 1965. The researchers were acutely aware of the need for a comparison group. They comment on a study of the same question conducted at UCLA: "Most importantly, he failed to use a control group of college students who were not varsity athletes. Thus, there is no way of knowing whether the mobility experienced by ballplayers in his study was a consequence of athletic participation or whether ballplayers and non-ballplayers alike experienced mobility during this period due to factors unrelated to athletic involvement" (p. 61). Sack and Theil addressed this problem by creating a comparison group of 444 Notre Dame nonathletes who graduated during the same time period.

Both groups were upwardly mobile. Their incomes, educational levels, and occupational levels consistently exceeded those of their fathers. But the groups were not equivalent with respect to family socioeconomic status—athletes tended to come from lower socioeconomic backgrounds. Controlling for this difference, the researchers found no significant differences between the groups in occupational attainment or income.

Can we safely conclude that athletic participation has no effect on social mobility? How well could the researchers control for the socioeconomic differential? Probably not too well because they had data for only 12 athletes from the highest socioeconomic level (compared with 57 nonathletes) and only 6 nonathletes from the lowest (compared with 31 athletes). Inclusion of a comparison group is only a first step. For a study to be credible, the comparison must be credible.

Whenever you form a comparison group without random assignment, you risk selection bias. You must work to minimize bias through study design. This is precisely what the remaining four types of comparison groups may help you to do.

Stratified Sample of Nonparticipants

Reconsider the study-skills course. If science majors and students with low SAT or ACT scores are more likely to enroll, the treatment group will have more students with these characteristics, and a simple random sample of nonparticipants will have the opposite balance—more nonscience majors and more students with high SAT or ACT scores. Comparison using group C eliminates this imbalance through stratified sampling. Stratification ensures group equivalence according to the stratifier and facilitates the detection of effects associated with the stratifier.

To create a stratified comparison sample, divide the population of comparison students into strata based on the background characteristics creating the potential selection bias. In this example, stratify by major and ACT score. Then draw separate random samples from each stratum. The easiest approach is to assign the same number of students from each stratum to the control group as are in the treatment group from that stratum. So if the treatment group has 40 science majors with low ACT scores, randomly assign 40 similar students to the comparison group.

This strategy's success depends upon using the "right" stratifiers. If the groups differ only with respect to the stratifiers, or correlates of them, this procedure minimizes bias. But if the groups differ according to other factors, even a rigorously implemented stratified sampling scheme will yield a nonequivalent comparison group. For example, suppose use of a personal computer is an important predictor of GPA, but you never thought of stratifying by it. If the groups are not comparable on this factor—perhaps students in the study-skills course are less likely to have personal computers—you may find misleading results and the course will appear less effective than it really is.

The challenge in creating a good comparison group using stratified sampling therefore comes down to anticipating the factors likely to differ across groups, or likely to affect the outcome. Common sense is helpful, as is a careful review of the literature. In the present example, you would want to stratify by factors previous researchers have found to be associated with GPA. Of all the comparison groups available, those created using stratified sampling are among the most effective. But their success always depends upon choosing good stratifiers.

EXAMPLE: *Using a stratified sample as a comparison group: Differences between Arab and Jewish students in Israel.*

Are college admissions tests more or less accurate predictors of academic performance for Arab students than for Jewish students in Israel? Moshe Zeidner (1986) investigated this question by examining test scores and freshman grades for a stratified random sample of 104 Arab and 308 Jewish students selected from a population of 1,017 Arab and 1,778 Jewish students at the University of Haifa. Although Arab students had lower freshman GPAs even after controlling for their lower entrance exam scores, the strength and magnitude of the relationship between admissions scores and GPA did not differ for the two groups.

Why did Zeidner use a stratified sample? Examining the population, he noted a marked gender imbalance: 59 percent of the Arab students were male as compared with 39 percent of the Jewish students. A simple random sample would have replicated this imbalance, and if gender was associated with GPA, the two groups would have been nonequivalent. He therefore stratified each group by gender, and selected equal numbers of male and female Arab and Jewish students for study.

Unfortunately, Zeidner may not have stratified by the most important variable. He considered stratifying by student major. His interest in this factor stemmed from course enrollment patterns for the two groups: many Jewish students major in quantitative areas such as math, statistics, computer sciences, and economics, and many Arab students major in nonquantitative areas. If major is an important predictor of GPA, as it is likely to be, the two groups probably are nonequivalent, so even the stratified random sample did not yield an ideal comparison group. Zeidner points out this limitation in his account.

Matched Comparison Groups

A matched comparison group is composed of people who correspond, *one-to-one,* to specific people in the treatment group. You construct a matched sample by arraying all members of the treatment group according to the characteristics you think might create selection bias. Then array the comparison population according to the same characteristics. Matches can be formed through several different algorithms, but the idea remains the same: For each student in the treatment group, assign a student to the comparison group who matches her on every background characteristic possible. Think of a matched sample as a stratified sample taken to the extreme—each student in the treatment group defines her own stratum.

Matching ensures equivalence between treatment and comparison groups according to every stratifier used in the matching process. If you matched by stratifiers strongly correlated with the outcome, then this is a powerful way of assigning a comparison group. But you can never be sure that you matched by *every* important stratifier. If you omitted any crucial stratifier, the two groups may differ on this dimension. And if this stratifier strongly influences the outcome, your omission can have serious consequences.

A deeper problem with matching is the inherent difficulty and laboriousness of the process. To find good matches, you need complete data for many more comparison students than you will ultimately study. Finding a match for extreme or unusual cases is particularly hard. Who would be a good match for a 69-year-old retiree entering college for the first time? And what do you do when you cannot find a good match—settle for a poor one, or set the treated case aside? Matching also complicates statistical analyses. Whenever you use a matched sample, your analyses must take the matching into account. If not, your tests of inference may be too conservative, failing to find an effect that is really there.

Most people who have tried constructing matched comparison groups ultimately conclude that it sounds easier and better than it actually is. We recommend this strategy only when you have easy access to all the data you might need on a very large pool of potential comparison cases, and when you are reasonably sure that you are matching on the "right" stratifiers. Only then can you fully realize the gains of matching.

EXAMPLE: *Using matched comparison groups: Academic performance of college athletes.*

Does playing varsity sports adversely affect student academic performance? Debra Stuart (1985) addressed this question by studying 91 freshmen who entered Iowa State University between 1977 and 1980 and who received scholarships for playing football. Concerned that race and major would be associated with grades, and that the distribution of students by these characteristics might differ by athletic status, Stuart selected a matched sample of 91 nonathletes for comparison. Nonathletes were defined as students who did not receive a grant-in-aid to play sports and who did not participate as a "walk-on." For each of the 91 athletes, a nonathlete of the same sex, year of entry, race, and major was randomly selected for study. Athletes arrived at school less well prepared than nonathletes; however, no differences in college performance were found.

Restricted Treatment and Comparison Groups

Consider a slightly different approach to creating comparability. Instead of studying *everyone* exposed to a treatment, study a *subgroup*. This is precisely what comparison using group E does—it focuses attention on a subgroup at high risk for academic failure. Narrowing the definition of *both* groups makes them identical with respect to the restricting factor. Eliminating variation in the outcome that might be associated with the restricting factor rules out a potential selection bias.

This procedure is not without problems, however. By excluding classes of participants, you change the target population you are examining. For example, in using group

E you will no longer be studying the effects of the study-skills course on all freshmen, but only on freshmen at high risk. This limits generalizability, because you cannot generalize from high-risk students to all students.

When you restrict attention to subgroups, you trade improved comparisons for weakened generalizability. You hope to learn something about a limited group, instead of nothing about a larger group. Of course this is a compromise, but often a wise one. We recommend using this strategy when the excluded classes are small, because the reduction in generalizability is also small and the potential gain in inference is large.

EXAMPLE: *Restricting attention to subgroups: On-campus versus off-campus living.*

Do commuter students have different college experiences from their peers who live on campus? Ernest Pascarella (1984) examined this question using data from students at 74 public and private four-year schools participating in the Cooperative Institutional Research Program. Rather than studying the entire group of 9448 students, Pascarella limited his work to 4191 students who: "1. entered a four-year college or university in 1975 as full-time students; 2. were attending the same institution at the time of the 1977 follow-up survey; and 3. had lived either on-campus during the 1975-1977 academic years, or with their parents during the same time period" (p. 250). His final sample included 3410 students who lived on campus and 781 students who commuted.

By restricting eligibility *for both groups* in this way, Pascarella ensured comparability with respect to many characteristics such as level of school and enrollment status. This limited his generalizability—he was unable to comment on the effects of commuting on part-time students, students at two-year schools, students living on their own, or students who changed living arrangements—but it enabled him to say something about the homogeneous group he chose. And Pascarella's large sample size allowed him to control statistically for any remaining differences between the groups. His trade of generalizability for comparability seems well justified.

Students Who Applied but Did Not Get In

Despite all attempts to ensure comparability, every comparison group considered so far suffers from a potentially serious flaw: students who decide they need a study-skills course may differ from those who decide they do not. Comparison using group F attempts to minimize this bias by comparing students who enrolled in the course with students who were interested in the course but could not enroll because of logistics.

This group, more than any of the other five, is likely to be similar to the treatment group on many characteristics associated with *motivation* to take a study-skills course. All other procedures manipulate objective criteria—high school achievement and proposed major. Comparison group F is equivalent to the treatment group with respect to a much more amorphous, but probably more important, factor—self-perceived need. No objective measure can account for differential perceptions. For this reason, group F may be the best comparison group among the six broad possibilities.

Many research questions are amenable to such comparisons. When evaluating the academic performance of athletes, compare them to students eligible for the team, perhaps even recruited, but who decided not to participate. When evaluating the effects of a new MBA program, compare matriculating students to students who were admitted but chose not to attend.

Despite the strengths of comparison using group F, it, too, is flawed, because students who manipulated their schedules so that they could attend the study-skills class may differ systematically from students who did not make the effort to do so. Perhaps those who chose not to attend did not feel they needed the course quite as much. Perhaps other demands on their time made enrollment impossible. Without random assignment, such rival hypotheses will always cloud your study's results (Hoaglin et al., 1982).

EXAMPLE: *Students who applied but couldn't get in: The effects of a career awareness course.*

David Carver and David Smart (1985) used this strategy when evaluating the effects of a career course for undecided freshmen at the University of Northern Colorado. (We described this study in Chapter 2, and refer the reader there for background information.) They selected the comparison group from a list of students who had expressed interest in taking the course but who could not enroll because of scheduling conflicts or unavailability of slots. The researchers believe that this process "ensured that the treatment and comparison groups were reasonably similar with respect to year in school, undeclared major status, and expressed interest in taking the . . . course" (p. 40). To back up this hypothesis, Carver and Smart compared the groups with respect to a host of characteristics, ranging from age, sex, and race to financial status, residence, and employment, and found no differences. Although random assignment would have improved the validity of their comparison, the researchers' comparison group seems well suited for their purposes.

What to Do in Practice

Finding a good comparison group is never easy. You must explore many options and evaluate their strengths, weaknesses, and feasibility. We reiterate that random assignment eliminates problems that can come back and haunt you. But if random assignment is not feasible, we make the following recommendations.

The best comparison group is composed of students as similar as possible to students in the treatment group. You need similarity across objective criteria, such as class year, sex, and academic achievement, and similarity across subjective criteria, such as motivation to learn, flexibility, and orientation to school. A group of students interested in or eligible for a special program, but unable to participate because of external factors, is probably your best bet. A well-chosen stratified sample, or restricted sample, of non-participants is second best. Consider matching only if you have easy access to all requisite information. Historical comparisons and simple random samples should be avoided.

Sometimes you can improve the quality of a comparison by combining two or more of these strategies. Study a stratified random sample of nonparticipants who expressed an interest in the treatment but were unable to participate. Or study a matched sample of nonparticipants restricted to students from the largest categories. Circumstances unique to a particular research situation may suggest other possibilities.

Whatever choice you make, *the burden of demonstrating comparability remains with you.* If the groups are non-comparable, your findings will not be persuasive. Make every effort to ensure equivalence through design. After doing so, use statistical analyses to determine whether any differences remain. If you find any, try to disentangle their effects using further statistical analyses.

Retrospective Case-control Studies

Sometimes a researcher, studying students or faculty with different *outcomes,* wants to find out, *retrospectively,* what predictors contributed to the difference. You might compare students who graduated with students who dropped out and ask what academic and personal characteristics were associated with their behavior. You might compare students who defaulted on their loans with students who repaid them and ask whether you could have predicted the chances of default. You might compare students who chose to attend your college with those who declined their admissions offer to see what makes students decide to attend.

These studies differ in a very important way from all the others described in this chapter. Instead of comparing people receiving different treatments (having different values of a predictor) and seeing whether they respond differently, you compare people displaying different responses (having different values of an outcome) and examine whether they differed according to the predictors. You move from outcomes to predictors, not from predictors to outcomes. When you use such a design, you are conducting a *retrospective case-control* or *ex post facto* study (Suchman, 1967).

Although case-control studies sound compelling on the surface, they usually lead to nothing but equivocal results. The problem is that they make you reason backwards. Take the case of college dropouts. Does outside employment, part time, increase the risk of dropping out? Suppose you interviewed a group of students who dropped out and asked them if they worked part time. Then you asked the same question of a comparison group of students at the same college who did not drop out. If the frequency of part-time work was higher among the dropouts, you might conclude that employment was responsible for students' dropping out.

But would you be right? Probably not, because many other plausible explanations of the difference loom large. Perhaps the two groups of students came from different socioeconomic backgrounds. Those who dropped out might have come from poorer families, less able to put their children through college, while those who stayed might have come from richer families, better able to support their children for four years. Maybe family socioeconomic background, and not part-time employment, is what actually affects persistence.

Once again, the problem is identifying an appropriate comparison group. Which persisting students should be in the comparison group? If you select a simple random sample of students who did not drop out, they are likely to differ from those who dropped out in many ways other than just the frequency of part-time work. You can attempt to control for differences using the strategies we describe in this chapter, but the basic problem will always remain: How can you be sure you controlled for all the important factors?

Retrospective case-control studies suffer from other problems as well. A major difficulty is that the passage of time clouds memories. If you ask seniors about their exposure to a treatment as freshmen, such as hours of part-time work or financial resources, you are likely to get imprecise answers lacking credibility. The problem worsens when the predictors you need to know about happened years earlier. Can *you* remember exactly how many hours per week you worked in your sophomore year of college? Written records may yield good information on some topics, but many types of information will have to be collected through retrospective interviews. The precision and credibility of such information is shrouded in doubt.

If retrospective case-control studies are so weak, why are they so common? The answer lies in their feasibility, especially when studying *infrequent occurrences*. To design a prospective study of a reasonably rare occurrence, such as defaulting on a student loan or dropping out, you must initially study a very large sample of students and then follow them over many years. After all, only a small percentage of any cohort will default on their loans or drop out of school. The rarer the event, the more students you must initially study.

A retrospective case-control study allows you to focus immediately on students known to have a particular characteristic. You do not have to study a large cohort and wait until the event of interest occurs. But convenience comes at a price. Inferences concerning the relationship between predictors and outcomes will always be limited by your ability to rule out rival explanations and to justify the accuracy of retrospective measurement (Judd and Kenny, 1981; Katzer, Cook, and Crouch, 1982).

EXAMPLE: *Conducting a retrospective case-control study: The role of financial support in predicting student attrition.*

Stanley Iwai and William Churchill (1982) conducted a retrospective case-control study at Arizona State University to determine whether students who withdraw from school use fewer sources of financial support than students who persist. Questionnaires were sent to 3322 students who withdrew between the first and second semesters of the 1975–76 academic year and to a "comparable" sample of 3909 students who persisted through the year. (No details are given on how comparability was achieved, but the factors dealt with were student gender, school year, and college of enrollment.)

As often happens in case-control studies, response rates were low and differed across groups: 32 percent of the persisters responded as compared with 18 percent of the withdrawers. And although response rates did not differ by gender, school year, or college of enrollment, they did differ by GPA—in both groups, students with high GPAs were more likely to respond. To compensate for this potential bias, Iwai and Churchill subdivided each group by GPA, splitting persisters into two subgroups (high and low) and withdrawers into three (high, low, and failing).

Controlling for GPA, school year, and gender, withdrawers reported using fewer sources of support than persisters. Iwai and Churchill provide three plausible explanations for this finding: (1) persisters are more motivated to succeed in school and so they seek out more sources of financial support; (2) persisters have personality characteristics (such as maturity) that promote finding and keeping a job or scholarship; and (3) persisters realize the advantages of not "putting all their eggs in one basket" and so try to maintain multiple sources of support.

Although each of these explanations may well be correct, consider two rival ones based on *methodology:* (1) because persisters are still using the support sources, they are unlikely to omit any when they answered the questionnaire, whereas students who withdrew from school may have forgotten the sources they once used; and (2) although withdrawers who responded to the survey may have had fewer sources of support, withdrawers who did not respond may have had many sources; perhaps they did not respond because they were disappointed that, despite all their support, they were unable to persist. The point here is that no matter how well done the retrospective analysis is, a critic will always be able to come up with possible alternative explanations for your findings. Therefore, if you cannot design and carry out a good, prospective randomized study, try to anticipate as many explanations for your findings as possible, and have data ready to inform those potential explanations.

Design Effects Can Swamp Treatment Effects

The key idea in this chapter is that research findings often differ dramatically depending upon what research design underlies them. Put simply, *research design matters*. Some cynical observers would even argue that how you choose to design your study has such a major influence on what you find that you can shape your findings by shaping your design.

We are far less cynical, and simply urge you to choose a good comparison group. We also urge you to develop a reasonable fallback position for situations in which you can't implement your first choice. We believe that knowing the implications of choosing different designs will help you to shape your work, and also to assess the work of others.

In this spirit, you should be alert for circumstances when a decision about design is so crucial that this decision has as much effect on your work's outcome as does the treatment you are examining. This sounds extreme. How could choice of a research design, a kind of abstruse step for many practitioners, be as important as the actual treatment? The following example shows how.

EXAMPLE: *Does the effectiveness of SAT coaching courses depend on how you study them?*

How helpful is coaching for SAT exams? In its publications, the College Board argues that coaching can help very little, and that long-term, sustained academic work is the best preparation. Meanwhile, coaching organizations such as Stanley Kaplan, Inc., and the Princeton Review advertise their programs as able to raise SAT scores by 150 points or more. What does the concrete evidence show?

Rebecca DerSimonian and Nan Laird (1983) undertook to review the evidence. They found mountains of it. Conflicts were widespread. During President Carter's administration the Federal Trade Commission conducted hearings to assess SAT coaching, and found it had "questionable value." In contrast, earlier reviews found that coaching can raise scores substantially.

DerSimonian and Laird located 19 studies of coaching for the verbal SAT exam and 17 for the math. After examining how each was done and its results, they concluded that each author's choice of research design is a better predictor of study results than anything else. We quote from their summary:

> Our analysis . . . shows on average a positive gain but also a large variation in the effect of coaching from study to study that cannot be explained by the method of evaluation. When coached students are simply compared to national norms, as in uncontrolled studies, the mean gains in verbal and math scores are about 40 to 50 points. For controlled, but unmatched and unrandomized studies, the mean gain is about 15 points for both math and verbal scores, and is reduced to about 10 points for matched and randomized studies.   (p. 13)

These findings are fascinating, for two reasons. First, they offer concrete evidence about how results can vary depending upon choice of research design. Second, they are a dramatic illustration of how design effects can swamp treatment effects. The numbers are compelling. Randomized studies find that coaching is worth perhaps ten to fifteen points, while research design effects are more than twice as big. Choosing a weaker study design makes the coaching look better.

How to Fix It

The only way to fix it is to make every effort, when designing your project, to anticipate the effects of your research design. If there is no evidence that research design affects results, you are fortunate. The best way to find out is to do a careful research review, of the kind we describe in Chapter 2. Your review should turn up design effects if they are substantial, as in the SAT coaching example. Your task is then to decide which design will most effectively isolate the treatment you are examining, and to implement that design if possible. A good presentation of results to colleagues will include your findings about any design effect, and your reasons for choosing a particular design for your work.

6

Outcomes are the yardsticks you use to judge a predictor's effects. By selecting good outcomes and credible methods for measuring them, you increase the quality of your findings and the chances that your results can inform educational practice.

Your research questions should guide you toward particular outcomes relevant to your purposes. For example, what outcomes are relevant if you are studying complaints about the teaching skills of foreign graduate students leading sections in the natural sciences? Two very different types of outcomes come immediately to mind: how much students in these sections *learn* during the semester, and how well such students *like* the course. If most students learn a lot but those with foreign teaching assistants do not take another science course because they hated their first one so much, isn't there a problem? Yet enjoyment alone also is insufficient—if most students love the sections taught by American teaching assistants but few students learn anything new, isn't there also a problem?

After selecting outcomes, you must measure them. One method of collecting information about student enjoyment is to ask the teaching assistants. But are instructor ratings reasonable indicators of student enjoyment? Would you be better off asking faculty members to observe and find out what they think? Would the best approach be to ask the students directly?

Choosing *what* to measure, and *how* to measure it, is not nearly as simple as it appears. In this chapter, we raise issues that should help you identify your options, evaluate which of them make the most sense, and determine which will generate the most compelling results. By the end of the chapter you should be familiar with:

- *Different kinds of outcomes.* Higher-education researchers use many different kinds of outcomes. Measures of academic achievement are most common, but you should consider other types of measures as well.
- *The distinction between achievement and learning.* Are you interested in knowing the status of people at a particular time, or are you interested in measuring their change, development, and growth?
- *The importance of validity.* Why are some measures more *credible* than others? A good instrument must be more than a catch-as-catch-can potpourri of items—it must be a systematic means of gathering data. What are the different types of validity, and how can you determine how valid your measures are for your purposes?

Different Kinds of Outcomes

Sometimes you will state your research questions in terms of specific outcomes. How well do our seniors applying to medical school perform on the MCATs? How many hours per week do freshmen spend on extracurricular activities? Has the persistence rate for women majoring in science increased as a result of the new advising program? All these questions specify a single outcome—MCAT scores, hours per week, persistence rate—and all you must do is find a good way of measuring each one.

More often, however, you will state your research questions in terms of general *domains* of measurement, not specific outcomes. You might ask what effect the new core curriculum has on academic achievement, but you must still decide what *kind* of academic achievement to measure—factual knowledge or general thinking skills? You might ask what effect participation in student government has on students' self-esteem, but you must still identify those dimensions of self-esteem that are of prime interest. On these occasions, selecting good outcomes is more complex, and to avoid omitting an important outcome, you should usually use more than one.

Outcome Domains

Higher-education researchers generally assess the effects of college and college programs using easily quantifiable indicators of academic achievement: course grades, persistence to graduation, standardized test scores, admission to graduate or professional school, and so on. There are many good reasons for the popularity of these outcomes, including their availability, face validity, precision, and close correspondence to clear college goals. When you are evaluating the effects of a new curriculum, academic achievement is certainly one good criterion for gauging success.

Although the popularity of these outcomes is well deserved, we urge you to consider measures from other domains as well. College affects students in myriad ways, and different experiences in college—friends, living arrangements, extracurricular activities, courses, and so on—affect different aspects of development. During their college years, students not only increase the breadth and depth of their academic and professional knowledge and skills; they also change in other ways. Some learn social skills. Some acquire leadership skills. Some modify their beliefs and values. Some refine their professional and personal goals and expectations and their attitudes toward themselves, others, and society. Some cultivate a stronger sense of self, with a clearer vision of their role in the world. Outcomes from these ancillary domains can round out your portrait of the effects of college (Bowen, 1977; Boyles, 1988; Volkwein, Carbone, and Volkwein, 1988).

Our purpose here is not to list all the potential outcomes you might want to use in any one project. Several excellent books describing the diversity of college outcomes are available, and we refer the reader to those by Peter Ewell (1984), Kenneth Feldman and Theodore Newcomb (1969); Robert Pace (1979; 1985); and Robert Klitgaard (1985). Our goal is simply to point out the many possibilities, and to call for a broader sweep of measures, moving beyond the important, but not exclusively important, academic domain.

EXAMPLE: *Using outcomes from different domains: Effects of individualized curricula on students.*

In the late 1960s, many colleges relaxed academic distribution requirements, allowing students to pursue individualized degree programs. Darwin Hendel (1985) of the University of Minnesota conducted a randomized experiment evaluating the effects of one such program, the Bachelor of Elected Studies (BES). Among the 428 students who applied to the BES program during 1974–75, 244 were randomly selected to participate and 184 were required to remain in departmental programs.

Hendel initially evaluated the success of the program using objective academic indicators. Across many academic dimensions, including total number of quarters enrolled, total number of credits completed, breadth and depth of courses taken, GPA, graduation rates, and enrollment in graduate or professional schools, Hendel found no differences between the two groups. He used this consistent pattern to argue that BES had no adverse academic effects.

But BES also had *positive nonacademic* effects that were found only because Hendel also conducted a follow-up survey focusing on student satisfaction. Five years after admission (or denial of admission) to the program, he sent questionnaires to all 428 students. Those admitted to BES reported higher levels of overall satisfaction with their undergraduate education, and of specific satisfaction with their program's role in helping them obtain a liberal education and learn about a particular discipline. By using both academic and nonacademic outcomes, Hendel was able to provide a fuller portrait of the effects of BES.

Will You Measure Status or Development?

Students' learning and development are central goals of college. Curricular and extracurricular activities are designed to foster and maintain changes in knowledge, attitudes, and beliefs, and it is these changes and their consequences that we hope will persist after graduation.

So, having decided on a set of outcomes, you must decide whether to study the status of students on these outcomes at one point in time or *changes* in status over a period of time. Are you interested in how much accounting business majors *know* at the end of freshman year (their status) or in how much accounting they *learned* during the year (their gain)? In the *level* of students' conversational skills in French by graduation, or in *changes* in these skills during four years of study?

The need to distinguish sharply between status and development is reflected in the recent call by Alexander Astin (1977), Ernest Pascarella (1987), and others for "value-added" analyses. Although the term *value added* has been used by different people to mean different things, the general idea remains the same: because students come to college with diverse backgrounds and skills, we should broaden our research focus from *achievement* at any one point in time (status) to growth over time (change) (Newcomb et al., 1967; Smart, 1985; Singer and Willett, 1988).

Despite a longstanding interest in student growth and development, only recently have educational researchers agreed on the right way to study it. Heated debate among methodologists about how change should be studied has led some authors to suggest (incorrectly) that it is so difficult to study development that researchers are well advised not to try.

But recent work by John Willett (1988), Anthony Bryk and Steven Raudenbush (1987), and others shows that the study of development is easy, *if you collect the right data.* These methodologists have shown that the central problem with studying student development stems from poor research design. Too many researchers try to examine development using data collected at only two timepoints, a problem because the accurate depiction of development requires data collected at three or more timepoints. The implications for design are clear: you must decide early whether you are interested in status or development, and if you choose development, you must design your study accordingly.

Designing a Study of Development

Cross-sectional data cannot describe student development over time. At an intuitive level, this statement seems tautological—to study people as they develop, you must observe them over a period of time and watch them grow. Questions concerning development must be studied longitudinally, using data collected on the same people on each of several occasions. The more occasions (or "waves") you include, the better you will do.

The weakest study of development involves data collected at *two* points in time, a pretest and a posttest. Subtracting pretest from posttest yields a *difference score* summarizing each student's growth during the research period. These difference scores become outcomes for subsequent data analysis.

Although two is the *minimum* number of waves necessary for studying development, two waves cannot portray the complex patterns of growth we expect of college students. Among the many problems with two-wave designs is their omission of data required for characterizing the *shape* of each student's growth trajectory. All you know is each student's status at two points in time; you do not know how they got from point A to point B. Did all the learning occur immediately after pretest, and did the student then coast for several years? Did most students grow at a steady pace, learning approximately equal amounts each year? Did some students peak at the end of junior year, only to fall off during senior year? With two waves of data, you will never know.

The best way to be sure you can comment cogently on development is to collect data at three or more timepoints. With three or more waves of data, you can construct a more fine-grained photograph of each student's development over time. Patterns of student growth can be seen even in simple plots of status versus time. Is growth linear or curvilinear? Do most students peak at some point, or do most level off over time? Are there ceilings on growth? What are they, and when do they occur?

If three waves are better than two, it should come as no surprise that four waves are better than three. In fact, the rule of thumb is "the more, the better." Additional waves of data allow you more accurately to represent and measure students' growth. Of course, advice like this is cheap; putting this advice into practice is expensive. But multiwave data collection is the only way to be sure that you can comment on development. If you want to study development, you must bite the bullet and collect data at three or more points in time (Rogosa and Willett, 1985; Willett, 1989; 1990).

EXAMPLE: *Studying development using multiwave designs: How do students' moral judgments change during college?*

Does attending college promote students' moral judgment, or do people offer increasingly sophisticated responses to moral dilemmas whether or not they go to college? James Rest (1988) investigated this question longitudinally by interviewing 102 people four times over a ten-year period. Initial data collection took place during the senior year of high school; follow-up data were collected two, four, and ten years after high school graduation.

Rest presents results for three subgroups of students, classified according to the amount of education they eventually completed: (1) *high:* college graduate; (2) *moderate:* two to four years of college; and (3) *low:* less than two years of college. At every timepoint, students in the high education group had higher mean levels of moral judgment than their peers in the other two education groups, suggesting that, even in high school, students who will go on to complete college differ from others with respect to moral judgment.

The differences in developmental trajectories were even more interesting. During the four years after high school graduation, mean moral judgment scores for all three groups steadily increased, steeply during the first two years and gradually during the following two years. But, ten years after high school graduation, the mean moral judgment scores for the high and moderate education groups remained stable and high, while the mean moral judgment score for the low education group fell considerably, nearly back to high school levels. Rest used this evidence to argue that college graduates have different developmental trajectories from noncollege graduates, and that college *does* promote moral development.

Short-term versus Long-term Effects

Researchers who find strong relationships between predictors and outcomes in the short term often want to know whether the effects persist over time. This issue arises for two very different reasons. One is to see whether an effect is "real," or whether it is attributable to the very process of research and experimentation (the so-called Hawthorne effect). Do the high volunteer rates following a public service publicity campaign persist once the campaign's novelty wears off?

The other reason to examine long-term effects is to see whether the effects persist *within people* over time. Often, new programs have good initial results but their benefits peter out over the years. The education literature is filled with evaluation reports documenting powerful short-term effects followed by gradual diminution of benefits. If you collect data only during intensive program participation, you will never know about long-term efficacy.

We do not mean to imply that short-term effects are insufficient for demonstrating program effectiveness. Rather, you should think about whether you are interested in the immediate impact of a program, or in the persistence of its effects.

EXAMPLE: *Short-term versus long-term effects: The efficacy of an intervention program for high-risk students.*

During the 1970s, many public colleges experimented with open admissions policies, creating what critics have called a revolving door. Poorly qualified students were admitted, they enrolled, and then they performed poorly, leading them to withdraw or be dismissed, never to complete their degree.

Stayner Landward and Dean Hepworth (1984) examined the efficacy of an intervention designed to break this pattern. Using high school grade point averages and ACT scores, they identified 224 high-risk freshmen enrolling at a large state university and invited them to participate in an Academic Enrichment Program (AEP), a two-credit, first-quarter course providing academic support and counseling. Thirty of the 91 students who volunteered were randomly assigned to participate. The remaining 61 formed one control group and the students who refused to participate formed a second control group.

The short-term success of the program was remarkable. Students who participated had a mean first-semester GPA of 2.14, as compared with 1.41 and 1.34 for the two control groups. Second-semester persistence also differed dramatically: 86 percent of the AEP students returned for the winter quarter as compared with 54 and 52 percent of the two control groups.

Based on these initial data, we might conclude that AEP was a great success. But a long-term perspective yields a different picture. By the second quarter, the mean GPA of program participants fell to 1.29, and was indistinguishable from the mean GPA of the two control groups. And by the third quarter, the three groups were virtually identical with regard to academic performance.

Are Your Measures Valid?

Having selected your outcomes and predictors, you must decide how to measure them. How should you measure the effectiveness of teaching, for example? By using instructor reports? Student ratings? Faculty ratings? Each of these sources would tell you something about teaching effectiveness, but how well does each one assess exactly what you want to know? Does each one cover *every* aspect of effective teaching? What dimensions does each overlook? Are you sure that ratings are the best way to proceed? Would you be better off using an entirely different approach, such as measures of student achievement or learning (the eventual "products" of teaching)?

Validity describes how well a measure actually assesses what you want it to. A valid measure of teaching effectiveness really tells you about effective teaching. Validity is a relative concept, describing the soundness and appropriateness of a measure *for your purposes.* Just because another researcher carefully established the validity of a measure for her purposes with students in her school does not make it valid for *your* purposes with students in *your* school. Measures are not universally valid; each time you use a measure with different people, for a different purpose, in a different context, or at a different time, you should reassess its validity.

EXAMPLE: *The importance of examining validity: Do self-reports of teaching effectiveness really reflect teaching effectiveness?*

Penelope Kegel-Flom (1983) studied 55 instructors at the School of Optometry at the University of California, Berkeley, who agreed to rate themselves and to have students and faculty colleagues rate them with regard to effectiveness of teaching. Three sets of ratings were obtained on the school's standard instructor-evaluation form, which consisted of one global rating of teaching and five five-item scales: professional breadth, instructor-student relationship, interactive teaching, feedback effectiveness, and instructor-patient relationship.

The lack of agreement among the three sources was remarkable. The average correlation between faculty and student ratings on the same scale was only .28, suggesting that faculty members and students use different criteria to judge an instructor's effectiveness. Acknowledging that the term "effective teaching" means different things to faculty and students, how valid are instructors' self-reports in comparison to both these sources? Kegel-Flom found that self-reports had virtually nothing to do with either student or faculty ratings—the average correlation between self reports and either student or peer ratings was .05. Although limited to a single school using a single rating form, Kegel-Flom's findings suggest that self-reports may not be valid indicators of teaching effectiveness.

Content Validity

A measure is *content valid* if its individual items, as a group, cover all the different domains you want to measure. A final exam in a course is content valid if it includes questions on *everything* discussed during the term in proportion to each topic's representation in the curriculum.

Student evaluations of teaching effectiveness are content valid if the form deals with *all* relevant aspects of effective teaching.

Methodologists distinguish between two types of content validity: face validity and sampling-content validity. *Face validity* is the weaker of the two. You establish face validity by having "experts" examine the measure and agree that it does assess what it is supposed to assess. The measure looks right, reads right, feels right.

Because face validity is in the eye of the beholder—what looks right to you may not look right to someone else—you should also consider *sampling-content validity.* You establish sampling-content validity by identifying all the specific domains of interest and by clearly showing how your items, taken together, cover them. Establishing the sampling-content validity of a final examination, for example, would require that you comb through the syllabus, lectures, and textbook and develop a pool of items representing the content of the entire course, paying systematic and proportional attention to the structure and flow of the curriculum (Banta, 1988).

EXAMPLE: *Examining content validity: Developing valid comprehensive examinations.*

Trudy Banta and Janet Schneider (1988) describe how the administration at the University of Tennessee, Knoxville, encouraged faculty members to develop content-valid comprehensive examinations for 11 different bachelor's and master's degree programs.

For each program, faculty committees began by defining the content areas to be included on the test, using final examination files, comprehensive examinations from other universities, item pools generated for previous tests, and placement examinations administered to graduate students. Once content areas were identified, faculty members began writing the actual examinations. The format of the examinations differed by program: two used only essays, five used only multiple-choice questions, and four used a combination of these approaches. Faculty members sought items requiring both simple cognitive skills (recall of information) and higher-order cognitive skills (problem solving, analysis, synthesis, and evaluation). All participating faculty were given two textbooks on test construction, and consulting time with a measurement specialist.

Three additional steps were taken to ensure the content validity of the examinations. First, two outside consultants reviewed each of the tests; this helped faculty establish face validity and identify ambiguous or unclear items. Second, several departments pilot-tested the instruments with selected students, a process that also led to item modification. Third, large samples of students in each of the eleven departments were required to take the examinations, with the guarantee that performance on the examination would not affect grades. These students were then asked to comment on the examinations, and discuss whether they thought the tests reflected the content of what they had learned in the program.

Banta and Schneider conclude with good advice for all higher-education researchers trying to develop valid comprehensive examinations: "Don't use questions from final examinations. Most of these are too narrow; coverage should be broader for a comprehensive examination. Use a measurement specialist to improve the quality of the items and to conduct item analyses after the test is given. Don't underestimate the difficulty of getting all faculty to agree on what should be learned by all students" (p. 81). Developing valid measures is a difficult, time-consuming process. But if your measures are not valid, what meaning can you ascribe to them?

Criterion Validity

Most outcomes and predictors can be measured using several different strategies, which vary in accuracy and cost. Although you always want the best data you can get, you must decide how much quality you really need, because better data usually come only at increased cost. It is often wise to use less expensive measures, as long as the compromise in quality is small relative to the cost saving. For example, many researchers ask students for their SAT scores on questionnaires rather than examining students' admissions folders, because such self-reports are usually highly correlated with actual SAT scores. *Criterion validity* describes how well measures of convenience actually assess the criterion of interest.

Methodologists distinguish between two types of criterion validity—*concurrent* and *predictive*—differing only in the *time* when the criterion is measured. If student reports of cumulative GPA are strongly related to actual cumulative GPA, the self-report has *concurrent validity*. If student reports of expected course grades at midterm are strongly related to actual final course grades, the self-report has *predictive validity*.

If your measure has been used before and its criterion validity was established at that time, it is probably safe to reexamine criterion validity during regular data collection. The easiest way to do this is by selecting a subsample of respondents and collecting data on both measures. For example, you could investigate the concurrent validity of student reports of SAT scores by checking admissions folders for a random sample of 100 students participating in the regular study. Or you could investigate the predictive validity of student midterm course grades by following a random sample of 50 students until the end of the semester, after your main project ends, and then gathering data on the criterion (actual course grade).

But if your measure is new, be sure to validate it *before* using it in a full-scale project. Why wait to find out that your measure may be invalid after it's too late to fix any problems? If you examine criterion validity *before* collecting data, you can use measures shown to have criterion validity with confidence, and you can improve invalid measures before investing additional time and effort.

Although criterion validity appears more objective than content validity, it, too, rests heavily on human judgment. The quality of your assessment of criterion validity depends entirely on the credibility of the criterion. What importance should you give to a relationship between an inappropriate criterion and a measure? A good criterion must be fair, reliable, relevant, and accessible.

Criterion validity must be established using a representative sample of respondents. A haphazard, convenience sample will not do. You should select respondents using the principles of probability sampling discussed in Chapter 3. After all, any demonstration of criterion validity is only generalizable to the main study if the respondents in the validity study are representative of the larger group.

Be sure that the full range of variation in the criterion is displayed in the validity subsample. If not, restriction of range, discussed in Chapter 4, can lead you to conclude (incorrectly) that a perfectly valid measure is invalid. For example, when investigating the predictive validity of midterm grades for final grades, you may get a low correlation simply because many students doing badly at midterm opt to drop the course. When you correlate the two sets of scores, you will have to set aside these students, decreasing the variation in the criterion and diminishing the correlation between measures. Similar range restrictions are created when students who are doing less well in school stop out, or drop out, before graduation. Don't incorrectly conclude that a perfectly good measure is invalid simply because of selective attrition.

EXAMPLE: *Taking advantage of good predictive validity: The relationship between research productivity and teaching effectiveness.*

John Centra (1983) examined the relationship between research productivity and teaching effectiveness in a sample of 2973 faculty members from 61 four-year colleges and universities. As part of normal course evaluations, each faculty member had students fill out the Student Instructional Report

(SIR), a comprehensive measure of teaching effectiveness whose items relate to six dimensions of teaching performance: course organization and planning, faculty-student interaction, communication, course difficulty, and workload.

Rather than verify the publication records of the nearly three thousand faculty participating in the study, Centra used faculty self-reports of research productivity. He supported this procedure as follows:

> Self-reported number of publications generally accurately reflects the actual number of articles published. In one sample of psychologists . . . the self-reported number of articles correlated .84 with entries in *Psychological Abstracts* (for a sample of 4-year college teachers the correlation was even higher at .97). The number of articles produced is also related generally to the quality of research and scholarship, as judged by the number of citations of published work. [Other studies] reported correlations in the .60 to .72 range between citation counts and number of publications.   (p. 382)

Although Centra did not investigate the predictive validity of self-reports in this specific sample, the evidence he cites is compelling.

Construct Validity

Construct validity refers to the degree to which a measure actually assesses the underlying theoretical construct it is supposed to assess. It is perhaps what first comes to mind when nonresearchers talk about validity. A valid measure of academic achievement will generate scores that actually represent academic achievement. If a student can get a high score using strategies unrelated to academic achievement (such as by guessing or by being good at test-taking), or if student characteristics unrelated to academic achievement affect performance (as might happen if a test is framed in language unfamiliar to the student), then the scores are not construct-valid indicators of academic achievement.

Construct validation is a never-ending process. You must

constantly look for evidence demonstrating that a measure assesses what you think it does. Construct validation is an art, relying heavily, sometimes too heavily, upon substantive analysis. You must link a solid theoretical foundation to empirical evidence supporting your argument.

Look for positive and negative evidence concerning validity. For example, suppose you developed a measure of career orientation consisting of thirty items generated systematically from a strong psychological and sociological framework. A logical analysis might suggest that the measure was construct valid. But if you find large cultural differences, with foreign students consistently scoring much lower than American students, your measure may not be as valid as you think.

Construct validity is usually investigated by testing theories about the measure's behavior under different circumstances. You might hypothesize about group differences, strong relationships that might exist with other measures, or weak relationships that might exist with still others. For a measure of prose writing skill, for example, you might hypothesize that journalism majors would score high, and that chemistry majors would score low. You might further hypothesize that the measure would not differ for men and women. Or you might predict that the measure would be strongly related to reading comprehension and vocabulary but unrelated to physical strength.

Unlike the demonstration of criterion validity, where the criterion may be remote or expensive to measure, you often have easy access to the measures with which the construct has a hypothesized relationship. As a result, construct validity may not necessarily have to be investigated using a subsample of respondents. If there is already strong evidence of construct validity, and you simply need supplemental evidence in your sample, you can investigate construct validity during your project using the entire sample of respondents. If you are unsure about the construct validity of your measures, however, take the time to study it before your major project begins. We describe the design of construct-validation pilot studies in Chapter 9.

Validity over Subsamples

Many studies sample respondents from different groups. Sometimes you use group membership to stratify the target population before drawing a sample, and interest centers on differences among groups. For example, you might compare writing samples obtained from a current sample of students with writing samples from students enrolled in earlier years or at similar schools.

Comparisons across groups are acceptable only if the same scores mean the same thing for people in all groups. If grade inflation has become a problem on your campus, today's A may not indicate the same level of performance as an A did in 1980. Just as you would not compare the heights of one group with the weights of another, neither should you compare groups using measures with different metrics. In technical terms, scores must be *equatable* across groups.

Scores are equatable only if the measure is valid in every subgroup. This is not simply a matter of giving the same instrument to everyone. People from different subgroups may interpret the same items differently. Such problems occur not only among different cultural groups (for whom language differences almost ensure that key words, phrases, and ideas will not translate), but also among groups that appear similar but do not really share the same perspective. Freshmen and faculty members are likely to interpret questions about college goals, for example, quite differently. Divergent perspectives may make your measures invalid.

How can you ensure validity across subgroups? Our advice is to pilot test your measures with people from *all* subgroups to be included in your study. Debrief pilot respondents, ask them to identify problematic items or instructions and to suggest alternative wording. It would be a shame, for example, if foreign students were unable to answer your questions about current events because the items included many acronyms (e.g., NATO, CIA, PRI) which do not translate the same way in all languages.

Validity when Studying Change

Researchers generally use one of two approaches for collecting developmental data—administering the same instrument repeatedly or administering "parallel" or "equivalent" forms. Validity issues are especially complex under either strategy, for your measures must be equatable not only across groups but across *time*.

Administration of physically different but psychometrically equivalent tests takes a major toll on the test-construction process, and we strongly urge you use parallel forms only when they have been developed and rigorously tested by organizations such as Educational Testing Service, American College Testing Program, and the Psychological Corporation, which specialize in the construction of tests.

EXAMPLE: *How much should you worry about pretest bias? The effects of coaching programs.*

Robert Bangert-Drowns, Chen-lin Kulik, and James Kulik (1983) examined 29 controlled studies of coaching programs designed to raise achievement test scores of applicants to college, and found a marked pretest sensitization effect. In the 16 randomized studies using only a posttest achievement measure, the average effect size for coaching was .18. In the 13 studies using both pretests and posttests, the average effect size was twice as large, .32. The authors conclude that giving a pretest to both the treatment and the control groups produces a greater comparative effectiveness of coaching. Perhaps for some students the experience of taking the pretest ties in to some of the coaching instruction and strengthens it.

What should you do about pretest effects? We have one concrete suggestion, one that assumes you are willing to make an effort to separate a pretest effect from a real treatment effect. You can do this by embedding a small second treatment group into a research design where possible. This second group is a randomly selected subset of the full treatment group. But students in this second group do not take a pretest. Adopting this plan will give you three groups to compare—a treatment group getting both pretest and posttest, a treatment group getting just posttest, and a control group getting both pretest and posttest. Comparing the first treatment group with the controls gives an estimate of the impact of the treatment. Comparing the two treatment groups gives a sense of whether or not, and how much, the simple step of taking a pretest influences students' posttest performance.

7

The dean decides to weigh instructional effectiveness more heavily when making tenure decisions. Two assistant professors with similar publication records are up for promotion. Students in their classes are surveyed and, on a scale 1 to 5, one receives a rating of 2.5, the other a rating of 3.5. Can the dean be sure that these professors actually differ? Could the ratings be so inaccurate that 2.5 is indistinguishable from 3.5? Should a tenure decision be based on such fallible measures?

Proponents of the interdisciplinary program for freshmen argue that their courses improve students' critical thinking skills. A randomized experiment reveals that students in interdisciplinary courses average 85 on a test of critical thinking skills and students in traditional courses average only 60. The difference seems large, but is not "statistically significant." Are interdisciplinary courses really no better than traditional ones, or is the test simply too inaccurate to pick up the difference? Should decisions about curriculum be based on such imprecise information?

Inaccuracy creeps into measurement in myriad ways. Measuring age and number of earned credits is relatively easy; measuring attitudes, behavior, and aptitudes is far more difficult. Consider instructional ratings, the mainstay of college assessment. Do all of the 20 questions on the student rating form assess the same instructional qualities equally well? Would the students' ratings change if you worded the questions somewhat differently? If the students filled out the forms a week later? A month later? At the beginning of class instead of at the end? At home instead of in class?

Few things can be measured perfectly. But by making judicious design decisions you can improve the quality of your measurements, and in this chapter we present several specific strategies for doing so. By the end of the chapter, you should:

- *Understand what influences measurement quality.* Quality is undermined by the presence of measurement error. Most errors come from one of three sources— flaws in the instrument and its administration, random fluctuations over time in the people being measured, and disagreement among raters or scorers. Learn what the sources of error are, and how they creep into your measurements.

- *Learn how to minimize the effects of measurement error.* Methodologists have developed many strategies for minimizing the effects of measurement error. We present six specific strategies we find useful and discuss when and how you can use them.

- *Know when to investigate measurement quality.* The quality of your data can be investigated before or during your study. Think about when you should investigate it before data collection, and when you can get away with embedding a study of measurement quality into your main project.

What is Measurement Error?

Ask any two students about the quality of a professor's teaching and you probably will get two different answers. Ask one of these students the same question after the course is over and you probably will get yet a third answer. Ask a professor about a student's aptitude twice, once early and once late in the term, and you probably will get two different answers. Has the professor's effectiveness changed? Has the student's aptitude changed? Perhaps, but not necessarily. The observed variation may be due to nothing more than *measurement error.*

Whenever you collect data, you are not necessarily recording the underlying "true" value of a characteristic (such as instructional effectiveness); you may be recording a combination of this true value and some accompanying measurement error. Remember when you didn't do well on a test simply because you slept poorly the night before? You told yourself, and perhaps your professor, that your observed score did not show what you really knew. Your score imprecisely reflected your true knowledge—it was contaminated by measurement error.

Measurement error arises from many sources. Uncontrollable fluctuations in people's psychological and physical condition during data collection, misinterpretations of the wording of the instrument, the impact of the particular time and conditions under which the instrument is given, and variations in its administration and scoring can all lead to unsuspected error. Even seemingly small details, like poor lighting or extreme temperatures, can distort responses.

Although the sources of error are diverse, the effects are the same—*measurement error makes observed scores falli-*

ble indicators of true scores. An instrument laden with measurement error does not yield the information you want—the underlying true scores. Some observed scores will be too high, others will be too low, and you will never know which is which.

The magnitude of the measurement errors determines the trustworthiness of your data. When errors are small relative to true scores, observed scores closely mirror true scores: the observed scores of people closely parallel their true scores. When errors are small and you compare the instructional ratings of different professors, you can be pretty sure that the professors do, in fact, differ in the way observed. The one with the higher rating really is more effective, at least as measured by *this* instrument. The observed variation in scores is worth knowing, reflecting real differences among people.

But when errors are large relative to true scores, your data are little more than "noise." The "signal" has been disturbed, made less intelligible and less informative; observed scores may not closely mirror true scores. If you had asked the questions slightly differently, given the instrument later in the term, or used different raters or scorers, you might have gotten dramatically different results. So not only would the scores of professors differ from scores at another time, the one you got *this time* might bear little resemblance to the *true score.* If this can happen, can you be sure that professors with different ratings do, in fact, differ by the amount observed? They may not even differ in the *direction* observed! Should tenure decisions rely on ratings so error-laden that the weaker of two professors might get a higher score simply because she handed out the forms at the beginning of class while the other professor handed them out at the end?

Even a well-planned study will fail if it relies on data that are riddled with measurement error. You can select a stratified random sample of students and randomly assign them to treatment and control groups, but if your instruments are heavily contaminated by measurement error, you may not detect an effect that really occurs. Once the data have been collected, it is too late to fix any problems, for they arose *during* data collection. *Statistical analysis cannot retrospectively repair a flawed instrument.*

But good design *can* prospectively minimize the influence of measurement error. By carefully constructing instruments, controlling the conditions under which they are given, deciding when they should be given, and choosing and training the people who score them, you can reduce the effects of measurement error. Of course, you will never eliminate all of it. By its very nature, measurement error is hidden. If you are unaware of a particular source of error, how can you be sure to alter those design features that could control it? And some sources of error are not easily controlled. But your inability to eradicate *all* error should not stop you from minimizing it as much as you can.

Reliability and Measurement Error

Rather than thinking about measurement error directly, researchers often evaluate their measurement in terms of its *reliability*. Reliability describes the extent to which two sets of measurements of the same characteristic on the same people duplicate each other. If an instrument yields identical duplicate measurements, then the rank-order of the people measured will be consistent, and we say that the measurement is reliable. The question "What is your date of birth?" is a reliable method for gathering data on age because most people give the same answer each time they are asked.

If an instrument yields inconsistent duplicate measurements when it is given at different times, under different conditions, or by different people, then it is not reliable. Another way of gathering age data is to ask "How old are you?" This question is not nearly as reliable as "What is your date of birth?" because people respond differently under different circumstances and people of the same exact age may give slightly different answers. For example, most people give their ages in whole numbers—a student will say she is 20 or 21, not 20 years, 6 months, 5 days. Asking for such accuracy could create arithmetic errors. With rounded numbers, some people round down, staying 20 until their twenty-first birthday, while others round up, becoming 21 once their twentieth birthday party is over. And rounding can be inconsistent. If asked at the end of an interview about drinking, a student who usually says "20" may say "21" simply because of the state drinking age. So what appears to be a direct and simple question may not yield high-quality data.

Three Ways of Estimating Reliability

Most estimators of reliability work by finding the correlation between duplicate measurements of the same characteristic. A variety of estimators are available, differing primarily in how the duplicate measurements are gathered. When you examine the consistency of responses given by the same people to the same instrument, or two parallel instruments, at different times, you estimate *test-retest reliability.* When you examine the consistency of ratings of the same stimuli (such as students' essays) by different judges or raters, you estimate *interrater agreement.* When you examine the consistency of peoples' responses to different items on the same instrument at the same time, you estimate *internal-consistency reliability.*

Estimating test-retest reliability and interrater agreement is fairly easy. For the former, give the instrument twice to a group of students and correlate the two sets of scores; for the latter, give the instrument once, have two raters score the data, and correlate the raters' scores.

Estimating internal-consistency reliability is a bit more difficult conceptually, because only one set of data is available—the responses of one group of people at one time. What is there to correlate?

Methodologists have developed an ingenious solution to this dilemma. Instead of two versions of the instrument being given (as when estimating test-retest reliability), the single instrument is split in half, the two parts are treated as equivalent, and the two half-test scores are correlated (with a small adjustment for total length of instrument). Of course, as your instrument gets longer, the number of ways to divide it skyrockets. And why divide it in half? Why not thirds, fourths, or fifths? Why not even treat each item as a separate mini-instrument, correlate the scores for all items, and use some sort of average correlation to estimate internal-consistency reliability? Broadly speaking, this logic leads to the three most popular estimates of internal-consistency reliability: the Kuder-Richardson coefficients (KR-20 and KR-21) and Cronbach's alpha.

Because different reliability estimators are sensitive to different sources of error, they will not necessarily agree. An instrument can have high internal consistency, for example, but low test-retest reliability. This will happen if all its items homogeneously assess a single characteristic at one instant, but if students are so variable from moment to moment that responses change when the same questions are asked at different times. Measures of mood and affect, for example, can be internally consistent, but often have low test-retest reliability.

This means you must examine several different reliability estimates before deciding whether your instrument is really reliable. Each separate estimate presents an incomplete picture. If the student rating forms handed out during the last two weeks of the term are to accurately assess perceived effectiveness of instruction, they must be internally consistent, stable across the two-week period, *and* reasonably similar across students within classes. Otherwise, no one administration of the forms will yield decent information for decisionmaking or research.

A Flaw in the Concept of Reliability

Measurement error is only one of two factors affecting reliability. In general, the less precision with which you measure each person, the bigger the variation attributable to measurement error and the lower your estimate of reliability. But the effect of measurement error on reliability is not absolute, because reliability indirectly compares the magnitude of variation in measurement error to the magnitude of variation among people's true scores.

A simple example illustrates this abstract concept. Suppose we give a test to two different groups of people. Suppose further that the average true score in both groups is identical, say 50, but the *range* of true scores is different: 45 to 55 in one group, 0 to 100 in the other. If the variation attributable to measurement error in both groups is identical, with errors ranging from −5 to +5, will the instrument be equally reliable in both groups? No, because *the effect of measurement error on reliability depends upon the amount of true variability in the groups being measured.* The test appears more reliable in the group with greater true variability, because the errors end up having little effect on the relative rankings of the people in the group. An error of 5 points moves the average student (with a score of 50) to 45 or 55. Either way, the student is still approximately "average." In the other group, a 5-point error moves the average student to either the highest or the lowest possible score. If an average student can get such extreme scores just because of measurement error, the instrument is certainly unreliable!

When the true scores of students in a sample are homogeneous, variability in true scores is low, and even a small amount of variation due to measurement error can make an instrument appear unreliable. When the true scores of people in a sample are heterogeneous, variability in true scores is high, and so even a large amount of variation from measurement error may not affect the appearance of reliability. If you study a sample of people whose true scores are homogeneous, reliability will necessarily be low. *So, if you use a normally reliable instrument in a restricted sample, it can appear very unreliable,* even though it is providing precise and accurate measurements of a group of students.

This can be a serious problem for researchers in higher education because of the intrinsic homogeneity of college populations. Although most schools seek diversity, admissions procedures usually reduce variability on some dimensions, certainly those of academic achievement and aptitude. If your research interest centers on these dimensions, it can be difficult to find or construct reliable instruments. But this may not mean that your measurements are imprecise; it may simply mean that all the students in your sample are similar.

Attrition exacerbates the problem of homogeneity, and nonrandom attrition makes it even worse. As Vincent Tinto (1975) notes in his classic paper on attrition, most students withdraw for specific reasons: "Academic dismissal is most closely associated with grade performance . . . [Voluntary] withdrawal, instead, appears to relate to the lack of congruency between the individual and both the intellectual climate of the institution and the social system composed of his peers" (pp. 116–117). Because students drop out nonrandomly—with the least successful or the socially ostracized being the first to leave—the consequences for reliability can be dramatic. Measures shown to be reliable for the entire freshman class may not be reliable for honor students or seniors. Measures shown to be reliable in a large state university may not be reliable in a small private college, even though the measurements may be equally precise on both campuses.

But the converse is also true: if you study a more heterogeneous sample, reliability will appear higher even though precision remains unchanged. When you select students from a target population in which true variability dwarfs variation from measurement error, you increase reliability. Of course, you should not modify your target population simply for this purpose. When studying the freshman foreign language program, do not include seniors simply to improve the reliability of a measure of language achievement. But do use a stratified sample to ensure that the full spectrum of population variability is represented in your sample.

Does the effect on reliability of heterogeneity in true scores make reliability a useless parameter to estimate? Not at all. In Chapters 3 and 5 we argued that increasing heterogeneity in your sample improves your chances of finding strong effects. Now we are arguing that you should also try to reduce measurement error. More true heterogeneity and greater precision—a winning combination. Both will increase reliability and improve the quality of your work. But remember: reliability is not necessarily the best indicator of your success, because it does not tell you separately about variation in true scores and variation attributable to measurement error—it tells you about them together.

One final note about examining measurement quality. Estimating the quality of your measurements is not an end in itself. You must *use* the information to improve your study. If an instrument has low test-retest reliability, this may be telling you that, because people's responses fluctuate randomly from day to day, you should gather data at several different times and take the average. To assess the prevalence of depression among freshmen, for example, have students fill out questionnaires several times during the year. The goal is not simply to find out how good your measures are, but to learn how to make them better.

EXAMPLE: *The effect of homogeneity on reliability: The reliability of the Law School Admissions Test (LSAT).*

Standardized tests such as those developed by the American College Testing Program (ACT) and the Educational Testing Service (ETS) usually have impressive reliability estimates. But if you use these tests with restricted populations, *your* estimate of reliability can be lower.

Brian Powell and Lala Steelman (1983) estimated the equivalent-forms reliability between scores on two different versions of the LSAT using 51 students enrolled in an LSAT preparatory training course. Students took the June and October 1980 versions of the LSAT on two consecutive days; testing order was determined by randomization. Finding an estimated correlation of .80 between scores on the two forms, the authors wrote: "The correlation of .80, although high, is slightly lower than the correlation found in the total test population. This occurs because . . . the sample's scores have less variability than the national scores" (p. 37).

Six Strategies for Improving Measurement Quality

You can vastly improve measurement quality through thoughtful design, instrument construction, and data-collection procedures. A haphazard collection of questions administered in catch-as-catch-can fashion to a convenience sample of students or faculty will not yield high-quality findings. The time spent creating good instruments and ensuring variability in true scores across people in the sample has an exceptionally high payoff. Here are six specific ways to design quality into your data collection.

Selecting and Revising Items

Most instruments—be they achievement tests, attitude scales, or rating forms—consist of many individual questions ("items"), each of which is a tiny indicator of the underlying construct. The SAT, for example, is composed of dozens of multiple-choice questions, each a little measure of a student's "scholastic aptitude." Total scores summarize responses to the individual items. The choice of individual items affects the quality of the total.

Each item must really assess what it is supposed to assess. Constructing a reliable, but invalid, measure makes little sense; you can reliably determine the number of students in a lecture hall, or pieces of chalk on the board, yet these are certainly not valid indicators of teaching effectiveness. But reliability is a necessary *precondition* for validity. *An unreliable measure cannot be valid.* If students' scores on a history test fluctuate widely depending upon how the questions are asked, the time of day the test is given, and who does the grading, the test *cannot* be a valid measure of knowledge of history.

For an instrument (or a subscale) to yield high-quality measurements of a single construct, it must be internally homogeneous and coherent. All items must be substantively and psychometrically equivalent; they must fit into the whole. Including items unrelated to the construct you are measuring adds irrelevant variation, increases measurement error, and reduces precision. Including reading comprehension items on a measure of students' moral judgment would undermine the quality of measurement because each student's score would now relate to reading comprehension, a construct perhaps irrelevant for moral judgment.

Always check your instrument's performance before using it on a large scale. Examine each item's behavior alone and in relation to all others. Administer the instrument to some colleagues, a small group of experts, or a small sample of students. Debrief each person, examining her answers and asking her why she gave each response. Ask for critiques of the instrument's structure and organization and of each item's content and wording. Clarify wording, fix the instrument's flow and structure, and replace any problematic items.

Increasing the Number of Items

If each item in an instrument is really measuring the same thing, why not use just one item? This would shorten the instrument, eliminate repetition, and reduce the burden on students and faculty. Data collection would be quicker, more efficient, and less expensive.

Unfortunately, the single-item test is especially susceptible to the influence of measurement error. Because each item is a fallible indicator of students' true scores, the score on any one item (even the "best" item) can be far from the true score. Across many similar items, some scores will be too high, others too low, but, on average, they should be near the true value—after all, they are all measuring the same thing. As long as any errors are unsystematic, independent of one another and the underlying true value, individual item scores will fluctuate randomly about the true score. Summing over many items cancels out the errors, yielding a total closer to the true score.

So one good way to improve measurement quality is simply to include more items in your instrument. As long as each item equivalently measures the underlying characteristic you are examining, the reliability of the total score will increase dramatically with additional items. This is an extremely effective strategy because as items are added, variation caused by measurement error is rapidly dwarfed by the increasing variability in true scores. (As items are added, variability in true scores increases multiplicatively, while variation caused by measurement error increases only additively.)

For similar reasons, you should try to gather several indicators of each characteristic you are measuring. Instead of using one self-report measure of student self-esteem, ask roommates and professors, too. When measuring achievement, give both multiple-choice and open-ended exams. Socioeconomic information should include data on the income, occupation, and education of both parents. If each indicator assesses the same characteristic, you will improve measurement quality when you combine the multiple indicators in your analyses.

Obviously, practical constraints and respondent tedium make it impossible to include hundreds of items to measure each characteristic. But reliability increases quickly when only a few items are added, and the effects of adding items are most dramatic when you begin with but one or two. For example, if the average correlation between items is .3, as is common in testing college students, adding two items to a two-item scale increases internal consistency reliability (Cronbach's alpha) from .46 to .63, but adding the same two items to a ten-item scale only increases it from .81 to .84.

EXAMPLE: *Longer versus shorter instruments: Measuring loneliness among college students.*

College can be a lonely time: students leave home and have new demands placed upon them. But can loneliness be quantified? Deciding the answer was yes, Dan Russell, Letitia Peplau, and Carolyn Cutrona (1980) developed the Revised UCLA Loneliness Scale. In this instrument, students are given 20 statements such as "I feel in tune with the people around me," "No one really knows me well," "I can find companionship when I want it," and "People are around me but not with me" and are asked to use a 4-point scale (1 = never, 2 = rarely, 3 = sometimes, 4 = often) to indicate how often they feel described by these statements. Reliability was estimated in two samples: 162 UCLA freshmen, and 237 students in psychology courses at UCLA or the University of Tulsa. Internal consistency was high in both (Cronbach's alpha = .94).

If you want to study loneliness at your school, do you really need all 20 items? The authors say perhaps not. Discussing this point, they suggest that if resources are limited, a 4-item scale might be reasonable. Using the "best" four items (the actual items cited above), the authors estimated Cronbach's alpha to be .75 in their sample of UCLA freshmen. Although the longer instrument is certainly more reliable, in some applications the 4-item scale could suffice.

Lengthening Item Scales

Many characteristics are measurable using commonly accepted scales—age, GPA, and high school rank, to name a few—but others, such as attitudes, opinions, and perceptions, are not easily quantified. No universal metric exists. What metric underlies satisfaction with roommate assignments? Realizing that most people can make more than yes/no distinctions—satisfaction is certainly a relative construct, varying along some continuum, from extremely dissatisfied to extremely satisfied—you can ask for ratings on short ordinal scales such as 1 to 3, 1 to 4, or 1 to 5.

The important point for measurement quality is that the scale's *length* is within your control. Construct the scale so that students or faculty can give as precise responses as they are able, allowing differences among them to shine through. For decades, 3-, 4- and 5-point scales have been popular, owing to tradition and an implicit belief that people cannot distinguish accurately among more than a handful of points on a scale. But surely few characteristics have such limited variability. Longer scales offer a greater range of possible responses. As long as students at your campus can distinguish among the options, the observed scores from longer scales are more likely to reflect any true variation that exists across students, making the measure more reliable.

We therefore recommend that you make your scales as long as your resources permit. Seven-point scales are better than 6-point scales, which are better than 5-point scales, and so on. Unfortunately, the ambiguity of this statement is necessary. We can't unequivocally say that the best scales have 7 points or 70 points: optimal length is determined by the nature of the characteristic you are examining and the extent to which students can discriminate among levels. At one extreme, you could argue that if the underlying characteristic is really continuous, the scale should be unbounded (of infinite length). But this is impractical, and might ultimately lead to poor measurement quality, for how could such a scale have identical meanings for, and be used equivalently by, everyone?

So boundaries are necessary, and your challenge is to select the "right" number of points. Think of extending the scale until your students can no longer discriminate between adjacent values—when they can no longer tell the third point from the fourth or the second. That's where you should stop, because it's where haphazard responses begin to add imprecision back into your measurements. When does this happen? In real terms, you'll never know—the best you can do is guess, and then test your hunch in a pilot study. But erring on the side of overextension is always preferable, because during analysis you can collapse scales that were too long, but you can never lengthen scales that were too short.

The principle of lengthening scales can be extended to questions you would use to assess characteristics such as the number of classes taken per semester or the number of hours spent studying each day. Colleagues often "precode" continuous responses using broad categories such as (a) less than 1.00; (b) 1.00–1.99; (c) 2.00–3.99; (d) 4.00 or more. Consider the advantages of a different approach. Invite students to answer using a continuous scale. Let them give as precise answers as they can. If they cannot give a precise answer, ask them to estimate. If they give a range, you can always use the range's midpoint. And if you still prefer precoded categories, at least use more of them. Coarsely categorizing continuous data eliminates important information. Using longer scales allows the real values to shine through and makes true differences among students more likely to be detected.

EXAMPLE: *Lengthening item scales: The effects of including plus and minus qualifiers on the reliability of student grades.*

Although plus and minus qualifiers are included in grading systems for many reasons often unrelated to measurement considerations, a side effect of this practice is to improve measurement quality. Why? Because qualifiers extend 5-point scales (A, B, C, D, F) to 13-point scales (assuming no qualifiers are added to F).

This effect is illustrated by Jason Millman, Simeon Slovacek, Edward Kulick, and Karen Mitchell (1983) in their study of the reliability of grades given to 124 civil engineering students who earned both bachelor's and master's degrees at Cornell University between 1976 and 1980. Reliability was estimated by correlating the students' grades in their major field with their combined GPA for these courses. At the undergraduate level, reliability based upon the 13-point scale was .777; with the 5-point scale, it was .745. But at the graduate level, where grades are more homogeneous (grades of C or lower are rare), the effect of scale length was more pronounced. Reliability using the 13-point scale was .736; using the 5-point scale it was .674. If you can get the data, longer scales are clearly preferable to shorter scales.

Administering the Instrument Systematically

The conditions of instrument administration—the room, the clarity and wording of instructions, the length of time given to complete questions—all affect measurement quality. If you allow administration conditions to vary across students, you can introduce large and irreversible measurement errors into your data.

All instructions must be clear and unambiguous. On self-administered instruments, include practice items so students can check their comprehension of the task. Interviewers should be carefully trained. They should not reword questions, lead students, or feel too relaxed about interpreting replies. Give them standardized probes to use when students hesitate and standardized replies to use when students ask questions. The goal is to make sure that every student receives an identical stimulus. You don't want any inconsistency that can increase variation due to measurement error and decrease precision. It would be unfortunate, for example, if students at the back of the room got low scores on a listening comprehension test simply because they could not clearly hear the taped passages.

The Timing of Data Collection

How do you decide *when* to collect data? Convenience is certainly one factor, but should it be the only one? If students' responses are unlikely to differ across time, the answer to this question is yes. As long as responses will be identical (or nearly identical) regardless of when you collect data, simply choose the most convenient opportunity. Make it easy on yourself.

But if responses are likely to differ, timing becomes crucial. If you are faced with different responses to the same question, which one best reflects the "true" underlying response? Unfortunately, you'll never know. The best you can do is: (1) determine whether there is a problem by giving the instrument several times and comparing the sets of responses; and (2) if the test-retest correlations are low, collect data at several times, hoping that the errors will cancel out, leading to a summary score more representative of the underlying true score.

But this strategy has a problem. Low test-retest correlations are not always due to measurement error; sometimes students genuinely *change* between measurement occasions. For example, measures of achievement *should* change during the semester. A low test-retest correlation for an achievement test does not always imply lack of precision for the individual measurements. If learning does occur, but people learn different amounts, the test-retest correlation will suffer but measurement precision may still be high. You may know everyone's true scores accurately on each testing occasion, but their differing growths may have shuffled their relative rankings so that the test-retest correlation is deflated. So if true scores actually change over time, a test-retest correlation cannot disentangle these changes from measurement error; it pools them together. You cannot be sure what part of the observed change over time is attributable to measurement error and what part to real change.

The potential impact of heterogeneity in real growth on test-retest correlations suggests that the length of time between administrations is important. When the gap is large, you may inadvertently leave room for real change that will be misinterpreted as error. Closing the time gap resolves this, but may be impractical. Not only can this abuse students' good nature by subjecting them to seemingly unnecessary reassessment with the same instrument, but memory can affect retest responses: "Oh, I remember, I said very satisfied." So you want to use a time gap short enough so that little real change can occur, but long enough so that students are willing to be retested.

EXAMPLE: *Estimating test-retest correlations: The stability of responses to the University Residence Environment Scales (URES).*

The 96-item URES is a popular instrument for assessing the social climate of university residences. Marvin Gerst and Rudolf Moos (1973) examined its internal consistency using 466 students and staff living in 13 dormitories at an unnamed private university. All ten scales were reasonably internally consistent, with KR-20s ranging from .76 to .87.

But is one administration of the URES sufficient for constructing a stable estimate of residence climate? Does a dormitory's climate change from day to day and week to week? To investigate these questions, the authors went to two dormitories (one male, one female) at an unnamed public university and gave the URES on three separate occasions to 83 students. They found that

> individuals living in these two dormitories perceived their respective environments in similar ways both one week and one month after an initial testing. The correlations . . . range from .67 to .75 after one week and from .59 to .74 after one month. While there is some decrease in the correlations from the one-week to the one-month testing, as would be expected, the drop-off is quite small indicating adequate individual stability of perceptions over 11% of the academic year. (p. 518)

And if responses are aggregated to the dormitory level, as is often done, the stability of the URES increases to well above .80. Gerst and Moos conclude that a single administration of the URES should be sufficient for gathering good data on residence social climate.

Use Multiple Raters or Scorers

When several professors grade the same essay, they should be reasonably consistent in their assessments. After all, if this did not happen, what meaning could be attached to course grades? Without common standards, all subjective evaluations are questionable.

But agreement usually goes only so far—beauty remains in the eye of the beholder. One professor might call a senior thesis innovative; a colleague might call it trifling and derivative. No matter how commonly held you believe your standards are, some disagreement is natural. So when using data that are dependent upon subjective judgment, you must identify the *criteria* to be used for rating and decide whether *multiple raters* are necessary. At issue is the magnitude of error introduced into the measurements because of raters themselves, over and above any imprecision associated with the *instrument*.

To illustrate, suppose you wanted to exempt students from a freshman expository writing course based upon essays written during the first week of school. Is it enough to have each student's essays read by only one professor? Perhaps, but not necessarily. Your answer depends on the magnitude of the disagreement among professors.

The first strategy for coping with disagreement among raters is to eliminate as much disagreement as you can before it arises. To do this, you must rid yourself, and your raters, of the assumption that we all share common standards. We might like to think we do, but empirical evidence suggests the contrary. We do not all agree on what constitutes a good essay. Gather the raters together and have them articulate, discuss, and refine their criteria. Have them focus on both broad and fine distinctions; they may agree on the difference between an A and an F, but the difference between an A− and a B+ is far trickier. Standardization is essential; without it, interrater agreement will suffer and imprecision will creep into your measurements.

Having developed standardized criteria, you must then decide how many colleagues will rate each paper. To decide, select a random sample of papers, have two or three professors read each one, and then estimate interrater agreement. Make sure the ratings are "blind"; don't let the raters see their colleagues' ratings. If interrater agreement is very high, then perhaps only one professor will need to read each paper; any one professor's evaluation is similar enough to all the others that one measurement yields a precise assessment. If interrater agreement is low, however, several professors should read each. This is a critical investment of resources; without it, your data may reflect little more than the individual biases of which professor read which paper.

EXAMPLE: *Estimating interrater agreement: Peer assessments of research, teaching, and service.*

Lawrence Root (1987) examined interrater agreement among a six-member Executive Committee that assessed the research, teaching, and service contributions of faculty members at the University of Michigan's Graduate School of Social Work. Ratings were made on an 8-point scale ranging from $0 =$ unsatisfactory to $7 =$ exceptional.

> The first step was an effort to standardize rating criteria. The Executive Committee implemented some basic training techniques in an effort to establish a common understanding of the ratings. The initial step involved reviewing and discussing the criteria . . . [Then cases] were selected to illustrate the levels of performance which had previously been associated with high and low ratings. This exercise was intended to encourage greater continuity and consistency over time as well as to clarify the criteria employed. (p. 74)

To increase standardization of the materials, faculty members were given a reporting form, which they could use if they wanted. Each faculty member's packet was then rated by every committee member.

Interrater agreement was generally high; with the exception of one rater, correlations between raters always exceeded .60. But consistency differed across faculty activities; the average correlation between research ratings was .850; between service ratings, .607; and between teaching ratings, .603.

Should all six raters continue to examine each faculty member's performance, or does the high level of interrater agreement suggest that fewer raters could suffice? Root addresses this very point: "One practical implication of the high interrater reliability is the possibility of a reduction in the number of raters with only a modest loss of composite reliability. Given the extensive time necessary for performing these assessments, reducing the number of raters represents a significant time savings" (p. 80). He suggests using three raters, arguing that the effect on research ratings would be small and the effect on teaching and service ratings would be tolerable. But, he concludes, "the question of 'how much reliability is enough' remains a matter of judgment" (p. 80).

Looking at Measurement Quality

No single study can establish the quality of an instrument for all purposes, in all settings, for all time. Measurement quality must be established in context, for a well-described use in a specific setting. Always gather such information either before or during your study.

To decide when to collect information about measurement quality, think about how much you already know about your instruments. If you or others have used them before with a sample from a similar population and they worked well at that time, take advantage of this previous work. Don't reinvent the wheel. Higher-education journals are filled with reports of measurement quality gathered during studies at various colleges, under various conditions, for various purposes. If your application is similar, measurement quality should be maintained. After all, if this were not the case, why bother using published instruments?

But be careful: Previous estimates of measurement quality are informative only if you use the instrument in a similar way, for a similar purpose, with similar people.

Rigidly structured administrations of published instruments are not as common as you might believe. Most researchers modify instruments, use them for slightly different purposes, or use them with somewhat different types of students. Even subtle differences can diminish the applicability of published estimates.

We therefore recommend that you always reestimate reliability and evaluate the precision of your instrument. Just because an instrument worked well when it was used at Ohio State does not guarantee it will work well at Michigan State. Even an instrument that worked well at your own college ten years ago may no longer perform as well today. If you modify an instrument or use it with different students or at a different time, you must reinvestigate its quality. This helps both you and other researchers; your study will extend knowledge about other situations in which the instrument may be useful.

When should you collect data on measurement quality? If you are confident the instruments will perform well in your project, then collecting data "along the way" should suffice. As long as you end up confirming your hunch, you will save time and money. Of course, the instruments may *not* perform as well as you expected. If this happens, there will unfortunately be little you can do about it.

So if your measures have not been used in a similar setting with similar students, and especially if they have never been used before, take the time to examine their performance *before* large-scale data collection. Collect data on measurement quality as part of a small-scale pilot study while investigating other aspects of design, such as sampling strategies, use of stratifiers, and the choice of an appropriate comparison group. Although pilot studies may appear unnecessarily expensive and time-consuming, they ultimately pay huge dividends, improving the quality of any final project. In Chapter 9 we present a detailed discussion of how to organize pilot studies.

EXAMPLE: *Deciding when to collect data on measurement quality: Examining the relationship between residence-hall environment and students' sense of competence.*

Steven Janosik, Don Creamer, and Lawrence Cross (1988) used a modified version of the University Residence Environment Scales (URES) to examine the relationship between students' sense of how well they fit into their dormitory and their sense of interpersonal and intellectual competence. They found that "higher sense of competence scores were associated with perceptions that residence life should provide greater emotional support, greater involvement of students in governance, and less competition" (p. 322).

Because of the well-documented reliability of the URES (see the example earlier in this chapter), the authors collected supplemental internal-consistency reliability data "along the way" using their full stratified random sample of 600 freshmen. The additional reliability information was especially important because they *modified* the URES, changing its true-false format into a 4-point scale ranging from strongly agree (1) to strongly disagree (4). They made this change with the hope of improving measurement quality.

But because their measure of perceived competence—the Sense of Competence Scale—was new, they conducted a pilot study with 97 students to investigate its performance. This 23-item instrument included 2 subscales: 13 questions designed to assess intellectual skills, and 10 designed to assess interpersonal skills. These subscales yielded estimated Cronbach's alphas of .76 and .79 respectively. Armed with this information, the authors were able to collect their data more confidently, and their findings are convincing.

HOW MANY PEOPLE
SHOULD YOU STUDY?

8

You've stated a research question clearly and reviewed previous research. You've identified the target population and developed a sampling plan. You've thought carefully about predictors and the comparisons inherent in them. You've selected instruments and improved them. You now face a crucial design question: How many people should you study?

When asked this question by colleagues—and we are asked this question more often than any other—we invariably respond "The more, the better." *The more people you include in your study, the better your chances of finding effects that really exist.* But, of course, this advice is too general to be practical. Research is time consuming, and you can't afford to use all your resources collecting data. You need to know not just that "more is better"; you need to know "how many is enough."

In this chapter, we provide guidelines to help you make this decision. We discuss conceptual issues involved in determining the minimum necessary sample size and we give some ballpark estimates of sample size we have found applicable in many research situations. By the end of the chapter, we hope you will:

- *Understand why we say "more is better."* Choosing your sample size is a crucial feature of design. If you don't collect data on enough people, an otherwise well-designed study may not yield statistically significant results, or results clear enough to guide policy decisions.
- *Know how other design features affect decisions about sample size.* The types of instruments you use, their reliability, the types of analyses they support, and expected attrition all affect how many people you should include in your study. Learn how to account for these factors when setting your sample size and how design modifications will allow you to get away with studying fewer people.
- *Get a feel for some ballpark estimates of sample size.* Even without mastering the technical details, you can get an intuitive sense of how big a sample is needed in many research settings.

Why Is Sample Size So Important?

To understand why sample size is so critical, it helps to think through exactly what you are doing when you analyze your data. If you've selected your sample from a clearly specified target population using probability sampling methods, you can be reasonably sure, *within the limits of sampling variation,* that what you find in the sample holds in the population—that your results can be generalized. When you generalize from the sample to the population, you are making a *statistical inference.*

Statistical inference is actually a four-step process leading to proof by contradiction. The first step is straightforward—state your research questions as research hypotheses, statements of the way you think things really are in the population. For example, when studying the effects of using computers to teach Russian, your research hypothesis might be that computer-aided instruction (CAI) is better than traditional "chalk-and-talk" methods. Specifically, you might hypothesize that students taught using CAI methods have higher Russian achievement test scores, on average, than students taught using traditional methods.

Second, reframe your research hypotheses as *null hypotheses,* statements of the way you think things *aren't* in the population, statements you might like to *reject* on the basis of sample data. In the Russian example, your null hypothesis might be that, in the population, students taught using CAI methods have Russian achievement scores *equal,* on average, to those of students taught using traditional methods. You don't really believe the null hypothesis; it is a straw man to be shot down. You hope the data will refute it, thereby supporting your CAI innovation.

Third, using an appropriate statistical test, determine how likely it is that you would have gotten the sample results you did if the null hypothesis were really true. That's what *p-values* tell you—the probability that you would have gotten a result as extreme as (or more extreme than) you actually did, if the null hypothesis were true. In a way, *p*-values tell you how closely the observed data match what you would have expected to find if the null hypothesis were true: if the observed data are inconsistent with the null hypothesis, the *p*-value is near zero; if the observed data are not inconsistent with the null hypothesis, the *p*-value is far from zero (and close to one).

Fourth, use the *p*-value to make an inference, reasoning as follows: If the *p*-value is near zero, the observed data are inconsistent with the null hypothesis, so the null hypothesis must not be true, and you reject it. Rejecting a statement of no effect implies a conclusion that there *is* some effect—that teaching method makes a difference. If the *p*-value is far from zero, the data are not inconsistent with the null hypothesis, so the null hypothesis *may* be true, and you can't reject it. You simply don't know whether teaching method and Russian achievement are or are not related. When a *p*-value is far from zero, it is telling you that, with the sample data you have, you can't answer your research question.

This four-step procedure forms the cornerstone of deductive empirical research. But it does have an inherent drawback: *you can never be* sure *your inferences are correct.* Because you do not study all students in the population, sampling idiosyncrasies can distort your results. You are making an informed guess based on limited evidence from a representative group of students. If sampling variation misleads you, you may be wrong. Sampling variation adds uncertainty to all statistical inference, for and against null hypotheses. Inferences are based on probabilities. *You reject a null hypothesis when you are reasonably sure it is false; you fail to reject it when you can't be sure it is false.* You are never certain; at best, you are very confident.

Kinds of Mistakes

Two types of mistakes are possible. You can reject the null hypothesis when it is really true, making a *Type I* or *alpha error,* or you can fail to reject the null hypothesis when it is really false, making a *Type II* or *beta error.* If CAI is really *not* more effective than traditional methods but *you say it is,* you are making a Type I error. If CAI *is* really more effective than traditional methods but *you don't say it is,* you are making a Type II error. The possibilities of such failures of inference—rejecting a null hypothesis that is really true and failing to reject a null hypothesis that is really false—will always remain with us. The best you can do is try to minimize them.

Type I errors are serious: no one wants to say an effect exists when, in fact, the opposite is true. To minimize the chances of such errors, you test null hypotheses at pre-specified *alpha levels,* such as .01 and .05. Conducting tests at low alpha levels doesn't *eliminate* the chance of making a Type I error, it just limits it to a comfortably small value. The most popular alpha level is .05, but this value is not absolute; it is simply a compromise between making a Type I error and never rejecting the null hypothesis at all. Most researchers feel secure in knowing that, with an alpha level of .05, they have only a 5 percent chance of rejecting the null hypothesis incorrectly.

Type II errors are also serious: if an effect exists, you want to have a good chance of finding it. Yet most researchers consider Type II errors less consequential, arguing that, if an effect exists, failing to find it in any one study is not too serious because eventually *someone* will find it! We disagree; the one study you have the biggest investment in is *your* study. Because you want your study to be able to say something definitive, *you must not shrug off Type II errors.* Only when their chances of occurring are low are you likely to find effects that really exist, allowing you to answer your research questions. When the chances of Type II errors are high, you face a dilemma if you are unable to reject your null hypothesis—you will not be able to say whether an effect does or does not exist. You court the risk that, after investing all your time and effort, your research questions will remain unanswered.

How can you minimize the chances that Type II errors will occur? One way is to test your null hypotheses at relaxed alpha levels, say .10 and .15. Using a relaxed alpha level makes you more likely to reject *all* null hypotheses, including ones that *should* be rejected, thereby decreasing the chances of a Type II error. But, of course, you are also more likely to reject null hypotheses that *should not* be rejected, thereby increasing the chances of a Type I error. Although using a relaxed alpha level does decrease the chances of Type II errors, this amounts to little more than statistical sleight of hand.

Type II errors should be minimized in another way—by design. The single most important design feature affecting the occurrence of Type II errors is sample size—*the more students you study, the lower your chances of making such errors*—but other features, such as the precision of your measures and attrition in your sample, also play a role. By making judicious design decisions, you can hold the probability of a Type I error to .05 or .10, while still minimizing the chances of a Type II error.

Statistical Power Analysis

The process of determining how many students (or faculty members) to include in your study in order to control the chances of a Type II error is known as *statistical power analysis*. Statistical power is defined as one minus the probability of a Type II error, and it is *the probability that you will detect an effect that is really there*. By increasing power, you decrease the chances of making a Type II error and increase the chances of finding real effects. If CAI methods are really better than traditional ones, you stand a better chance of finding out.

In theory, simply decide how much power you want and set your sample size (and other design features) accordingly. If you think a 20 percent chance of Type II errors is tolerable, design your study to have a power of .80; to be more sure, design your study to have a power of .90. But increased power comes at increased cost—*you increase power by including more people in your study*. To increase power to .99 usually requires so many people as to be impractical (often several thousand), whereas powers from .70 to .90 can be had with more manageable sample sizes (often from one hundred to several hundred). Although there is no consensus about the power you should routinely adopt when planning your study (as there is with the .05 alpha level), we recommend that you design your study to have *at least moderate power,* between .70 and .90. This limits your chances of making a Type II error to a tolerable level, from .30 to .10, without breaking the bank.

Four factors directly influence the sample size you will need to attain the level of statistical power you have chosen: (1) the minimum effect size you want to have a good chance of finding; (2) the statistical analyses you will use; (3) the precision of your measures; and (4) how many students will drop out after the sample has been selected. In the following four sections, we discuss these factors, show how they are related to decisions about sample size, and provide some ballpark estimates of sample size for different types of studies you might design.

EXAMPLE: *Designing a study with good statistical power: Do college admissions decisions differ by an applicant's race or gender?*

Elaine Walster, T. Anne Cleary, and Margaret Clifford (1970) were among the first researchers to attend specifically to the concept of statistical power while designing a higher-education research project. To investigate whether the gender or race of an applicant affects college admission decisions, they conducted an ingenious experiment. They took the college applications of three real high school seniors in Wisconsin (with three very different levels of academic achievement as measured by high school grades and ACT scores), and systematically manipulated the students' reported gender and race. For each of the three students, *four* different applications were created: one making the student a black male, one making the student a black female, one making the student a white male, and one making the student a white female.

The researchers then randomly selected a sample of 240 colleges from *Lovejoy's College Guide* and sent each of the 12 applications to 20 randomly selected colleges from this sample. By looking at the variation across the 240 admissions decisions, the researchers hoped to ascertain whether

males were preferred over comparable females, and whether black applicants were preferred over white applicants—reasoning that, after all, the
three sets of 80 applications were identical except for reported gender and
race. The researchers did *not* find the effects they expected: although for
the "low ability" application males were preferred over females, there were
no statistically significant differences in admissions decisions according to
the applicant's race.

How much faith can we place in Walster, Cleary, and Clifford's results,
especially the finding of no difference by race? We believe the results are
especially compelling because the researchers studied so many schools,
making it difficult to argue that the null findings might be a consequence of
low statistical power. The researchers address this very point directly, noting
that the

> sample size can markedly affect the probability of obtaining statistical
> significance . . . [We specified] magnitudes of effects that are either
> important or unimportant and control[led] the probabilities of making
> correct decisions by solving for the sample size . . . In this study we
> decided that a mean difference relative to underlying variability of 0.5
> would be important to detect with a probability of .90. In addition,
> alpha was set at .05. Specifying these parameters led to the choice
> of a sample size of 240.   (p. 238)

Had Walster, Cleary, and Clifford studied only a few schools, their null
findings with respect to race might easily have been attributed to low statistical power. With such a large sample size, however—240 colleges—we
find the authors' argument compelling that either there are no differentials
by race, or if there are such differentials they are small in magnitude.

What Size Effect Do You Want to Detect?

In Chapters 2 and 4, we introduced the idea of effect size
and discussed why bigger effects are easier to detect than
smaller effects. If you are searching for large effects, and
they really exist, the null hypothesis is *so wrong* that you
can see just how wrong it is by studying only a few people.
If CAI methods are really so much better than traditional

ones, even a small study will reveal the difference. But when you are searching for small effects, even if they really exist, the null hypothesis of no effect is so close to the truth that you must include many students in your study before being able to reject it. After all, if the null hypothesis is *nearly* true, it *should* be difficult to reject, even if you study hundreds of students.

So before determining how many students to include in your study, you must decide how big an effect you want to find. Although this may seem like putting the cart before the horse—if you already know the effect size, why do the study?—it actually is not. When specifying an expected effect size, you are simply indicating *the minimum effect size you consider worthy of your time.* You are deciding on the smallest effect of computer-aided instruction you care about. Is a difference of 5 points in Russian achievement big enough to warrant your interest, or are you interested only in differences of at least 15 points?

It is difficult to decide just how large an effect you care about. But rough guidelines are available, and by using them carefully you can come to a reasonable working decision.

Some helpful advice is given by Jacob Cohen (1988), who provides three rules of thumb:

- A *small* effect is undetectable by the naked eye: a difference of .20 standard deviations between two group means, a correlation of .10 between a predictor and an outcome, or the difference between 50 and 45 percent. A small effect corresponds to the mean difference in heights between 15- and 16-year-old girls—two groups that differ, but not by much.

- A *medium* effect is large enough to be detected by the naked eye: a difference of .50 standard deviations, a correlation of .30, or a difference between 50 and 35 percent. A medium effect corresponds to the mean difference in infant mortality between blacks and whites in the east south central states.

- A *large* effect would not be missed by even a casual observer: a difference of .80 standard deviations, a correlation of .50, or a difference between 50 and 25 percent. A large effect corresponds to the mean difference in height between 13- and 18-year-old girls.

Cohen's guidelines are widely accepted by empirical researchers, and you may find them useful if you have no other information to go on.

A better way to decide on a minimum effect size is to think about *practical significance,* the real-world meaning you can give to effects of various sizes. Practical significance is very different from statistical significance. If you include enough students in your sample, for instance, a difference of 5 points on the SAT will become statistically significant, but for an individual student, an admissions officer, or even a researcher, this difference is probably trivial. A difference of 50 SAT points is another matter.

Practical significance is in the eye of the beholder. You must know your outcomes and how big an effect your predictors are likely to have in relation to them. Because practical significance depends upon the research context, only *you* can judge if an effect is large enough to be important. Don't waste time worrying about minuscule effects; *design your study so that it is powerful enough to detect effects of practical significance.* After all, if an effect is so small that it is barely detectable by the naked eye or an expert judge, should you be spending your time studying it?

A third way to decide on the minimum effect size of interest is to use your research review, especially if you have conducted or have found a meta-analysis. In a meta-analysis, an effect size is estimated for each study; taken together, the distribution of estimated effect sizes gives a rough indication of what the next study is likely to find.

Meta-analyses often reveal a sobering fact: effect sizes are not nearly as large as we all might hope. Table 8.1 presents average estimated effect sizes from six meta-anal-

TABLE 8.1. A SUMMARY OF TYPICAL EFFECT SIZES: MEAN EFFECT SIZES IN SIX META-ANALYSES OF HIGHER EDUCATION.

Topic and author	Number of studies in review	Mean effect size*
Financial aid and persistence (Murdock, 1987)	46	.13
Computer-based teaching (Kulik, Kulik, and Cohen, 1980)	59	.25
Programs for high-risk students (Kulik, Kulik, and Schwalb, 1983)	60	.27
Student feedback on instruction (Cohen, 1981)	22	.38
Coaching for non-SAT aptitude tests (Kulik, Bangert-Drowns, and Kulik, 1984)	24	.43
Keller's personalized system of instruction (Kulik, Kulik, and Cohen, 1979)	75	.49

*Standardized mean difference (see Chapter 2 for details).

yses in higher education, on topics ranging from the effects of programs for disadvantaged students to the relationship between student feedback on instruction and teaching performance. All six meta-analyses concluded that the average effect was different from zero—that the outcomes and predictors were related (that treatment and control groups differed)—but the average effect sizes were in the small to medium range. Because small to medium effects are the norm, make sure your study has enough power to detect them. Only then will you be able to do credible research.

Once you have decided on the smallest effect that interests you, it's easy to figure out how many students you should include in your study. Several books can help you with computational details (see, for instance, Cohen, 1988; or Kraemer and Thiemann, 1987). In this chapter, we simply present some ballpark estimates of sample size that you may find helpful.

Table 8.2 presents the total sample sizes needed to detect "small," "medium," and "large" effects at three levels of statistical power (.70, .80, and .90). Sample sizes are presented for the two major ways of denoting effect size: a correlation coefficient (applicable when examining the relationship between a continuous outcome and a continuous predictor) and a standardized difference between group means (applicable when comparing outcomes between two groups). In all cases, we assume that two-tailed statistical tests are being conducted at the .05 alpha level.

Small effects are difficult to detect. Regardless of the type of effect you are studying and the amount of power you want, you must study several hundred or a thousand students to have a reasonable chance of detecting them. But don't be dismayed. You may never want to design a study to detect small effects because they are not usually of much practical significance.

Medium-sized effects, in contrast, can be detected with a moderate-sized sample, usually between 100 and 200, depending upon the power you want. One popular guideline is that you should include enough people to have a reasonable chance (power of .80 or so) of detecting medium-sized

TABLE 8.2. HOW MANY STUDENTS SHOULD YOU SELECT? SOME BALLPARK ESTIMATES OF TOTAL SAMPLE SIZE.

Type of effect size	Statistical test used	Statistical power	Anticipated effect size		
			Small	Medium	Large
Correlation coefficient	Pearson correlation	.90	1,047	113	37
		.80	783	85	28
		.70	616	67	23
Standardized mean difference	Two-group t-test	.90	1,052	170	68
		.80	786	128	52
		.70	620	100	40

Note: Two-tailed test, alpha = .05.

effects. This allows you to strike a balance between the detection of tiny effects and blockbuster effects, while still keeping your budget in check.

Large effects are easy to detect, even using small samples. If you were comparing achievement scores among students using two different computer-based curricula, for example, you would have a 90 percent chance of detecting differences between the groups with as few as 68 students altogether (34 students per group).

Many of our colleagues examining these ballpark estimates of sample size think about detecting only large effects. They consider designing a study with 20 or 30 students, supporting their decision with lofty talk of practical significance. Don't fall into this trap. Few important effects are actually that large, and if your study has power to detect only large effects, you have little chance of finding the more realistic small and medium-sized ones. After the data are in, and you cannot reject your null hypothesis because your sample is too small, you will have simply missed an opportunity.

EXAMPLE: *Making a preliminary calculation of sample size: The effectiveness of mastery learning systems for teaching calculus.*

Samuel Thompson (1980) conducted an experiment at the U.S. Air Force Academy comparing the calculus achievement scores of students taught using conventional lecture-discussion-recitation (LDR) strategies and individualized mastery (IM) strategies. He stratified 840 freshmen into four ability groups based on their high school GPA and college admissions test results, and within each stratum he randomly assigned equal numbers of students to the two teaching methods.

Thompson's excellent study is well worth reading. He paid careful attention to many methodological details. For example, comparability between the two instructional groups was enhanced by scheduling classes at the same time of day, randomly assigning professors to teaching methods, and having both groups use the same textbook. Observer bias was controlled by having each exam graded blindly by two instructors, one from each instructional group.

But why did Thompson study 840 students? Examining Table 8.2, we see that with that many people he had enough power (between .80 and .90) to detect even small effects—a difference of .20 standard deviations between the two groups. He detected no statistically significant differences in calculus achievement between the two groups: "with the same level of instructional effort, individualized mastery instruction and conventional instruction produced indistinguishable results in mathematics achievement. This result emerged from an experiment in which the design, methodology, and statistical power were sufficient to detect achievement differences of any practical significance" (pp. 371–372). Because he designed a study with a good chance of detecting even small effects—that is, because he studied 840 people—Thompson's findings are especially persuasive.

What Type of Analysis Will You Use?

Statistical power is actually a property of an analytic technique and a corresponding statistical test, *not* of research design. Most hypotheses can be tested in several ways, and some statistical tests are intrinsically more powerful than others. A more powerful test allows you to detect effects of identical size in smaller samples. This means if you can answer your research questions using more powerful tests, you can get away with studying fewer people.

So before deciding on a final sample size, you must think about how you will analyze your data. In general, we have avoided discussing analytic dilemmas in this book, because they often are tangential to the development of good design and considering them would complicate matters. We raise the topic now because, when statistical power is under discussion, analysis *becomes* a design issue.

The sample sizes presented in Table 8.2 assume that you

will use simple parametric analyses—Pearson correlation coefficients for examining the relationship between continuous predictors and outcomes, and two-sample t-tests for testing differences between group means. If you think that you will use other analytic techniques, you must modify your target sample size accordingly. We turn now to two fundamental choices that directly affect power and sample size: the use of analyses that incorporate covariate information, and the use of parametric versus nonparametric tests.

Including Covariates in Your Analyses

In Chapter 4, we described the important role of covariates: predictors not of direct substantive interest but likely to be associated with the outcome. In a study of the effectiveness of different ways of teaching calculus, for example, scores on a calculus pretest, or on the mathematics portion of the SAT, might be important covariates. In a study of the impact of athletic participation on college GPA, high school GPA might be an important covariate. Covariates are predictors that you expect to be related to the outcome, and whose impact you would like to disentangle from the impact of the predictors in which you are really interested.

Covariates can be incorporated into your data analyses as extra predictors in multiple regression analysis and analysis of covariance. Including extra predictors in this way enables you to *increase* statistical power. Adding a predictor means using more information; more information means more power. With more powerful analyses, you can study fewer students or faculty members and still detect effects of the same size, or you can study the same number of people with higher power.

Table 8.3 presents the smaller sample sizes needed when

TABLE 8.3. HOW MANY STUDENTS SHOULD YOU SELECT WHEN CO-VARIATE INFORMATION IS AVAILABLE? BALLPARK ESTIMATES OF SAMPLE SIZE, ADJUSTED FOR COVARIATE INFORMATION.

Statistical method	Statistical power	Anticipated effect size					
		Small: (correlation =)		Medium: (correlation =)		Large: (correlation =)	
		.20	.50	.20	.50	.20	.50
Multiple	.90	998	778	103	79	32	24
regression	.80	742	578	77	59	25	18
	.70	590	460	61	47	20	14
Analysis of	.90	1,010	594	164	128	66	52
covariance	.80	756	444	122	96	50	38
	.70	594	350	96	76	40	30

Note: Assuming a two-tailed test, alpha = .05, and that the covariate and other predictors are uncorrelated.

the correlational analyses and t-tests of Table 8.2 are replaced by multiple regression analysis and analysis of covariance. Sample sizes are given for two situations: when the correlation between the covariate and the outcome is .20, and when it is .50.

Comparing parallel entries in Tables 8.2 and 8.3 shows just how helpful covariate information can be. Even when the relationship between the covariate and the outcome is fairly weak (such as a modest correlation of .20), you can reduce your target sample size by up to 15 percent, depending upon the effect size you are looking for, the amount of power you want, and the type of analysis you anticipate. When the association between the covariate and the predictor is stronger (such as a correlation of .50), you can reduce your target sample size by as much as 40 percent.

The more covariate information you can include, the more power you gain. The sample sizes given in Table 8.3 assume that you are including only one covariate, and that it has a correlation of .20 or .50 with the outcome. Since both multiple regression and analysis of covariance allow you to include as many covariates as you want, you can increase your power (or decrease your target sample size) by including additional covariates. For example, if several covariates jointly predict 50 percent of the variation in your outcome, you can cut your target sample size in half.

But the gains in power (or reductions in sample size) derived from the use of covariate information are realized only if you use good covariates. Choice of covariates is largely a substantive challenge—there should be a compelling reason for including the covariate when disentangling the effects of other predictors. But over and above these substantive issues, good covariates should also meet two statistical criteria: they should be highly correlated with the outcome, and relatively uncorrelated with each other (so that they are not redundant in their prediction of the outcome). By using covariates that meet these criteria, you can gain considerable power.

Parametric versus Nonparametric Tests

Just as you can *increase* statistical power by adding information to your analyses through covariates, so can you *reduce* statistical power by setting aside information. Although this may seem a foolish thing to do—why would you ever want to reduce power?—it is exactly what happens when you use *nonparametric* statistical techniques such as Spearman's rank-order correlation, the Wilcoxon test, the Kruskal-Wallis test, or contingency-table techniques to analyze your data.

Why are nonparametric and contingency-table techniques less powerful than their parametric counterparts? The reason is simple: they ignore important information. Nonparametric techniques replace continuous scores with ranks; contingency-table analyses ignore even the ordering among people, basing results only on the way people are spread out among categories. These substitutions diminish the amount of information contained in the specific data values, leading to reductions in variability and ultimately producing a decrease in power. Parametric techniques such as correlational analysis, multiple regression analysis, and analysis of variance and covariance are intrinisically more powerful simply because they exploit *all* available information in continuous data.

If parametric techniques are so much better, why does anyone ever resort to nonparametric and contingency-table analysis? The reason is that the increased power of parametric techniques comes at a price: parametric analyses require stringent distributional assumptions. In fact, it is the building in of these assumptions that adds information to the analyses. The assumptions differ across analytic techniques, but one common assumption is that, in every possible subgroup of the population of students or faculty members, the outcome must be normally distributed. If assumptions like this are met, parametric analyses are indeed more powerful. But if the assumptions are not met, the differential advantage of parametric analyses disappears, and they may give you the wrong answer. If this is the case, then you can resort to nonparametric and contingency-table analysis.

So to use the most powerful analytic tools available, you must ensure that all assumptions—including the all-important distributional assumptions—will be met. How can you do this? Two strategies are helpful: use instruments that yield data that are continuous (not categorical), and select outcomes that are normally distributed. Many of the strategies offered in Chapter 7 for improving the quality of your measures will ensure that your data meet these criteria. For example, totaling several items rather than using a single item to measure an outcome will increase the chances that your data will be continuous and normally distributed. Your choice of measures can therefore have a big effect on statistical power.

EXAMPLE: *Increasing statistical power by using covariates and parametric tests: The effect of a university rape-prevention program.*

Recent increases in reports of sexual assault on the nation's campuses have led some schools to initiate rape-prevention and awareness programs. Lynn Borden, Sharon Karr, and A. Toy Caldwell-Colbert (1988) investigated the effectiveness of one such program using 50 male and 50 female undergraduates at Emporia State University in Kansas. Following a pretest administration of two standardized instruments—an Attitudes Toward Rape Questionnaire and the Rape Empathy Scale—half the men and half the women in the sample participated in a 45-minute seminar on rape awareness and prevention. Although students were not randomly assigned to treatment and control groups, assignment was made on the basis of class-section meeting times, a factor the authors viewed as unrelated to attitudes toward rape. A follow-up posttest was given to both groups four weeks later.

The authors were unable to find that the rape prevention seminar had any statistically significant effect on students' attitudes toward rape. But this may not mean that the program is ineffective. As shown in Table 8.2, a total sample size of 100 provides power of only .70 to detect medium-sized effects. It may be that the rape-prevention program is actually modestly helpful, but that the sample size simply did not give sufficient statistical power to detect a true positive effect. Lack of statisical power always looms large as a possible explanation for null findings.

Nevertheless, the researchers adopted two excellent strategies to increase the statistical power of their study. First, they incorporated covariate information into their analyses—the students' gender, pattern of church attendance, and personal acquaintance with a rape victim. Second, they used sophisticated parametric analysis (multivariate repeated measures analysis of variance), a statistical procedure that was appropriate because of the high quality of the instruments they used. Even though both of these strategies increased the study's statistical power, the researchers still could not find a statistically significant effect for the program.

Borden, Karr, and Caldwell-Colbert were surprised by their null findings.

They concluded: "The nonsignificant results for the program were not anticipated because the university rape prevention program has received strong support and praise by students, as well as faculty. Indeed, there has been a steady request for the program throughout the community, indicating that it was successful in conciousness raising . . . More applied research on college campuses is needed" (p. 135). When anecdotal evidence conflicts with findings from a study, the study can override the anecdotal evidence only if it is carefully designed and has high enough power.

Instrument Precision and Sample Size

The ballpark estimates of sample size presented so far assume that your instruments are free of measurement error. But, as we discussed in Chapter 7, this is rarely the case. If your instruments have some error, you will have less power than you think. You will be less likely to detect effects that really exist, regardless of their size and your analytic technique. So before choosing a final sample size, you must consider the possibility of measurement error.

Probably the best approach to dealing with the effects of measurement fallibility on sample size is to try and improve your measures so much that you need not bother making any adjustments at all. Design away as much error as you can. The time spent improving your instruments before using them is time well spent. *Precision of your instrument is a controllable cost factor.* Don't try to save money by collecting data using less time-consuming, but less precise, instruments. Although *per-person* data collection may be cheaper, *total* data collection usually ends up being more expensive because you must collect data for more people to compensate for the imprecision of the instrument. Otherwise you sacrifice statistical power, and the savings are illusory.

Nevertheless, despite your best efforts, some measurement error may persist. If you suspect this will happen—and experience shows that it usually does—be sure to increase your target sample size accordingly. The sample sizes given in Table 8.2 are for studies that use perfectly reliable instruments (reliability = 1.00). Table 8.4 presents target sample sizes for studies that use fallible instruments, with real-world reliabilities of .60 and .80. To find a target sample size for another reliability value, simply interpolate between the two sets of numbers.

Comparison of parallel entries in Tables 8.2 and 8.4 shows the advantage of using precise measurements. As reliability decreases, your sample size must rise dramatically to ensure the same level of statistical power. For example, if your outcome is perfectly reliable (Table 8.2), you need only 113 students to have a 90 percent chance of detecting a medium correlation (.30) between it and any predictor. But if the reliability of your outcome is .80 (Table 8.4), you must study an additional 27 students to have the

TABLE 8.4. HOW MANY STUDENTS SHOULD YOU SELECT WHEN MEASUREMENT IS NOT PERFECTLY RELIABLE? BALLPARK ESTIMATES OF SAMPLE SIZES YOU NEED, ADJUSTED FOR MEASUREMENT FALLIBILITY.

		Anticipated effect size					
		Small: (reliability =)		Medium: (reliability =)		Large: (reliability =)	
Statistical test used	Statistical power	.60	.80	.60	.80	.60	.80
Pearson correlation	.90	1,741	1,306	189	140	65	47
	.80	1,302	977	142	106	49	36
	.70	1,025	769	112	83	39	29
Two-group t-test	.90	1,754	1,316	282	212	112	84
	.80	1,312	984	212	160	84	64
	.70	1,032	774	166	126	66	50

Note: Assuming a two-tailed test, alpha = .05.

same amount of power. If its reliability is .60, you must include yet another 49.

Notice that the effect of measurement fallibility on power and on sample size is most dramatic when you are looking for small effects. If you wanted a 90 percent chance of detecting a small correlation of .20, for example, the necessary increases in sample size (over what you would need if your measures were perfectly reliable) are 259 and 694 for reliabilities of .80 and .60, respectively. The bottom line: *measurement imprecision exacts a very high toll.* Try and eliminate all the error that you can.

What If Students Drop Out?

Not everyone you select for your study will agree to participate. Not everyone who agrees to participate will follow through on this intention. Not everyone who begins to participate will persevere until the end of the study. Some students drop out or are dismissed, others transfer, and many may simply forget to show up for testing and interviews. Faculty members and administrators change jobs or aren't on campus on a certain day. From the standpoint of statistical power, the reason for refusal and attrition is not important, but the disappearance of people from your sample is.

Don't be tempted to select an initial sample size just large enough to provide a specific amount of statistical power. It is not the initial sample size that counts, but the final one. You must incorporate realistic rates of refusal and attrition into your calculations of sample size.

The estimates given in Tables 8.2, 8.3, and 8.4 are the sample sizes you need to have in your *final* analyses. Because of attrition and refusal, you must increase your initial sample size to compensate for people who will disappear from your sample before analysis. If roughly 10 percent refusal and 40 percent attrition are likely, for example, you should double your initial sample size.

What rates of refusal and attrition should you expect? No single rule of thumb is particularly helpful because, even among similar studies, these rates differ widely. Some researchers have been very successful in limiting refusal and attrition. For example, in a longitudinal study of withdrawals from the University of California at Berkeley in the class of 1974, Carl Simpson and his colleagues (1980) obtained an initial response rate of 92 percent in November 1971 and a follow-up rate of 80 percent almost two years later in June 1973.

But others have not been so lucky. In a study of influences on academic growth among students at a large public university in the Northeast, Patrick Terenzini and Thomas Wright (1987) got an initial response rate of 50 percent of the 1980 entering class. On follow-up at the end of each of the four subsequent academic years, this sample fell by about 35 percent per year. By the end of the study, only 19 percent of the original sample remained.

We suggest that you make an educated guess based upon the experiences and advice of colleagues. Look for similar studies and examine their rates of refusal and attrition. Model your follow-up procedures on studies that got high rates of cooperation. Ask your registrar and personnel officers what they think you will find. Consult the admissions and student records offices. Check how many students transfer into, and out of, your school each year. Check how many students are accepted into each program and how many drop out before graduation. Check the Year Abroad programs. Consult employment and financial services offices to determine the transience of faculty and staff. If in doubt, err on the conservative side, assuming slightly *more* refusal and attrition than you really expect. After all, you can always choose to not follow up all participants, but you cannot so easily add new students to your sample once your study has begun.

EXAMPLE: *How much attrition should you anticipate: What have other researchers found?*

Common sense suggests that the longer your study, the more attrition you should expect. If you design a study with a four-year postgraduate follow-up, anticipate sizable attrition rates. Many graduates will move, others will lose contact with the alumni office, and some will not return your questionnaire. If you design a study that can be completed within a single semester, you can reduce attrition dramatically.

Many researchers have been successful at limiting attrition. Table 8.5 gives the percentage of students successfully followed over time in 10 studies we described elsewhere in this book. Not surprisingly, researchers who use short follow-up periods are particularly successful at maintaining contact with students. For example, in their one-semester studies of aca-

TABLE 8.5. HOW HARD IS IT TO KEEP ATTRITION LOW IN LONGITUDINAL STUDIES? FOLLOW-UP RATES IN TEN LONGITUDINAL STUDIES.

Author	Length of follow-up	% successfully contacted
Abrams and Jernigan (1984)	1 semester	96
Andrews (1981)	1 semester	93
Muehlenhard, Baldwin, Bourg, and Piper (1988)	4 months	87
Landward and Hepworth (1984)	1 quarter	96
	2 quarters	54
	3 quarters	50
Pascarella, Terenzini, and Wolfe (1986)	1.5 semesters	53
Simpson, Baker, and Mellinger (1980)	1 month	92
	2 years	80
Theophilides, Terenzini, and Lorang (1984)	1.5 semesters	35
	2 years	27
Terenzini and Wright (1987)	1 year	65
	2 years	42
	3 years	27
	4 years	19
Stuart (1985)	2 years	76
Hendel (1985)	5.5 years	67

demic programs, both Abrams and Jernigan (1984) and Andrews (1981) were able to retain over 90 percent of the respondents in their original samples.

Some researchers have been successful at limiting attrition even when following students for longer periods of time. After two years, for example, Simpson, Baker, and Mellinger (1980) maintained an 80 percent success rate, and Stuart (1985) maintained a 76 percent success rate. And after 5.5 years, Hendel (1985) succeeded in contacting 67 percent of his original sample, even though many of the students had graduated and left the state.

Table 8.5 illustrates that students *can* be followed over long periods of time. But this can take a real effort—many respected investigators have been unsuccessful at keeping attrition low. Rather than base your sample-size estimate on an unrealistically optimistic follow-up rate, use a conservative plan and work hard to be pleasantly surprised.

SHOULD YOU TRY IT OUT
ON A SMALL SCALE?

9

Does studying harder and longer improve students' grades, or does it have little or no effect? Surely, well-directed hard work should reap just rewards. But in a 1972 survey of University of Michigan undergraduates, Howard Schuman, Edward Walsh, Camille Olson, and Barbara Etheridge (1985) found no relationship between GPA and student reports of time spent studying. In an effort to understand this counterintuitive finding, they embarked on a multi-year sequence of studies, each effort building upon the previous one.

In their first project, Schuman and his colleagues developed a self-report index of number of hours spent studying. They validated the index as a measure of "effort" and related it to student GPA obtained from university records. They found only a weak association between effort and grades, even after including other predictors such as class attendance and academic ability as covariates. But capitalizing on a finding from their first study (that hours studied varied by major), and assuming that grading practices probably differed by major, they conducted a second study, investigating the association between effort and grades *within* individual courses. In subsequent studies, they improved their approach by measuring students at several times during the semester and cumulating data over time.

Why did Schuman and his colleagues conduct several studies? Since they knew their research questions from the start, why didn't they design a single full-blown study? They had a good reason: *many features of their design could not be determined without prior exploratory work.* They needed to develop and test instruments for measuring effort and grades, to figure out what other predictors might mediate the relationship, and to identify good stratifiers for sampling. So they conducted a series of small studies, each a pilot for the next. They moved from obtrusive to unobtrusive measures, from simple random samples to stratified random samples, and they incorporated more covariates into their analyses.

Trying out your ideas on a small scale is an excellent precursor to any large-scale study. In this chapter, we discuss the role of small-scale studies and show how you can profitably use them. By the end of the chapter, we hope you will:

- *Understand why small-scale studies are useful.* Know the advantages and disadvantages of trying out ideas on a small scale, and be able to weigh the benefits against the costs.
- *Learn when small-scale studies are most useful.* Identify facets of your design that need empirical clarification, and decide whether a small-scale study could help you.
- *Know how to design a small-scale study to investigate facets of your design that require clarification, while deliberately ignoring other facets.* Understand when to forfeit generalizability for empirical gain.

The Advantages of Pilot Studies

To plan your research project, you must think carefully about a broad spectrum of issues: research questions, target populations, subgroups of the population that require special attention, outcomes, predictors, covariates, appropriate comparisons, and high-quality instruments. Throughout this book, we have asked questions that should help you nail down many of these details. In an ideal world, the procedure we have outlined would be effective. It is systematic, thorough, and careful.

But between the image and the reality falls the shadow. Nothing comes quite that easy. Perhaps you can easily identify the target population, the predictors, and the instrumentation, but you just cannot decide which of several dozen possible outcomes to measure. Or perhaps it is easy to identify the outcome—such as whether a student ultimately graduates, or whether writing has improved, or whether students' world outlook has changed—but you have no idea how big an effect you expect to find, so that it is difficult to determine how many students you must study.

Should you abandon all hope, throw up your hands, and move on? Or make these important decisions arbitrarily? Of course not. If you cannot specify some particular design feature clearly, you should consider testing several of your ideas in an *exploratory pilot study*. A small-scale pilot is often just the thing to help organize and improve a larger, more rigorously defined future study.

When Is a Pilot Study Most Useful?

No design is ever so complete that it cannot be improved by a prior, small-scale exploratory study. Pilot studies are almost always worth the time and effort. *Carry out a pilot study if* any *facet of your design needs clarification.*

Pilot studies are planned in much the same way as full-blown studies. Think of them as microcosms of the future study. In a pilot, you should still try to do the best you can—if not, how will you be able to believe its results? A pilot is not a small ad hoc exercise sloppily performed—it is a preliminary study that informs a future effort by systematically examining specific facets of the eventual design. In a pilot, you make a deliberate tradeoff—you compromise methodological rigor across some dimensions to help clarify others. For example, if you use a pilot to examine the predictive power of several different covariates and predictors, you may study only one or two outcomes. Because other facets of the final design have already been nailed down, you compromise on them in the pilot in order to focus on issues you are unsure about. In a pilot, *you deliberately forfeit generalizability for information.*

Because pilot studies usually involve intentionally flawed designs, don't use them to try to test specific research hypotheses. Use pilot-study results to shape future research and to *generate* hypotheses; your pilot is exploratory and inductive, not confirmatory and deductive. Pay attention to any general lessons that emerge, but do not try formally to generalize the results.

The crucial advantage of a pilot study is that by forfeiting depth you buy breadth. A pilot study permits you to use different kinds of information to strengthen the overall picture. Be sure to gather qualitative data during your pilot. The insights of students and faculty members should be collected, especially if your sample size is small. Adopt a spirit of *formative evaluation* to help you adjust your design for the next time around.

By cautiously deciding where you can afford to compromise in your pilot study, you can save both money and time. By paying careful attention to the *process* of the pilot as well as its *product,* you can generate new ideas and validate old ones. You can more easily make future planning decisions. You can avoid making many costly mistakes.

Although you can pilot almost any facet of your research design, we believe there are three specific types of pilots you are likely to find particularly useful: (1) a pilot in which new instruments are constructed and refined; (2) a pilot in which a relational study shapes a future experiment; and (3) a pilot in which an informal, small-scale version of a future experiment is tested. We discuss these three types of pilot studies in the following three sections.

Piloting Instruments

As Schuman and his colleagues discovered in their study of student effort and grades, few things can be measured perfectly. Most data are gathered with fallible measuring instruments. When you select outcomes and predictors, you must ensure, by careful development of your instruments, that the quality and credibility of your measures are the best they can be, and you must gather evidence to demonstrate that you have been successful. Even when you use published instruments, you should still demonstrate their utility in your application because, even if the publishers have declared the instruments valid and reliable in one population, their findings may not be generalizable to the students and the campus *you* are studying.

The best way to confirm the credibility and quality of your measurements is to precede your study with a pilot that examines the performance of your instruments. A *measurement pilot* need not fully mimic your ultimate project. It should focus specifically on issues of measurement: validity, reliability, and precision. For instance, you may not include the eventual "treatment" in your pilot unless the treatment itself is likely to affect measurement.

One facet of a measurement pilot must not be compromised: the sample design. Be sure the sample in your pilot fully represents your chosen target population. You must evaluate your instruments in a context that makes the results of the pilot directly generalizable to your ultimate study. Reliability and validity coefficients must be portable between the pilot and future studies. Do not validate your instruments for a sample of freshman volunteers if you intend ultimately to study a sample of seniors. At a minimum, make sure the full range of students and faculty members in the target population is represented in your pilot-study sample; at a maximum, actually take a random sample from the target population. Make sure any stratifiers to be applied later or important subgroups you will ultimately include or omit are *treated exactly the same way in the measurement pilot as in the final study.*

Pilot studies typically involve fewer people than full-blown studies. Because an instrument pilot is not intended to support inferences about the effects of predictors, it does not require a magnifying glass of the same power. By studying fewer people you save time and money, especially when the coding of instruments is complicated or time-intensive. It is not the *size* of your pilot sample, but its *representativeness,* on which you should focus.

Measurement pilot studies can address many questions about the construction, modification, and evaluation of your measuring instruments. Some of the things you can achieve in a measurement pilot are listed below.

You can create an entirely new instrument. In the pilot study, you can write new items. You can try out new methods of collecting data. You can base new instruments on information you have gleaned from a literature review or on instruments others have used for similar tasks. You can check whether practice items are necessary. You can discuss your instruments with colleagues, using their opinions to modify the format and structure of the instrument and to add weight to your ultimate claims of validity.

You can make sure that instruments are clear and un-ambiguous. Will students misinterpret items or misunderstand instructions? Do raters fully understand what they should be doing? Is it clear to interviewers what questions they should ask, and how they should probe and follow up?

Before, during, and after the pilot, use informal conversations with respondents to improve your instruments. Check that your instruments are measuring what you think they are measuring. Think of the pilot as a proving ground for your instruments and as a training ground for you and for your colleagues and co-workers—a place where unforeseen problems can occur and be dealt with, without danger to ultimate findings.

If the instrument asks for ratings, observations, or opinions on an arbitrary scale, you can find out whether your response scales are reasonable. Should you use 5-point or 9-point scales? Should you include a "no opinion" option? Longer scales are better, but only if students can really distinguish their levels. If students cannot distinguish an 8 from a 9, a 1 from a 2, or if everyone answers "don't know," then your attempt at detail may be worthless. Try out different types of scales. Ask respondents what they thought about the scales. Raters can reevaluate the meaning of the fiducial marks on the scale, and having them talk can help you improve the final instrument.

You can check out the impact of the physical environment on measurement. To improve the quality of your data, you must control extraneous, nonsystematic variation that creeps in and distorts measurement. A pilot study can help you identify potential sources of error and give you an opportunity to try out ways of limiting their effects. Can classroom observers actually see the events they are supposed to record? Do they have enough time to keep an accurate record? Can students at the back of the room hear the tape recording in your test of oral comprehension? Do you need to provide pencils, scratch paper, calculators, a quiet room? For each problem that you can foresee, the pilot study is likely to reveal three others you will have to deal with eventually.

You can monitor the functioning of your instrument as a whole, and of each of its items and subsections separately. Use a pilot to modify, delete, or replace defective items or subsections. Is each section of the instrument doing what it was supposed to? "Item analyses" to answer these questions can be informal or formal. In an informal item-analysis, simply ask students or faculty to critique the structure and organization of your instrument, and the content and wording of the items. In a formal item-analysis, you can estimate specific statistics that summarize the performance of the items individually and of the instrument as a whole.

You can estimate the reliability and precision of your instrument. What is the test-retest reliability of your instrument? What is its internal-consistency reliability? What proportion of the error variation is due to discrepancies in measurement from occasion to occasion? What proportion is due to inexplicable variations between raters, between observers? Is your instrument long enough? Is it unnecessarily long? If you include more items, will the instrument become too tedious to complete? In a measurement pilot, you can check all these things and make suitable changes. You can collect information on reliability and precision that you can later use to adjust the statistical analyses in the final study.

You can investigate the validity of your measurement. Discussions with respondents will help you establish content validity. You can use the broad-based measurement of a few people on related measures to support construct validity. You can decide whether multiple measurements are required on each individual—several measurements with the same instrument, or single measurements with several instruments? You can establish the relative difficulty of different types of instrument administration. Data that are difficult or expensive to gather in a large sample can be relatively cheap to collect in a small pilot, and can provide a criterion measure for other, less complicated, methods of measuring the same construct. The small pilot sample may be relatively easy to follow up over time.

If you are interested in growth and change, you can estimate the number of "waves" of data you will need in your final study. In the pilot study, you can measure change for a small sample of students or faculty members over an extended period of time. You can use this information to judge the credibility and quality of the measurement of change. By plotting an individual growth curve for each person, you can figure out whether the changes are likely to be linear or curvilinear. You can choose a suitable mathematical representation for individual growth. You will be able to decide whether you need many, or few, data points in your final study to be sure you measure change well.

EXAMPLE: *Piloting instruments: Developing a measure of perceived effectiveness of teaching for use in schools of nursing, dentistry, and medicine.*

Maria Feldens and James Duncan (1986) were interested in discovering what dimensions of teaching effectiveness college students consider important, in order to develop programs for improving the quality of teaching. They designed a study to identify characteristics of effective university teachers, as perceived by students attending the nursing, dentistry, and medical schools at the Universidade Federal do Rio Grande do Sul-UFRGS in Brazil.

Their first goal was to develop a measure of desirable characteristics of teachers. Unable to find a suitable instrument in the literature, they created one using two consecutive pilot studies. For the first pilot they selected a group of 175 nursing, dental, and medical students similar to those who would participate in the final study. They asked students to jot down 5 behaviors they thought characterized a "good" teacher and 5 they thought were not appropriate in a university teacher. Based on these data and a literature review, the researchers made up a questionnaire. It listed 80 descriptions of teacher behavior and asked respondents to indicate, on a 5-point scale, to what extent they thought each behavior was manifested by effective university teachers. The instrument also included sections where respondents could identify especially good teachers by name, and make unsolicited comments and suggestions.

The questionnaire was then given to a second pilot sample of 50 students taken from among those who would participate in the final study. Feldens and Duncan also asked 4 university professors to react to the instrument. From the data gathered during this phase, the researchers modified the questionnaire to "enhance the simplicity and clarity of the items and increase their meaning and relevance for the investigation" (p. 643).

The final instrument, composed of 72 5-point items and a set of demographic questions, was completed by a stratified random sample of 392 nursing, dental, and medical students attending UFRGS. Analyzing this final round of data, Feldens and Duncan demonstrated that effective teachers were perceived to be willing to explain subject matter during the lesson; to be able to give clear explanations; to enjoy their jobs; to stimulate student interest; to have a thorough understanding of the subject matter; to be consistent in their evaluation of student work.

Feldens and Duncan benefited enormously from their pilot studies. While they began with some good ideas for their ultimate design, others had yet to be nailed down. For example, although they knew that their study would be descriptive, that the target population was all nursing, dental, and medical students at UFRGS, that professional program was a key stratifier, and that their goal was to describe teaching effectiveness as perceived by students in the target population, they had no instrument for measuring teaching effectiveness. They needed to construct one, to check its performance, and modify its content.

Feldens and Duncan were careful to conduct their pilot studies using samples of students selected to represent their target population. The purposeful matching of pilot and final samples ensured that the instrument they constructed was appropriate for *the particular population they wanted to examine.* By systematically constructing their instrument using a carefully planned sequence of data-gathering, *they built quality and credibility into their instrument from the very beginning.* Qualitative data from open-ended questionnaires and the literature review, in addition to the opinions of both students and professors, allowed them to identify the key components of "perceived teaching effectiveness," and ensured content and construct validity for the instrument. The second-phase selection of 72 items ensured that the items were homogeneous and the instrument internally consistent. The rewriting of the items for simplicity and clarity reduced measurement error in each item and in the questionnaire as a whole, and increased the precision of the final instrument.

Relational Studies

Suppose you want to evaluate the effectiveness of your campus writing center by discovering whether students who have used the center write more effectively than those who have not. You are interested in the relationship between a dichotomous predictor—whether a student has used the center or not—and an outcome such as the quality of expository writing (or perhaps the "value added" to that quality).

One important issue is whether you are interested in *correlation* or in *causality*. Do you want to know whether attendance at the writing center *causes* improvement in expository writing? Or will you be satisfied with a survey that indicates whether students who have attended the center write better than similar students who have not? If your focus is on causality, you must design an experiment. If your focus is on correlation, your study can be relational.

Given a free hand on campus, you might randomly select students and randomly assign half of them to use the writing center and half to some alternative, using a pretest and a posttest to detect changes in the quality of their writing. A prospective experiment like this would support causal inference. But, faced with practical or ethical constraints, you might simply conduct a relational study of students, some of whom have and others of whom have not used the writing center. In this case your findings might be influenced by selection bias, and your results might confound the center's effectiveness with preexisting differences among participants. Under even more severe constraints, you might be unable to study currently enrolled students and therefore have to resort to a mail survey of alumni (to find out if they attended the center while they were enrolled) in conjunction with a detailed examination of their transcripts (to obtain their grades). Neither of these last two designs would support causal inference.

Relational studies are often good pilots for future experimental work. A relational pilot is usually inexpensive and easy to carry out, and allows you to explore alternatives for the future experiment. You can examine relations among a large variety of different outcomes, predictors, and covariates. Perhaps you are not sure exactly what outcomes you want to measure, or what predictors (such as cumulative GPA, or entering SAT score, or gender, or major) to include. The relatively low cost of a relational pilot study (using data from surveys, questionnaires, and other self-reports) allows you to investigate a relatively large and diverse sample of participants. The pilot study can help you to specify an appropriate target population, and to make preliminary investigations of the way effects differ by subgroup. You may be able to use the pilot to identify the influence of different components of the treatment; for example, perhaps some students have attended only remedial classes at the writing center, while others have been in peer-counseling groups.

One particular way a relational pilot can help is by quickly giving you an idea of how large an effect you might find in an ultimate experiment. Relational pilots are often conducted to find out whether it is reasonable to expect to find any effect of a treatment at all. If you can't find an association between a treatment and an outcome in a relational pilot, then you may decide it's not worthwhile to launch your full-blown experiment.

EXAMPLE: *Piloting an experiment with a relational study: The effects of teaching style and achievement orientation on academic achievement.*

In constructing his California Psychological Inventory (CPI), Harrison Gough (1957) identified two types of achievement motivation: *Ac motivation* (achievement via conformance), which facilitates achievement in settings where conforming behavior—acceptance of regulations, a high degree of self-discipline, and so forth—is rewarded; and *Ai motivation* (achievement via independence), which facilitates achievement in settings where independence, individuality, and creative innovation are rewarded.

Is student achievement related to type of achievement motivation? Does this relationship differ according to the type of class in which the students sit—conforming or independent? Arguing that traditional college curricula reward conforming behavior while curricular reforms emphasize independent behavior, George Domino (1968, 1971) conducted two studies—one relational, one experimental—to answer these questions.

The relational pilot. Domino began with a survey of 348 full-time juniors attending a California college. Using scores on Ac and Ai subscales, he identified four subgroups of 22 students: HiAc-HiAi, HiAc-LoAi, LoAc-HiAi, LoAc-LoAi. He collected data on students' GPAs from the registrar and coded the environment of their classes as either conforming or independent. Domino found what he expected: HiAc-HiAi students did well everywhere, but, "for the HiAc-LoAi and LoAc-HiAi students, there was a distinct and understandable interaction between achievement and the demands of the environment" (1968, p. 259).

Domino's relational pilot helped to shape his subsequent experiment. He criticized the use of student GPA cumulated over four semesters as a measure of achievement, noting that "equivalent grades in different courses do not represent equivalent performances" (p. 256). He recognized that "some disciplines are more amenable to one type of presentation [conforming versus independent] than the other" (p. 258), and questioned whether his findings might be an artifact of subject-matter differences. He recognized the limitations of his sample, commenting that his results "derive from a particular college setting and may not be generalizable to other educational institutions" (p. 259).

The follow-up experiment. In his second study, Domino selected 100 students from the entering class of a large university, hoping to examine generalizability. The students were selected from a pool of 900 freshmen, according to their scores on the CPI: 50 HiAc-LoAi and 50 LoAc-HiAi. Within achievement-motivation types, students were randomly assigned to four sections of an introductory psychology class: two LoAc-HiAi groups (Sections 1 and 2) and two HiAc-LoAi groups (Sections 3 and 4). The four groups had equal numbers of men and women and comparable average SAT scores, and were homogeneous in their Ac and Ai motivation. The psychology instructors cooperated with Domino by teaching Sections 2 and 3 in a conforming manner and Sections 1 and 4 in an independent manner. Students and instructors were "blind" to the motivation scores.

By using four sections of introductory psychology, Domino avoided the potential artifacts that might have been due to subject-matter differences. Randomization and blinding ensured that this experiment could support statements of causality rather than just correlation.

At the end of the semester all students took a final examination measuring factual knowledge (200 multiple-choice items) and a test of convergent and divergent thinking (6 essay questions). The essays were graded by three external psychologists. Students were also asked to indicate their satisfaction with the course and the instructor. Finally, for each student Domino collected the course grade given by the instructor (without regard to the final examination), and a two-year cumulative GPA (not including the course).

Expanding his pool of outcome measures enabled Domino to widen his notion of academic achievement (with factual knowledge and originality being separated) and to include a new measure of satisfaction. He also was able to lessen his reliance on GPA, the only outcome in the pilot study. He continued to control for gender and general aptitude, as he had done in the pilot.

His findings were clear, and were supported very strongly by the findings of his pilot, thereby increasing generalizability. He found interactions between motivation and teaching style for factual content on the multiple-choice items, factual knowledge in the essays, perceived teacher effectiveness, and course evaluation, but not for original thinking, overall grade, or cumulative GPA. He concluded:

> Despite the artificiality of having the same instructor role-play both independent and conforming teaching styles, the results quite clearly indicate a very definite interaction between student achievement orientation and teaching style. If it can be argued that educational aims should include both the imparting of factual knowledge and some degree of satisfaction on the part of students, then one method of achieving these aims is to match student achievement orientation with teaching style. (1971, p. 429)

Informal Small-scale Experiments

Sometimes it is useful to pilot a future experiment not as a relational study but as a small-scale version of your ultimate experiment. Such a pilot usually compromises on sample selection or random assignment. You might use a small nonrandom convenience sample—say one or two sections of a course, the faculty in a small department, or a few departments in a single institution—to see whether you can actually implement the innovation you wish to study. Or you might try a small-scale experiment simply to see whether, once implemented, your innovation has any effect at all.

But if you are to enroll students in an ad hoc fashion, how should you select them? Should you just pick an instructor or a class haphazardly? If you do, you can argue that if the innovation is successful when a "typical" professor teaches "average" students, there is a reasonable chance it will work in other sections with other students. But what do you mean by average? A preferable first step is to use a best-case scenario. Select a section, instructor, or group of students you hope will be particularly receptive to your innovation. Then if your innovation doesn't work in this ideal environment, it probably is not worth pursuing. If it does work, you will have taken an important first step—you will have shown that the innovation can be implemented in your college and that, at least in an ideal setting, it does have an effect.

Generalizing from the results of such a pilot is chancy because the study is intentionally biased. You may not have controlled exactly who got the treatment and who did not—did students select themselves into sections, were they assigned at random, or were they "tracked"? You may not have controlled the nature of the innovative treatment—is its effect separable from that of the style of the instructor?

How can you take these uncertainties into account in a small-scale project? Qualitative inquiry should always play a role in broadening your findings. Build in systematic observation. You may be able to discriminate between the effects of your new curriculum and those of a teacher's enthusiastic personality. On the quantitative side, your small-scale study can capitalize on naturally occurring variations within your program. For example, if you have included several sections or classrooms in your pilot, perhaps you can tease out confounded effects by comparing classes. Does the innovation have the same effect across each of the classrooms? If the trial runs across semesters, or successive groups of students, is there consistency over time and across cohorts?

EXAMPLE: *Using a small-scale informal experiment to shape the design of a future experiment: Improving the teaching of expository writing.*

During the 1987–88 academic year, Norman Katz, an instructor of expository writing at Harvard University, decided to make a major change in his curriculum. Previously, he had taught students to write using traditional literary tools, asking them to write essays and to critique other pieces of writing. Arguing that writing is not content-free, Katz thought that students might improve more rapidly if writing assignments incorporated their substantive interests.

He decided to conduct a small-scale pilot to see if there was anything to this idea. His fundamental question: Does the interaction between expository writing and economics affect student performance in either or both areas? Katz invited freshmen who were taking introductory economics to participate in his 2 writing sections (out of the 60 sections of the writing course). Because all of the students shared a common background, the teaching of expository writing skills could be built around substantive ideas in economics.

Katz advertised his sections widely among freshmen. From among the volunteers, he randomly picked 15 candidates to participate in each of his two sections. Three outside readers from the English department and three from the economics department graded student papers, unaware of the innovation. The former group gave holistic judgments of writing quality; the latter evaluated the quality of the students' economic arguments.

In the opinion of the expert judges, the expository writing of students in the innovative sections was better than that of students in other sections of the writing course. It was also slightly better than the writing of other students who were taking both expository writing and economics courses, but who were not receiving the special instruction that capitalized on that fact. The effect was small but consistent. And qualitative feedback from students in Katz's sections indicated that they had enjoyed the innovative approach and felt it strengthened their knowledge of economics (Katz, 1988).

Katz's findings are not easily generalizable, because the pilot was not a true experiment. The pilot was intentionally flawed; Katz willingly sacrificed generalizability for manageability, breadth for depth. The first limitation is that freshmen *were not randomly selected.* Although they were randomly *assigned* to groups once they had volunteered, they originally selected themselves. If students who volunteered for the new curriculum were systematically different—either better or worse at writing—from their peers who were also eligible but who did not volunteer, can the effect of Katz's innovative curriculum be separated from this possible bias?

The nature of the "treatment" was not clearly defined. What exactly was the treatment? Could it be replicated by others? Can anyone other than Norman Katz actually offer it? Indeed, Katz modified his curriculum slightly in the spring of 1988, his second time around, learning from his first experience in the fall of 1987.

The findings may be attributable to the Hawthorne effect. It is possible that the students either knew, were told, or figured out they were part of an innovation, and worked extra hard at their writing. Katz therefore asked, will this happen if the new curriculum is implemented in a more widespread way?

Do these questions invalidate the small-scale study? Absolutely not. Much was learned. First, Katz was able to show his colleagues that he could easily implement this new curriculum in the classroom. He was able to show that freshmen were interested in the new curriculum—in fact, he had many more applicants than he could accommodate. Second, he was able to show the new approach was empirically promising, even though its effects could not be definitely separated from other, possibly confounding effects. He certainly showed it was worth trying the new approach again with a more rigorous design. Third, he was able to refine his ideas as to what treatment would make the most sense. Initially, he simply wanted to "use economics to teach writing better." By the end of two semesters, he had developed methods and materials that could be systematically modified and made available to other investigators, in other disciplines, on other campuses. Fourth, he developed a clearer idea of how the new approach was affecting student production, originality, and satisfaction. In follow-up studies, more rigorous measures of these constructs could be applied. There are undoubtedly other ways in which Katz's small-scale study shaped future work. He simply took the first step. More rigorously designed studies will seek to build on his example in the future.

Generalizing from a Small Study

It is nice to think that when a pilot study or small-scale project is designed well its findings can be generalized to a larger population, and that they will hold up. Usually they can and they will. But sometimes outcomes from a small study won't generalize, even when the work is excellent. It helps to keep this caveat in mind and to think about it. The basic question you should ask is, can the findings of the small study be generalized to a larger population without changing crucial features of the population?

You can ask this question about a small experiment, and you can ask it about small-scale survey results. Let's begin with an experiment. Suppose an innovative program is designed at a large university to train Ph.D. recipients for private-sector employment. The goal is to give people with Ph.D.s in English more employment options. The first questions you ask are: Can we do this training successfully? Will the graduates find good jobs?

You design a small randomized controlled pilot study. From a pool of 30 Ph.D. candidates expressing interest in the private sector, 15 are randomly assigned to get the new program, while 15 don't get it. One year later, you compare results for the two programs. The results are clear. The 15 Ph.D.s from the new program are all employed in private-sector jobs with good salaries. They report they are happy. Their supervisors are satisfied with their performance. The control group is not nearly as well-off: many have not found private-sector jobs at all. So a solid conclusion is that your program is highly effective—it has achieved its goals.

Now you must ask about generalizability. Will these findings, if translated into a program for a much larger population, still hold up? Translating them into widespread implementation suggests you will offer this training to all Ph.D. students in the humanities who want it. At a large university, this may be hundreds of people. In fact, if your colleagues at other universities hear about your successful project, they may adopt it too.

What will probably happen? The new, expanded program may well fail. A year later, many Ph.D.s who have received the training may still be unemployed. Why? Because while there is a strong and immediate private sector demand for 15 English Ph.D.s, there may *not* be a demand for 1000. So the successful and well-evaluated small study may have results that break down when generalized.

This illustrates an important concept in research on colleges. With some education programs or services, the benefit the program confers to any one recipient depends upon how many other people participate in the same program. The value to an individual participant depends upon program size. In this case, the more widely the new training or curriculum is offered, the lower the expected benefit to any one participating student.

EXAMPLE: *Implementing findings from a survey of students' use of time.*

Thomas Angelo (1989) organized an in-depth survey of how students spend their time at Harvard University. From the registrar's full list of 6400 students, he chose a 6 percent random sample, or 385 students. Using repeated callbacks, Angelo completed interviews with 365, for a response rate of 94 percent. A subgroup of 42 of these students were asked to keep detailed logs of how they spent their time—to track, hour by hour for one full week, time spent studying and on other academic pursuits, time spent on extra-curricular activities or part-time jobs, time spent socializing, and time spent on athletics.

Angelo then met with each of the 42 students individually, with two goals. One was simply to debrief, to understand in detail how each student spent his or her time. The second was to discuss with students how they might use their time more effectively. More than half of the students reported later that the full process was highly useful to them, and that they would make some changes in their schedules. A special finding was that many students wish to build some athletics or physical exercise into their daily activities, but want to do it at a time when university athletic facilities are little used, to minimize waiting time.

The students noticed that an optimum time for athletics is early afternoon, when the facilities are hardly used. Several of the 42 in this study actually changed their schedules to participate in athletics in early afternoon, and were very pleased with the change. But what if these findings were disseminated and generalized to all 6400 undergraduates? Even if only a small fraction of them acted on the findings and went to do athletics in the early afternoon, the result would be severe strain on the facilities. Far too many students would show up at the same time. This small study illustrates how the implementation of a small-scale research result can work beautifully, while wider implementation may cause the good results to break down.

WHERE SHOULD YOU GO FROM HERE?

10

The university work environment appears ideal for carrying out research and evaluation. Faculty members understand the value of doing research. Some are involved in it themselves. And the college or university community has a well-defined, easily counted, and accessible population—faculty, students, and staff.

Yet to our friends and colleagues at the university, these advantages are occasionally obscured by all the potential problems. Will the students object to participating in research? After all, they are paying tuition to be educated, not to be experimented upon. Will administrators value your findings, and use them to improve policy? If research projects on campus simply result in researchers talking to one another, without ever promoting improvement in teaching, advising, or admissions, then the policy value of such work will be negligible.

It may be useful to end our book by sharing some of the lessons we have learned in our large, collaborative assessment seminar, in which we have worked with colleagues to carry out more than twenty projects (Light, 1990). Our experiences may help you to anticipate some of the opportunities and constraints that will undoubtedly arise in your own work.

Our experience has taught us that research in higher education offers several different opportunities, in addition to the obvious one of doing important work. It offers an *opportunity for collaboration* among disparate groups—faculty, administrators, and students—who do not always get together naturally. The research process is a useful mechanism for bonding people together with a common goal. It also offers an opportunity for *administrative leadership*. In our seminar at Harvard, President Bok took a crucial leadership role. Because of his strong public statements and financial support, many who might otherwise have decided they were too busy joined the group.

Getting Started

When we started inviting our colleagues, both faculty members and administrators, to participate in our seminar, many asked: "What is the goal of this enterprise?" or "What do you want to come out of this?" An additional question, unspoken by most participants, was: "I'm busy—is it worth spending my already overcommitted time on this?"

Such questions were a surprise to us. Our colleagues seemed to be asking for a specific set of goals in advance. We, in contrast, had hoped that seminar participants would develop their own goals for research on college effectiveness and would work collaboratively to achieve them. These early questions forced us to think about how to present the concept of *systematically embedding research into day-to-day university activities*.

We found that an analogy to medical practice was helpful. Imagine a distinguished physician, perhaps the director of a hospital or a medical association, or a physician
with a large private practice. Because she cares about keeping her patients strong and well, preventing illnesses, and
detecting and curing troubles at an early stage, she issues
a public statement. In her statement, she invites all her
patients to come in for regular checkups. The goal is to
keep the patients functioning as well and as effectively as
possible. In the context of higher education, this is a role
college deans and university presidents can adopt—writing
to faculty members in an annual report, urging them to
think about how their institution is working well, and how
it might be strengthened.

Back to our physician. She invites her patients in, and
they come in voluntarily, because they share her goal of
good health for all. She is not checking their blood pressure
to threaten or criticize. Checkups are part of a routine for
the maintenance of good health. Similarly, research in colleges and universities can be constructive rather than
threatening, if it is a *collaborative process*. It must be organized and run by people who want the institution to
function well, who have a vested interest in the maintenance of its academic, social, and psychological health.
That certainly includes faculty at all levels.

The analogy with health care can be extended. Blood
pressure readings are not perfectly reliable—they vary
from day to day, hour to hour—and yet the data are useful
for guiding broad decisions. When such data are collected,
the doctor must ask: "What is the most useful way to report
these blood pressure readings to patients?" Is it to say: "You
pass—see you next year?" Or, "You fail—take this medi-
cation for the rest of your life?" No, measuring blood pressure is an opportunity to educate patients, to bring about
improvements in their daily lives and diets, to build on
existing strengths and rectify weaknesses. The same is true
of research in colleges. If used wisely, it can lead to im-

provements throughout the entire fabric of an institution. Research in higher education should avoid simple pass-fail judgments. It should collect extensive data in as full and as rich a way as possible. Findings must be shared in a spirit of research for improvement, to encourage innovation, and ultimately to strengthen the experiences of all who participate.

Lessons from Our Seminar

We had many expectations before embarking on our seminar, not all of which were met. We would like to share six expectations, three fulfilled and three unfulfilled, in the hope that others can benefit from our experience.

Our first correct expectation was that, despite the sense of some cynics that most faculty members are not eager to innovate and simply want to be left alone, many faculty members are delighted to innovate. This is especially true *if they feel there is institutional support and institutional reward*. Our seminar offered a forum for sharing ideas about new teaching devices, new teaching techniques, and ways of evaluating whether innovative teaching was working well. The availability of modest financial support, initially from the president's office and later from the Fund for Improvement of Postsecondary Education (FIPSE), the Sloan Foundation, and the Mellon Foundation, was crucial to the implementation of the many good ideas that were generated.

Our second correct expectation was that a group of distinguished, busy people would faithfully attend meetings to plan, advise, and comment on ongoing projects. We assumed that to maintain participants' interest the research enterprise had to be an enjoyable, intellectually rewarding activity in its own right. We invited senior administrators from twenty colleges and universities, and a mix of senior and junior faculty. Everyone attended regular evening meetings over several years. The attraction of the meetings changed over the several years of the seminar. At the outset, the activity was designing and organizing research projects. In the second year, the actual implementation of surveys and teaching innovations began, and participants paid more attention to supervising projects out in the field. Still later, attention was directed to using substantive findings in decisionmaking at the participating schools.

Our third correct expectation was that a tendency would develop for participants to reward adventuresome faculty and administrators undertaking systematic evaluation. Rather than focusing only on successful innovations, which is most people's natural tendency, we made a special point of honoring colleagues who tried a new idea and systematically assessed its effectiveness. They were honored regardless of whether the innovation turned out to be a blockbuster. This concept of *rewarding the process of innovation and systematic evaluation* took hold quickly.

A corollary of this expectation is that most improvements turn out to be modest. It is unrealistic to think that in a short time student learning in a course can be tripled, or that a 55 percent dropout rate for women in the physical sciences can be reduced to zero. Rather, we should treasure small gains. Modest gains built upon steadily over time rapidly compound to become big improvements.

We faced several surprises as well. We *incorrectly* expected that many faculty members would eagerly participate in some of the actual evaluation work, especially when the seminar was so well supported. We were a bit naive. Most senior faculty have their research agendas well set, and many junior faculty did not see a clear connection between this work and their professional futures. Finding faculty members to do the nitty-gritty work was difficult. Spending time on broad-based research in higher education is, for most members of the faculty, not a clear career path into any discipline, and therefore the seminar activities were an "extra."

Our second incorrect expectation was that students would be leery of participating in the research. We were utterly mistaken. Students turned out to be enthusiastic, unthreatened participants and, in the end, made the whole enterprise go. They volunteered eagerly to do much of the evaluation work, the day-to-day data collection, the organization, coding, and data analysis. When our seminar began there were no student participants. By the end of the second year, more than a dozen undergraduate and graduate students were actively involved. Several of the undergraduates have completed honors theses based on seminar projects, and several graduate students are writing doctoral theses arising from the seminar.

When asked why they are such enthusiastic participants, students give several reasons. First, participating in research on higher education is one of their few chances to shape their own environment and that of future college students. Second, they find the financial support useful. Third, they benefit from faculty supervision when carrying out this work and learn much from the interaction. The caveat here is that if students are heavily involved their efforts must be supervised. This requires a major commitment on the part of faculty members to assure a high-quality training experience as well as the production of high-quality work.

Our third incorrect expectation was that larger-scale, elaborate studies would be especially interesting to most participants. We misjudged this badly, and now believe that less can be more. Sometimes a small effort with a quick turnaround, if well done, is the most effective research of all. This is especially true when the findings from a project may affect a policy decision and the person in charge of policy has specially requested research to help shape the decision.

Decisions You Must Make

Constitute a Team for Each Project

For each project, we urge you to create a team that includes at least one administrator, one faculty member, and one student. This increases the chances that your research will have an impact on policy, and that students will be supervised.

We saw this illustrated in a seminar project to evaluate women's persistence in the physical sciences at Harvard, Yale, and Dartmouth colleges. The admissions office at each of these colleges wanted the work done, so the administrative supervision at each college came from the dean of admissions, or a person designated by the dean. Similarly, at each college key faculty members in science were interested in the project and became involved in its design and execution. Students did the detailed work of collecting and analyzing data from admissions records, departmental records, and in-depth student interviews.

Top-Down versus Bottom-Up Initiative

Two dramatically different methods for organizing research projects can work, and you should think carefully about which will work best on your campus. In a top-down initiative, a campus leader specifies a problem that needs solving or a program that needs improvement, and members of a research team get to work on it. At Harvard, President Bok wrote to all seminar participants, inviting them to consider how students allocate their time to extracurricular activities and to part-time jobs. His basic question was "how much is too much?": at what point does extensive involvement begin to affect academic performance? Many seminar participants found these questions important at their colleges too, and a project was undertaken to answer them (see Angelo, 1989).

In contrast, a bottom-up initiative comes from a particular faculty member, or department, or student group, or administrative office. Most seminar participants found bottom-up initiatives more inviting. For example, a senior professor asked whether different sectioning strategies in his large course would affect the involvement and learning of his students. Seminar participants guessed that any findings from his course would very likely generalize to other courses. As a result of one professor's question, a large study was organized to try out different sectioning methods, and the results were shared widely throughout the community (see Bushey, 1989).

Capitalizing on Existing Resources

We learned quickly that each research team tends to assume they must begin their work from the very beginning. They assume they are starting from ground zero, with little other work to build on. But you should remember that this often is not necessary. You may be able to build upon existing campus records and research results, thus saving both money and time (Braskamp, 1982; Ewell, 1988).

For example, in a survey already in progress to ask Harvard alumni to reflect on part-time work and involvement in extracurricular activities, a set of questions about foreign languages was added. What languages had these alumni studied in college? How much had they used the languages after graduation? What suggestions about studying languages did they have for current undergraduates and for faculty in language departments? Adding these questions to an existing survey not only saved time and money but also made it possible, as a bonus, to tie the respondents' answers about language to their answers to questions about their other activities in college.

Who Is Your Audience?

You will probably plan a different project if your work is designed to improve your own teaching effectiveness in your Russian course, than if your goal is to change the way American college students learn Russian. A recurring question in our seminar was: "How generalizable must my results be to be useful for others?"

While it is appealing to imagine that your study will change national education policy, often this view is a barrier to even *starting* a project. If you are thinking about national policy, you must plan a far more complex design than if you want to try out a small project in one class or at one college. We strongly encourage you to clarify in your own mind exactly who your audience is, and then to take the first step on a small scale, rather than letting concerns about generalizability immobilize you (Adelman, 1983; Ewell, 1987).

Projects pursued in our seminar were diverse, and different projects addressed different audiences. We have identified five specific audiences you might consider for your work:

1. *Your own course.* How effective is your course? How should you improve it next time you teach it?

2. *Colleagues in your department.* Perhaps your project builds on expert knowledge from your own teaching, but you feel your colleagues would benefit from systematic research results. Then you should try to make your project depend as little as possible on your personal teaching idiosyncrasies.

3. *Students.* Many projects are undertaken to provide better information to students, in the style of *Consumer Reports*. For example, a finding that involvement in extracurricular activities or part-time work up to twenty hours per week has no ill effect on academic performance may be helpful to students thinking about how to allocate their time. If students are your target audience, make sure you

carry out your work on a generalizable sample, and search for particular combinations of activities or commitments that students should avoid. For instance, you may find that physics or chemistry majors should not spend twenty hours per week on external activities because of the extra demands of laboratory work.

4. *The president or a dean.* If you organize your project for senior administrators, we urge you to consult regularly with them to determine how you can present results in the most useful way. Results that are crystal clear to one audience may be murky to another.

This happened in the Harvard seminar when data from a new way of teaching expository writing skills to students in an economics course were analyzed by a statistician. He enthusiastically performed elegant regression analyses to summarize student performance in sections with innovative instruction. Results were presented as a series of regression coefficients with their standard errors. When the statistician presented these data to his colleagues in statistics and economics, the audience found them clear and exciting. But when a group of deans from several colleges saw the regression coefficients (corrected for bias using two-stage least squares), they listened politely until the end of the presentation, and then asked for a far less technical summary of the main findings with policy implications for the colleges.

5. *A professional journal.* If your goal is to disseminate results to colleagues throughout the nation in a professional journal, you will probably want to make your findings as generalizable as possible and use cutting-edge statistical techniques. The formal refereeing process is a good way to assure that the methodological quality of your work is strong, and a professional journal is an effective way to reach a large audience.

We are especially enthusiastic about publishing results from college research in professional journals because they help to increase our cumulative national knowledge base.

In Chapter 2 we argued that each innovation or new project should incorporate and build upon the lessons of the old. Projects for the 1990s should be more advanced than those of the 1980s. Remember that your new project will be a stepping-stone for someone else to take the innovation even further. Sharing your findings helps to generate cumulative knowledge and steady progress (Adelman, 1986; Bloom, Cordray, and Light, 1988).

Planning a Longer-term Research Program

We began our assessment seminar by inviting colleagues from other colleges and universities to tell about their experiences with research and evaluation on their campuses. A crucial theme that came up over and over was the lack of follow-up. Participants told about interesting first steps that didn't lead to a second step, and that ultimately had little impact on their college. We encourage you to keep these comments in mind, and to plan a *series* of studies that, over time, will slowly but steadily strengthen your college in a specific area (Ewell, 1984; Ewell, 1988).

To illustrate, admissions deans from Harvard, Yale, and Dartmouth began their analyses of women's persistence in science with a careful look at existing data. What fraction of undergraduate women, they asked, who initially indicated a clear interest in the sciences, actually stayed with that interest through graduation? Each college got an answer, and in each case it was between 40 and 50 percent.

But they didn't stop with these findings. As a follow-up, the deans initiated interviews with both men and women who had indicated an interest in science. Students who dropped out were interviewed in depth and asked why they left. Students who chose to stay were also interviewed, and asked to share their perceptions of why they stayed while many of their fellow students did not.

The deans learned a lot. They found that nearly all of

the switching goes on during freshman year. While several faculty members in science were aware of this, it was not widely known. A second finding was that introductory courses are the crucial decision point for nearly every student who considers majoring in a science. If these courses are not well taught, many students decide to switch. A third finding was that women who switch give different reasons from men who switch. When asked, women who had switched gave reasons such as "I'm not mathematically strong enough," or "I found the work personally unfulfilling and lonely," or "The work demanded a stronger science background than I had, and I'm not a natural scientist." All of these responses show a tendency to *internalize* the decision to switch, to put the onus on themselves. Men, in contrast, give many more *external* reasons: "My advisor thought I would be a great social scientist," or "My obligations to the varsity swimming team kept me from working late in the lab."

This illustration drives home the value of a longer-term research program. Step one, finding the proportion of switchouts from the sciences, produces interesting information. Step two builds upon this knowledge, and asks why students switch. Step three, organizing changes in the science departments to strengthen introductory courses and student advising, is the policy step that ultimately can make a difference at a college.

In a well-designed long-term plan, you will move steadily from collecting data to initiating policy change, and then to evaluating what improvement, if any, you have accomplished. A long-term research program, building systematically from abstract learning to concrete changes in policy, should strengthen any college.

REFERENCES

Abedi, J., and E. Benkin. 1987. The effects of students' academic, financial, and demographic variables on time to the doctorate. *Research in Higher Education,* 27, 3–14.

Abrams, H. G., and L. P. Jernigan. 1984. Academic support services and success of high-risk college students. *American Educational Research Journal,* 21, 261–274.

Adams, L. L., and D. Gale. 1982. Solving the quandary between questionnaire length and response rate in educational research. *Research in Higher Education,* 17, 231–240.

Adelman, C. 1983. The major seventh: standards as a leading tone in higher education. In J. R. Warren, ed., *Meeting the New Demand for Standards.* San Francisco: Jossey-Bass.

Adelman, C. P., ed. 1986. *Assessment in American higher education: issues and contexts.* Washington, D.C.: Office of Educational Research and Improvement, U.S. Department of Education.

Alderman, D. L., and D. E. Powers. 1980. The effects of special preparation on SAT-verbal scores. *American Educational Research Journal,* 17, 239–251.

Andrews, J. D. W. 1981. Teaching format and student style: their interactive effects on learning. *Research in Higher Education,* 14, 161–178.

Angelo, T. A. 1989. What matters: a report of the Harvard Assessment Seminar survey of student involvement in extracurricular activities and part-time work. Document of the Harvard Seminar on Assessment. Cambridge, Mass., January 1989.

Astin, A. W. 1970. The methodology of research on college impact. Parts 1 and 2. *Sociology of Education,* 43, 223–254; 437–450.

———— 1977. *Four critical years.* San Francisco: Jossey-Bass.

———— 1985. *Achieving educational excellence: a critical assessment of priorities and practices in higher education.* San Francisco: Jossey-Bass.

Ayres, Q. W., and K. W. Bennett. 1983. University characteristics and student achievement. *Journal of Higher Education,* 54, 518–532.

Bangert-Drowns, R., C. C. Kulik, and J. Kulik. 1983. Individualized systems of instruction in secondary schools. *Review of Educational Research,* 53, 143–158.

Banta, T. W. 1988. Implementing outcomes assessment: promise and perils. *New Directions for Institutional Research,* 59. San Francisco: Jossey-Bass.

Banta, T. W., and J. A. Schneider. 1988. Using faculty-developed exit examinations to evaluate academic programs. *Journal of Higher Education,* 59, 69–53.

Basow, S. A., and N. T. Silberg. 1987. Student evaluations of college professors: are female and male professors rated differently? *Journal of Educational Psychology,* 79, 308–314.

Baxter, E. 1985. Verbal inactivity in tutorial groups, under conditions of varying preparation and leadership. *Higher Education,* 14, 723–740.

Bean, J. P. 1985. Interaction effects based on class level in an explanatory model of college student dropout syndrome. *American Educational Research Journal,* 22, 35–64.

Bean, J. P., and B. S. Metzner. 1985. A conceptual model of nontraditional undergraduate student attrition. *Review of Educational Research,* 55, 485–540.

Belland, J. C., W. D. Taylor, J. Canelos, F. Dwyer, and P. Baker.

1985. Is the self-paced instructional program, via micro-computer-based instruction, the most effective method of addressing individual learning differences? *Educational Communication and Technology Journal,* 33, 185–198.

Bennett, C. A., and A. Lumsdaine. 1975. *Evaluation and experiment.* New York: Academic Press.

Berg, K. M. 1988. The prevalence of eating disorders in coed versus single-sex residence halls. *Journal of College Student Development,* 29, 125–131.

Bloom, H. S., D. S. Cordray, and R. J. Light, eds. 1988. Lessons from selected program and policy areas. *New Directions for Program Evaluation,* 37, 1–120.

Bok, D. 1986. *Higher learning.* Cambridge, Mass.: Harvard University Press.

Boli, J., H. Katchadourian, and S. Mahoney. 1988. Analyzing academic records for informed administration. *Journal of Higher Education,* 59, 55–68.

Borden, L. A., S. K. Karr, and A. T. Caldwell-Colbert. 1988. Effects of a university rape prevention program on attitudes and empathy toward rape. *Journal of College Student Development,* 29, 132–137.

Bowen, H. 1977. *Investment in learning: the individual and social value of American higher education.* San Francisco: Jossey-Bass.

Boyer, E. L. 1987. *College: The undergraduate experience in America.* New York: Harper and Row.

Boyles, C. V. 1988. Help wanted: a profile of institutional research, 1970–1985. *Research in Higher Education,* 28, 132–142.

Braskamp, L. A. 1982. Evaluation systems are more than information systems. In R. Wilson, ed., *Designing American program review. New Directions for Higher Education,* 37.

Braxton, J. M. 1983. Teaching as performance of scholarly based course activities: a perspective on the relationships between teaching and research. *Review of Higher Education,* 7, 21–33.

Bruton, B. T., and R. Crull. 1982. Causes and consequences of student evaluation of instruction. *Research in Higher Education,* 17, 195–206.

Bryk, A., and S. Raudenbush. 1987. Applications of hierarchial linear models to assessing change. *Psychological Bulletin,* 101, 147–158.

Burda, P. C., and A. C. Vaux. 1988. Social drinking in supportive contexts among college males. *Journal of Youth and Adolescence,* 17, 165–171.

Bushey, B. 1989. Report of an educational innovation: sectioning in a large core course and the extent of student learning and involvement. Qualifying Paper, Harvard Graduate School of Education.

Bynum, J. E., and W. E. Thompson. 1983. Dropouts, stopouts and persisters: the effects of race and sex composition of college classes. *College and University,* 59, 39–48.

Campbell, D. T., and J. C. Stanley. 1963. *Experimental and quasi-experimental designs for research.* Boston: Houghton Mifflin.

Caporael, L. K. 1985. College students' computer use. *Journal of Higher Education,* 56, 172–188.

Carroll, J. G. 1980. Effects of training programs for university teaching assistants. *Journal of Higher Education,* 52, 167–183.

Carver, D. S., and D. W. Smart. 1985. The effects of a career and self-exploration course for undecided freshmen. *Journal of College Student Personnel,* 26, 37–43.

Centra, J. A. 1983. Research productivity and teaching effectiveness. *Research in Higher Education,* 18, 379–389.

Centra, J. A., R. L. Linn, and M. E. Parry. 1970. Academic growth in predominantly Negro and predominantly white colleges. *American Educational Research Journal,* 7, 83–98.

Chickering, A. W., and J. McCormick. 1973. Personality development and the college experience. *Research in Higher Education,* 1, 43–70.

Cohen, J. 1988. *Statistical power analysis for the behavioral sciences.* 2nd ed. Hillsdale, N.J.: Erlbaum.

Cohen, P. A. 1981. Student ratings of instruction and student achievement: a meta-analysis of multisection validity studies. *Review of Educational Research,* 51, 281–309.

Cook, T. D., and D. T. Campbell. 1979. *Quasi-experimentation: design and analysis issues for field settings.* Boston: Houghton Mifflin.

Cooper, H. M. 1984. *The integrative research review: a social science approach.* Beverly Hills, Calif.: Sage Publications.

Cooper, H. M., and R. Rosenthal. 1980. Statistical versus traditional procedures for summarizing research findings. *Psychological Bulletin,* 87, 442–449.

Cote, L. S., R. E. Grinnell, and L. D. Tompkins. 1986. Increasing response rates to mail surveys: the impact of adherence to human-like procedures and techniques. *Review of Higher Education,* 9, 229–242.

Cox, D. R. 1958. *Planning of experiments.* New York: John Wiley and Sons.

Crooks, T. J., and M. T. Kane. 1981. The generalizability of student ratings of instructors: item specificity and section effects. *Research in Higher Education,* 15, 35–313.

Cruse, D. B. 1987. Student evaluations and the university professor: caveat professor. *Higher Education,* 16, 723–737.

Dalgaard, K. A. 1982. Some effects of training on teaching effectiveness of untrained university teaching assistants. *Research in Higher Education,* 17, 39–50.

Dawber, T. R. 1980. *The Framingham Study: the epidemiology of atherosclerotic disease.* Cambridge, Mass.: Harvard University Press.

DerSimonian, R., and N. Laird. 1983. Evaluating the effect of coaching on SAT scores: a meta-analysis. *Harvard Educational Review,* 53, 1–15.

De Volder, M. L., W. S. De Grave, and W. Gijselears. 1985. Peer teaching: academic achievement of teacher-led versus student-led discussion groups. *Higher Education,* 14, 643–650.

Dillon, J. T. 1984. The classification of research questions. *Review of Educational Research,* 54, 327–361.

Domino, G. 1968. Differential predicting of academic achievement in conforming and independent settings. *Journal of Educational Psychology,* 59, 256–260.

—— 1971. Interactive effects of achievement orientation and teaching style on academic achievement. *Journal of Educational Psychology,* 62, 427–431.

Dooley, D. 1984. *Social research methods.* Englewood Cliffs, N.J.: Prentice-Hall.

Dowalby, F. J., and H. Schumer. 1973. Teacher-centered versus student-centered mode of college classroom instruction as related to manifest anxiety. *Journal of Educational Psychology,* 64, 125–132.

Dukes, F., and G. Gaither. 1984. A campus cluster program: effects on persistence and academic performance. *College and University,* 59, 150–166.

Easton, J. Q., and T. R. Guskey. 1983. Estimating the effects of college, department, course, and teacher on earned credit rates. *Research in Higher Education,* 19, 153–158.

Ellis, L., and D. Mathis. 1985. College student learning from televisea versus conventional classroom lectures: a controlled experiment. *Higher Education,* 14, 165–173.

Elmore, P. B., and K. A. LaPointe. 1975. Effect of teacher sex, student sex, and teacher warmth on the evaluation of college instructors. *Journal of Educational Psychology,* 67, 368–374.

Erdle, S., and H. G. Murray. 1986. Interfaculty differences in classroom teaching behaviors and their relationship to student instructional ratings. *Research in Higher Education,* 24, 115–127.

Erdle, S., H. G. Murray, and J. P. Rushton. 1985. Personality, classroom behavior, and student ratings of college teaching effectiveness: a path analysis. *Journal of Educational Psychology,* 77, 394–407.

Erwin, T. D. 1983. The influences of roommate assignments upon students' maturity. *Research in Higher Education,* 19, 451–459.

Ewell, P. T. 1984. *The self-regarding institution: information for excellence.* Boulder, Colo.: National Center for Higher Education Management Systems (NCHEMS).

—— 1987. Principles of longitudinal enrollment analysis: conducting retention and student flow studies. In J. A. Muffo and G. W. McLaughlin, eds., *A primer on institutional research.* Tallahassee, Fla.: Association for Institutional Research.

—— 1988. Implementing assessment: some organizational issues. In T. Banta, ed., *Implementing outcomes assessment: promise and perils. New Directions for Institutional Research,* 59. San Francisco: Jossey-Bass.

Feldens, M. D. G. F., and J. K. Duncan. 1986. Improving university teaching: what Brazilian students say about their teachers. *Higher Education,* 15, 641–649.

Feldman, K. A. 1971. Using the work of others: observations on reviewing and integrating. *Sociology of Education,* 44, 86–102.

—— 1983. Seniority and experience of college teachers as related to evaluations they receive from students. *Research in Higher Education,* 18, 3–68.

Feldman, K. A., and T. Newcomb. 1969. *The impact of college on students.* San Francisco: Jossey-Bass.

Ford, S. F., and S. Campos. 1977. Summary of validity data from the admissions testing program validity study service. In *On further examination: Report of the advisory panel on the Scholastic Aptitude Test score decline.* Princeton, N.J.: College Entrance Examination Board.

Foy, J. M., and D. W. Waller. 1987. Using British school examination as a predictor of university performance in a pharmacy course: a correlative study. *Higher Education,* 16, 691–698.

Fretz, B. K. 1981. Evaluating the effectiveness of career interventions. *Journal of Counseling Pyschology,* 28, 77–90.

Friedman, C. P. 1982. Factors affecting adoption of instructional innovations: an example from medical education. *Research in Higher Education,* 16, 291–302.

Friedman, M., and C. Stomper. 1983. The effectiveness of a faculty development program: a process-product experimental study. *Review of Higher Education,* 7, 49–65.

Fuqua, D. R., B. W. Hartman, and D. F. Brown. 1982. Survey research in higher education. *Research in Higher Education,* 17, 69–80.

Gaski, J. F. 1987. Comments on "Construct validity of measures of college teaching effectiveness." *Journal of Educational Psychology,* 79, 326–330.

Gerst, M. S., and R. H. Moos. 1973. Social ecology of university student residences. *Journal of Educational Psychology,* 63, 513–525.

Girves, J. E., and V. Wemmerus. 1988. Developing models of graduate student degree progress. *Journal of Higher Education,* 59, 163–189.

Glass, G. V. 1976. Primary, secondary, and meta-analysis of research. *Educational Reseacher,* 5, 3–8.

Glass, G. V., B. McGaw, and M. L. Smith. 1981. *Meta-analysis of social research.* Beverly Hills, Calif.: Sage Publications.

Goldman, R. D. 1972. Effects of a logical versus a neuronic learning strategy on performance in two undergraduate psychology courses. *Journal of Educational Psychology,* 63, 347–352.

Goldstein, E. 1979. Effect of same-sex and cross-sex role models on the subsequent academic productivity of scholars. *American Psychologist,* 34, 407–410.

Gosman, E. J., B. A. Dandridge, M. T. Nettles, and A. R. Thoeny. 1983. Predicting student progression: the influence of race and other student and institutional characteristics on college student performance. *Research in Higher Education,* 18, 209–236.

Gough, H. 1957. *The manual for the California Psychological Inventory.* Palo Alto, Calif.: Consulting Psychologists Press.

Greenwald, A. G. 1975. Consequences of prejudice against the null hypothesis. *Psychological Bulletin,* 82, 1–20.

Hackman, J. D. 1983. Seven maxims for institutional researchers: applying cognitive theory and research. *Research in Higher Education,* 18, 195–208.

Hedges, L. V. 1983. Combining independent estimators in research synthesis. *British Journal of Mathematical and Statistical Psychology,* 36, 123–131.

———— 1986. Issues in meta-analysis. In E. Z. Rothkopf, ed., *Review of Research in Education,* no. 13. Washington, D.C.: American Educational Research Association.

Hedges, L. V., and I. Olkin. 1985. *Statistical methods for meta-analysis.* New York: Academic Press.

Hendel, D. D. 1985. Effects of individualized and structured college curricula on students' performance and satisfaction. *American Educational Research Journal,* 22, 117–122.

Hoaglin, D. C., R. J. Light, B. McPeek, F. Mosteller, and M. A. Stoto. 1982. *Data for decisions: information strategies for policy makers.* Cambridge, Mass.: Abt Books.

Hogan, R. R. 1985. Response bias in a student follow-up: a comparison of low and high return surveys. *College and University,* 61, 17–25.

Hunter, D. E., and G. D. Kuh. 1987. The "write wing": characteristics of prolific contributors to the higher education literature. *Journal of Higher Education,* 58, 443–462.

Iovacchini, E. V., L. M. Hall, and D. D. Hengstler. 1985. Going back to college: some differences between adult students and traditional students. *College and University,* 59, 43–54.

Iwai, S. I., and W. D. Churchill. 1982. College attrition and the financial support systems of students. *Research in Higher Education,* 17, 105–113.

Jackson, G. B. 1980. Methods for integrative reviews. *Review of Educational Research,* 50, 438–460.

Jacobson, M. J., and M. H. Weller. 1987–1988. A profile of computer use among the University of Illinois humanistic faculty. *Journal of Educational Technology Systems,* 16, 83–98.

Jaeger, R. M. 1984. *Sampling in education and the behavioral sciences*. New York: Longman.

Janosik, S., D. G. Creamer, and L. H. Cross. 1988. The relationship of residence halls' student-environment fit and sense of competence. *Journal of College Student Development, 29,* 320–326.

Jensen, E. J. 1984. Student financial aid and degree attainment. *Research in Higher Education, 20,* 117–127.

Judd, C. M., and D. A. Kenny. 1981. *Estimating the effects of social intervention*. Cambridge: Cambridge University Press.

Kagar, D. M., and V. Fasan. 1988. Stress and the instructional environment. *College Teaching, 36,* 75–81.

Kasten, K. L. 1984. Tenure and merit pay as rewards for research, teaching, and service at a research university. *Journal of Higher Education, 55,* 500–514.

Katz, N. 1988. A report on an innovation for teaching freshmen expository writing: tying the instruction to basic economics. Report of the Harvard Seminar on Assessment. Cambridge, Mass.: Harvard Graduate School of Education.

Katzer, J., K. H. Cook, and W. W. Crouch. 1982. *Evaluating information: a guide for users of social science research*. 2nd ed. Reading, Mass.: Addison-Wesley.

Kegel-Flom, P. 1983. Personality traits in effective clinical teachers. *Research in Higher Education, 19,* 73–82.

Kish, L. 1965. *Survey sampling*. New York: John Wiley and Sons.

Kleemann, G. L., and R. C. Richardson, Jr. 1985. Student characteristics and perceptions of university effectiveness. *Review of Higher Education, 9,* 5–20.

Kleinbaum, D. G., L. Kupper, and H. Morgenstern. 1982. *Epidemiologic research*. New York: VanNostrand Reinhold.

Klitgaard, R. 1985. *Choosing elites*. New York: Basic Books.

Konnert, W., and R. Giese. 1987. College choice factors of male athletes at private NCAA division III institutions. *College and University, 62,* 33–44.

Kraemer, H. C., and S. Thiemann. 1987. *How many subjects: statistical power analysis in research*. Beverly Hills, Calif.: Sage Publications.

Kramer, G. L., N. R. Arrington, and B. Chynoweth. 1985. The academic advising center and faculty advising: a comparison. *NASPA Journal, 23,* 24–35.

Krathwohl, D. R. 1985. *Social and behavioral science research: a new framework for conceptualizing, implementing, and evaluating research studies.* San Francisco: Jossey-Bass.

Kuh, G. D., J. P. Bean, R. D. Bradley, M. D. Coomes, and D. E. Hunter. 1986. Changes in research on college students published in selected journals between 1969 and 1983. *Review of Higher Education,* 9, 177–192.

Kulik, C. C., J. Kulik, and B. Shwalb. 1983. College programs for high risk and disadvantaged students: a meta-analysis of findings. *Review of Educational Research,* 53, 397–414.

Kulik, J. A., R. Bangert-Drowns, and C. C. Kulik. 1984. Effectiveness of coaching for aptitude tests. *Psychological Bulletin,* 95, 179–188.

Kulik, J. A., C. C. Kulik, and P. A. Cohen. 1979. A meta-analysis of outcome studies of Keller's personalized system of instruction. *American Psychologist,* 34, 307–318.

——— 1980. Effectiveness of computer-based college teaching: a meta-analysis of findings. *Review of Educational Research,* 50, 525–544.

Lacefield, W. E. 1986. Faculty enrichment and the assessment of teaching. *Review of Higher Education,* 9, 361–379.

Landward, S., and D. Hepworth. 1984. Support systems for high risk college students: findings and issues. *College and University,* 59, 119–128.

Langenbach, M., and L. Korhonen. 1988. Persisters and nonpersisters in a graduate level, nontraditional, liberal education program. *Adult Education Quarterly,* 38, 136–148.

Lawrence, J. H., and R. T. Blackburn. 1988. Age as a predictor of faculty productivity. *Journal of Higher Education,* 59, 22–38.

Lentz, L. P. 1983. Differences in women's freshman versus senior career salience ratings at women's and coeducational colleges. *Review of Higher Education,* 6, 181–193.

Light, R. J. 1979. Capitalizing on variation: how conflicting reseach findings can be helpful for policy. *Educational Researcher,* 8, 3–8.

——— 1983. *Evaluation studies review annual,* 8. Beverly Hills, Calif.: Sage Publications.

——— 1984. Six evaluation issues that synthesis can resolve better than single studies. *New Directions in Program Evaluation,* 24, 57–74.

——— 1990. *The Harvard Seminar on Assessment: Final Report.* Cambridge, Mass.: Harvard Graduate School of Education.

Light, R. J., and D. B. Pillemer. 1984. *Summing up*. Cambridge, Mass.: Harvard University Press.

Light, R. J., and P. V. Smith. 1971. Accumulating evidence: procedures for resolving contradictions among different studies. *Harvard Educational Review,* 41, 429–471.

Lin, Y. G., W. J. McKeachie, and D. G. Tucker. 1984. The use of student ratings in promotion decisions. *Journal of Higher Education,* 55, 583–589.

Loo, C. M., and G. Rolison. 1986. Alienation of ethnic minority students at a predominantly white university. *Journal of Higher Education,* 57, 58–77.

Lucas, C. J., and C. D. Schmitz. 1988. Communications media and current-events knowledge among college students. *Higher Education,* 17, 139–149.

Lunneborg, C. E., and R. W. Lunneborg. 1969. Deviations from predicted growth of abilities for male and female college students. *Journal of Educational Measurement,* 6, 165–172.

Lynd, R. S., and H. M. Lynd. 1929. *Middletown: a study in contemporary American culture*. New York: Harcourt Brace.

Mahler, S., and D. E. Benor. 1984. Short and long term effects of a teacher-training workshop in medical school. *Higher Education,* 13, 265–273.

Marlin, J. W., Jr. 1987. Student perception of end-of-course evaluations. *Journal of Higher Education,* 58, 704–716.

Marsh, H. W. 1980. The influence of student, course, and instructor characteristics in evaluation of university teaching. *American Educational Research Journal,* 17, 219–237.

——— 1984. Students' evaluations of university teaching: dimensionality, reliability, validity, potential biases, and utility. *Journal of Educational Psychology,* 76, 707–754.

McBean, E. A., and W. C. Lennox. 1985. Effect of survey size on student ratings of teaching. *Higher Education,* 14, 117–125.

McClure, R. H., C. E. Wells, and B. L. Bowerman. 1986. A model of MBA student performance. *Research in Higher Education,* 25, 183–193.

McGee, G. W., and R. C. Ford. 1987. Faculty research productivity and intention to change positions. *Review of Higher Education,* 11, 1–16.

McLaughlin, G. W., M. B. Zirkes, and B. T. Mahan. 1983. Multicollinearity and testing questions of sex equity. *Research in Higher Education,* 19, 277–284.

Mevarech, Z. K., and S. Werner. 1985. Are mastery learning

strategies beneficial for developing problem-solving skills? *Higher Education,* 14, 425–432.

Millman, J., S. P. Slovacek, E. Kulik, and K. J. Mitchell. 1983. Does grade inflation affect the reliability of graders? *Research in Higher Education,* 19, 423–429.

Mitchell, R. 1989. A progress report on the New Pathways program at Harvard Medical School. Boston: Harvard Medical School.

Moline, A. E. 1987. Financial aid and student persistence: an application of causal modeling. *Research in Higher Education,* 26, 130–147.

Mosteller, F. M., and J. W. Tukey. 1977. *Data analysis and regression.* Reading, Mass.: Addison-Wesley.

Muehlenhard, C. L., L. E. Baldwin, W. J. Bourg, and A. E. Piper. 1988. Helping women "break the ice": a computer program to help shy women start and maintain conversations with men. *Journal of Computer-Based Instruction,* 15, 7–13.

Muffo, J. A., S. V. Mead, and A. E. Bayer. 1987. Using faculty publication rates for comparing "peer" institutions. *Research in Higher Education,* 27, 163–173.

Murdock, T. A. 1987. It isn't just money: the effects of financial aid on student persistence. *Review of Higher Education,* 11, 75–101.

Neff, L. 1988. Acquaintance rape on campus; the problem, the victims, and prevention. *NASPA Journal,* 147–152.

Neuman, S., and A. Ziderman. 1985. Do universities maintain common standards in awarding first degrees with distinction? The case of Israel. *Higher Education,* 14, 447–459.

Newcomb, T. M., K. Koenig, R. Flacks, and D. D. Warwick. 1967. *Persistence and change: Bennington College and its students after twenty-five years.* New York: John Wiley and Sons.

Newton, L. L., and G. H. Gaither. 1980. Factors contributing to attrition: an analysis of program impact on persistence patterns. *College and University,* 55, 237–251.

Norton, L. S., and J. Hartley. 1986. What factors contribute to good examination marks? *Higher Education,* 15, 355–371.

Nye, P. A., T. J. Crooks, M. Powley, and G. Tripp. 1984. Student note-taking related to university performance. *Higher Education,* 13, 85–97.

Oakes, D. 1974. Selection biases in clinical trials. Memorandum NS-270, June 4, 1974. Cambridge, Mass.: Department of Statistics, Harvard University.

O'Hanlon, T., and L. Martensen. 1980. Making teacher evaluation work. *Journal of Higher Education,* 51, 664–672.

Pace, C. R. 1979. *Measuring outcomes of college.* San Francisco: Jossey-Bass.

———— 1985. Perspectives and problems in student outcomes research. In P. T. Ewell, ed., Assessing Educational Outcomes. *New Directions for Institutional Research,* 47. San Francisco: Jossey-Bass.

Pace, C. R., and J. Friedlander. 1982. The meaning of response categories: how often is "occasionally," "often," and "very often"? *Research in Higher Education,* 17, 267–281.

Pascarella, E. T. 1984. Reassessing the effects of living on campus versus commuting to college: a causal modeling approach. *Review of Higher Education,* 7, 247–260.

———— 1987. Are value added analyses valuable? In *Proceedings of the 1987 ETS Invitational Conference: Assessing the Outcomes of Higher Education.* Princeton, N.J.: Educational Testing Service.

Pascarella, E. T., J. C. Smart, and C. A. Ethington, 1986. Long-term persistence of two-year college students. *Research in Higher Education,* 24, 47–71.

Pascarella, E. T., and P. T. Terenzini. 1983. Predicting voluntary freshman year persistence/withdrawal behavior in a residential university: a path analytic validation of Tinto's model. *Journal of Educational Psychology,* 75, 215–226.

Pascarella, E. T., P. T. Terenzini, and L. M. Wolfe. 1986. Orientation to college and freshman year persistence/withdrawal decisions. *Journal of Higher Education,* 57, 155–175.

Pervin, L. A. 1967. A twenty-college study of student by college interaction using TAPE (transactional analysis of personality and environment): rationale, reliability, and validity. *Journal of Educational Psychology,* 58, 290–302.

Pocock, S. J. 1983. *Clinical trials: a practical approach.* New York: John Wiley and Sons.

Powell, B., and L. C. Steelman. 1983. Equity and the LSAT. *Harvard Educational Review,* 53, 32–44.

Regan, M. G., and H. E. Roland. 1982. University students: a change in expectations and aspirations over the decade. *Sociology of Education,* 55, 223–228.

Rest, J. 1988. Why does college promote development in moral judgment? *Journal of Moral Education,* 17, 183–194.

Riecken, H. W., and R. Boruch. 1974. *Social experimentation: a method for planning and evaluating social intervention.* New York: Academic Press.

Rock, D. A., J. H. Centra, and R. L. Linn. 1970. Relationships between college characteristics and student achievement. *American Educational Research Journal,* 7, 109–121.

Rogosa, D. R., and J. B. Willett. 1985. Understanding correlates of change by modeling individual differences in growth. *Psychometrika,* 50, 203–228.

Romine, B. H., J. H. Davis, and W. S. Gehman. 1970. The interaction of learning, personality, traits, ability, and environment: a preliminary study. *Educational and Psychological Measurement,* 30, 337–347.

Rooney, G. D. 1985. Minority students' involvement in minority student organizations: an exploratory study. *Journal of College Student Personnel,* 26, 450–456.

Root, L. S. 1987. Faculty evaluation: reliability of peer assessments of research, teaching and service. *Research in Higher Education,* 26, 71–84.

Rosenfeld, R. H., and J. A. Jones. 1987. Patterns and effects of geographic mobility for academic women and men. *Journal of Higher Education,* 58, 493–515.

Rosenthal, R. 1978. Combining results of independent studies. *Psychological Bulletin,* 85, 185–193.

—— 1984. *Meta-analytic procedures for social research.* Beverly Hills, Calif.: Sage Publications.

Rosenthal, R., and D. B. Rubin. 1986. Meta-analytic procedures for combining studies with multiple effect sizes. *Psychological Bulletin,* 99, 400–406.

Russell, D., L. A. Peplau, and C. E. Cutrona. 1980. The revised UCLA loneliness scale: concurrent and discriminant validity evidence. *Journal of Personality and Social Psychology,* 39, 472–480.

Rutman, L. 1984. *Evaluation research methods: a basic guide.* 2nd ed. Beverly Hills, Calif.: Sage Publications.

Sack, A. L., and R. Thiel. 1979. College football and social mobility: a case study of Notre Dame football players. *Sociology of Education,* 52, 60–66.

Schaffner, P. E. 1985. Competitive admission practices when the SAT is optional. *Journal of Higher Education,* 56, 55–72.

Scheers, N. J., and C. M. Dayton. 1987. Improved estimation on academic cheating behavior using the randomized response technique. *Research in Higher Education,* 26, 61–69.

Schenrich, V., B. Graham, and M. Drolette. 1983. Expected

grades versus specific evaluations of the teacher as predictors of students' overall evaluation of the teacher. *Research in Higher Education,* 19, 159–173.

Schneider, B. E. 1987. Graduate women, sexual harassment, and university policy. *Journal of Higher Education,* 58, 46–65.

Schrager, R. H. 1986. The impact of living group social climate on student academic performance. *Research in Higher Education,* 25, 265–276.

Schuckman, H. 1987. Ph.D. recipients in psychology and biology: do those with dissertation advisors of the same sex publish scholarly papers more frequently? *American Psychologist,* 42, 987–992.

Schuman, H., E. Walsh, C. Olson, and B. Etheridge. 1985. Effort and reward: the assumption that college grades are affected by quantity of study. *Social Forces,* 63, no. 4, 945–965.

Seneca, J. J., and M. K. Taussig. 1987. The effects of tuition and financial aid on the enrollment decision at a state university. *Research in Higher Education,* 26, 337–362.

Shapira, R., E. Etzion-Halery, and A. Barak. 1986. Political attitudes of Israeli students: a comparative perspective. *Higher Education,* 15, 231–246.

Shaw, G. B. 1911. *The doctor's dilemma, getting married, and the shewing up of Blanco Posnet.* New York: Brentano's.

Silverman, R. J. 1987. How we know what we know: a study of higher education journal articles. *Review of Higher Education,* 11, 39–59.

Simpson, C., K. Baker, and G. Mellinger. 1980. Conventional failures and unconventional dropouts: comparing different types of university withdrawals. *Sociology of Education,* 53, 203–214.

Singer, J. D. 1982. Estimation of means and variances in studies of hierarchical data. Technical Memorandum NS-431. Cambridge, Mass.: Department of Statistics, Harvard University.

—— 1987. An intraclass correlation model for the effects of group characteristics on individual outcomes in studies of multilevel data. *Journal of Experimental Education,* 55, 219–228.

Singer, J. D., and J. B. Willett. 1988. Uncovering involuntary layoffs in teacher survival data: the year of leaving dangerously. *Educational Evaluation and Policy Analysis,* 10, 221–224.

Singleton, R., Jr., and E. R. Smith, 1978. Does grade inflation decrease the reliability of grades? *Journal of Educational Measurement,* 15, 37–41.

Slavin, R. E. 1983. When does cooperative learning increase student achievement? *Psychological Bulletin,* 94, 429–445.

Smart, J. C. 1985. *Higher education: handbook of theory and research.* Vols. 1, 2, and 3. New York: Agathon Press for the American Educational Research Association.

Spady, W. 1970. Dropouts from higher education: an interdisciplinary review and synthesis. *Interchange,* 1, 109–121.

Stafford, K. L., S. B. Lundstredt, and A. D. Lynn, Jr. 1984. Social and economic factors affecting participation in higher education. *Journal of Higher Education,* 55, 590–608.

Stampen, J. O., and A. F. Cabrera. 1988. The targeting and packaging of student aid and its effect on attrition. *Economics of Education Review,* 7, 29–46.

Stark, J. S., M. A. Lowther, and B. M. K. Hagerty. 1986. Faculty roles and role preferences in ten fields of professional study. *Research in Higher Education,* 25, 3–30.

———— 1987. Faculty and administrator views of influences on professional programs. *Research in Higher Education,* 27, 63–83.

Stevenson, M., R. D. Waller, and S. M. Japely. 1985. Designing follow-up studies of graduates and former students. In P. T. Ewell, ed., *Assessing educational outcomes.* San Francisco: Jossey-Bass.

Stuart, D. L. 1985. Academic preparation and subsequent performance of intercollegiate football players. *Journal of College Student Personnel,* 26, 24–129.

Suchman, E. A. 1967. *Evaluative research: principles and practices in public service and social action programs.* New York: Russell Sage Foundation.

Sudman, S. 1976. *Applied sampling.* New York: Academic Press.

Terenzini, P. T. 1982. Designing attrition studies. In E. Pascarella, ed., *New directions for institutional research: studying student attrition.* San Francisco: Jossey-Bass.

Terenzini, P. T., and T. M. Wright. 1987. Influences on students' academic growth during four years of college. *Research in Higher Education,* 26, 161–179.

Theophilides, C., and P. T. Terenzini. 1981. The relation between nonclassroom contact with faculty and students' perceptions of instructional quality. *Research in Higher Education,* 15, 255–269.

Theophilides, C., P. T. Terenzini, and W. Lorang. 1984. Freshman and sophomore experiences and changes in major field. *Review of Higher Education,* 7, 261–278.

Thompson, S. B. 1980. Do individualized mastery and traditional instructional systems yield different course effects in college calculus? *American Educational Research Journal,* 17, 361–375.

Tinto, V. 1975. Dropout from higher education: a theoretical synthesis of recent research. *Review of Educational Research.* 45, 89–125.

Tukey, J. W. 1980. We need both exploratory and confirmatory. *American Statistician,* 34, 23–25.

Volkwein, J. F., D. A. Carbone, and E. A. Volkwein. 1988. Research in higher education: fifteen years of scholarship. *Research in Higher Education,* 28, 271–280.

Voorhees, R. A. 1987. Toward building models of community college persistence: a logit analysis. *Research in Higher Education,* 26, 115–129.

Wallace, W. 1971. *The logic of science and sociology.* Chicago: Aldine-Atherton.

Walster, E., T. A. Clearly, and M. M. Clifford. 1970. The effect of race and sex on college admission. *Sociology of Education,* 44, 237–244.

Weber, L. J., J. K. McBee, and J. E. Krebs. 1983. Take-home tests: an experimental study. *Research in Higher Education,* 18, 473–483.

Weiss, C. H. 1972. *Evaluation research: methods for assessing program effectiveness.* Englewood Cliffs, N.J.: Prentice-Hall.

Weller, L. D. 1986. Attitudes toward grade inflation: a random survey of American colleges of arts and sciences and colleges of education. *College and University,* 61, 118–127.

Whitla, D. K. 1988. Coaching: does it pay? Not for Harvard students. *College Board Review,* no. 148, 32–35.

Willett, J. B. 1988. Questions and answers in the measurement of change. In Ernst Rothkopf, ed. *Review of Research in Education,* 15, 345–422.

——— 1989. Some results on reliability for the longitudinal measurement of change: implications for the design of studies of individual growth. *Educational and Psychological Measurement,* in press.

——— 1990. Measuring change: the difference score and beyond. In H. J. Walberg and G. D. Haertel, eds. *International en-*

cyclopedia of educational evaluation. Oxford: Pergamon Press.

Willson, V. L., and R. R. Putnam. 1982. A meta-analysis of pretest desensitization effects in experimental design. *American Educational Research Journal*, 19, 249–258.

Wilson, K. M. 1981. Analyzing the long-term performance of minority and nonminority students: a tale of two studies. *Research in Higher Education*, 15, 351–375.

Winston, R. B., Jr., G. S. Huston, and S. S. McCaffrey. 1980. Environmental influences in fraternity academic achievement. *Journal of College Student Personnel*, 21, 449–455.

Wolfe, L. M. 1985. Postsecondary educational attainment among whites and blacks. *American Educational Research Journal*, 22, 501–525.

Wortman, C. B., and V. C. Rabinowitz. 1978. Random assignment: the fairest of them all. In *Evaluation Studies Review Annual*. Beverly Hills, Calif.: Sage Publications.

Yess, J. P. 1981. The influence of marriage on community college student achievement in specific programs of study. *Research in Higher Education*, 14, 103–118.

Young, M. 1986. Religiosity and satisfaction with virginity among college men and women. *Journal of College Student Personnel*, 27, 339–344.

Yule, G. U. 1926. Why do we sometimes get nonsense correlations between time series? A study in sampling and the nature of time series. *Journal of the Royal Statistical Society*, 89, 1–22.

Zeidner, M. 1986. Are scholastic aptitude tests in Israel biased toward Arab college student candidates? *Higher Education*, 15, 507–522.

Zelen, M. 1979. A new design for randomized clinical trials. *New England Journal of Medicine*, 300, 1242–1245.

INDEX

Abedi, Jamal, 45
Abrams, H. G., 209–210
Academic performance: and athletics, 3, 87–90, 101, 130, 132, 200; and advising programs, 4, 15, 16, 82, 101; and testing formats, 6, 32; and computer use, 6, 127; of MBA students, 46–47; and fraternity membership, 76–77, 85–86; effect of employment on, 78, 84, 97, 238, 239; and freshman qualifications, 81–82; and SAT scores, 82, 83, 139, 140; and dropout rates, 135–136, 169; measures of, 142, 143; effect of studying on, 211–212; and motivation of students, 222–224. *See also* Grades
Achievement motivation study, 222–224

ACT (American College Testing program) scores, in research design, 122, 126, 127, 149, 154, 159, 171
Adelman, C. P., 9, 241
Admissions policy, 149–150, 192–193
Advising programs: effect on academic performance, 4, 15, 16, 82, 101; attitudes toward, 64–65; for SAT, 82, 139, 140
Aggregation levels in research studies, 15–16
Alpha (Type I) errors, 189–190, 191, 192
American Psychological Association, 18
Analysis: statistical, 7, 17, 84, 88–90, 95, 165; data, 25–26, 28, 199–205; quantitative, 28, 29; meta-, 28–32, 195–196; statistical power, 82, 191–